S0-BZB-670

GENERAL THEOLOGICAL SEMINARY
KELLER
LIBRARY
NEW YORK

SACRED WITNESS

SACRED WITNESS
RAPE IN THE HEBREW BIBLE

SUSANNE SCHOLZ

FORTRESS PRESS
MINNEAPOLIS

BS
1199
.R27
537
2010

SACRED WITNESS
Rape in the Hebrew Bible

Copyright © 2010 Fortress Press, an imprint of Augsburg Fortress. All rights reserved. Except for brief quotations in critical articles or reviews, no part of this book may be reproduced in any manner without prior written permission from the publisher. Visit http://www.augsburgfortress.org/copyrights/ or write to Permissions, Augsburg Fortress, Box 1209, Minneapolis, MN 55440.

Unless otherwise noted, Scripture quotations are taken from the *New Revised Standard Bible*, copyright © 1989 by the Division of Christian Education of the National Council of Churches of Christ in the USA. Used by permission. All rights reserved.

Introducing the Women's Hebrew Bible, Introduction in Feminist Theology 13 by Susanne Scholz, copyright © 2007 by Susanne Scholz. Used by permission of T&T Clark

A full bibliography for *Sacred Witness* is available at www.fortresspress.com/Scholz.

Cover image: *Bathsheba*, Yisehak Fine Arts
Cover design: Laurie Ingram
Book design: Christy J. P. Barker

Library of Congress Cataloging-in-Publication Data
Scholz, Susanne, 1966–
  Sacred witness : rape in the Hebrew Bible / Susanne Scholz.
    p. cm.
  Includes bibliographical references and indexes.
  ISBN 978-0-8006-3861-0 (alk. paper)
  1. Rape in the Bible. I. Title.
  BS1199.R27S37 2010
  221.8'3641532—dc22
                              2009041997

The paper used in this publication meets the minimum requirements of American National Standard for Information Sciences—Permanence of Paper for Printed Library Materials, ANSI Z329.48-1984.

Manufactured in the U.S.A.

14   13   12   11   10   1   2   3   4   5   6   7   8   9   10

Dedicated to
Women and Girls of Congo

In memory of
Gretel Markwirt (1909–1999)
Aisha Ibrahim Duhulow (1995–2008)

CONTENTS

ACKNOWLEDGMENTS

This book has been in the making since I taught a course entitled "Rape in Religion and Society" in the fall of 2001. It was then that I discovered the need for a book solely devoted to the wide spectrum of biblical rape texts in conversation with feminist perspectives on rape. I was not a newcomer to examining rape in the Hebrew Bible thanks to my previous monograph, *Rape Plots: A Feminist Cultural Study of Genesis 34*, Studies in Biblical Literature 13 (New York: P. Lang, 2000). I have long argued that the topic is highly relevant: rape statistics are staggering;[1] crimes of rape are omnipresent in peacetime and in war; and a general reticence to talk about rape is common. On more than one occasion, I have learned that rape is a conversation stopper, but it is a topic that simply will not go away, as frequent news reports on rape disturb me regularly. I strongly believe the topic of this book relates directly to the welfare of women and girls, boys, and men everywhere.

For this reason I dedicate this book to the women and girls in Congo who have suffered unimaginable pain as a result of the brutal war rapes in that country since 1994. The United Nations characterizes the situation in Congo as "the worst sexual violence in the world."[2] Women and girls, especially in eastern Congo, are "sadistically attacked" by all manner of male groups, including soldiers from different armies. Women and girls are "butchered by bayonets and assaulted with chunks of wood" so that "their reproductive and digestive systems are beyond repair." One doctor who works in a hospital in South Kivu Province, the epicenter of Congo's rape epidemic, exclaimed: "We don't know why these rapes are happening, but one thing is clear. . . . They are done to destroy women."[3]

This book is written in memory of two women. One of them is Aisha Ibrahim Duhulow (1995–2008), whose life was much too short and whose last moments of life were beyond horrific. On October 27, 2008, about fifty Somali men stoned this thirteen-year-old girl to death in a stadium packed with one thousand spectators. Accused of "adultery," she had been previously raped by three men while she traveled to visit her grandmother.[4] I read about her several weeks after her death and tried to imagine her last moments—impossibly horrific—when so many men threw stones at her. I attempted to picture the fury in their faces, the last faces Aisha saw, while she begged for her life until she could not do so anymore. She had survived gang rape, sought protection from the "authorities," as the *New York Times* explained, but to no avail. The same authorities "then accused her of adultery and sentenced her to death."[5] I honor Aisha and what she had to endure in her young life.

The other woman is my great-aunt, Gretel Markwirt (1909–1999), who survived a gang rape by nine soldiers in 1945, as World War II ended. She was German and the soldiers were Russian. Gretel told several of my female family members about her ordeal just a few years before her death. When the soldiers came into the house where she lived at the time with her husband and eleven-year-old daughter, she submitted to the gang rape in the hope of preventing them from going upstairs and finding her daughter. Her husband, Schorsch, was forced to watch. Tante Gretel, thirty-six at the time, survived this extreme violation but never forgot it.[6] Many women of her generation and background hid such experiences in their hearts. Over the years, I have collected countless stories, newspaper clippings, and rape statistics. May the women of Congo, Aisha, and Gretel stand as representatives of "real-life" rape stories in our time.

I have come to recognize during the many years of working on this topic that there is hardly any woman who does not have her own tale of rape in one form or another. Did not all of us grow up with the unspoken warning not to walk outside at night? I remember the worried fear when, as a child and then a teenager, I came home in the evening. "I should not be here anymore," was a succinct but palpable feeling I had about being in a public place after dark, which was inevitably followed by a sense of relief to have made it back home as planned. Although I do not recall any explicit talk about rape when I was growing up, the rule "Do not go into a park at night" was enough to put me on my guard—as it was, I am sure, for most women. And I remember for sure that male acquaintances usually insisted upon walking me home in the evening—though it never came up that most rapists are in fact acquaintance rapists, men whom we know. Again, the word "rape" was never explicitly uttered. Yet did we not all know somehow that the persistent danger of "rape" was the reason behind the extra care to get me home safely? Nowadays I wonder why I never had a course, or even one single discussion, on rape or sexual violence during my many years of academic training. Informal inquiries suggest to me that not much has changed since I left high school. Rape is not addressed as a subject matter in school even today. When I taught a course on rape in 2001, my students reported that they had never had a single discussion of rape in the context of the classroom or any other academic setting. Since the class was not part of the regular curriculum, it has probably not been taught again there, nor have I had the opportunity to teach a course on rape elsewhere.

I want to thank the following individuals for their help and support during the last decade. Many thanks to the editor at Fortress Press, Neil Elliot, who found merit in this project, granted the book contract, and generously granted the additional time needed to complete the manuscript. Thanks also to Susan Johnson, editor at Fortress Press, who helped to move this book to the finishing line, and to Andrew De Young, Project Manager at Fortress Press. Many thanks to the various libraries that opened their doors to me and allowed access to their valuable resources, including the many interlibrary loans that helped a great deal. I thank the McQuade Library at Merrimack College, the Stevens Memorial Library in North Andover, the Burke Library at Union Theological Seminary and Columbia University, the Andover-Harvard Theological Library at Harvard Divinity School, the Flora Lamson Hewlett Library at the General Theological Union, the University Library at the Chinese University of Hong Kong, the Hessische Landesbibliothek Wiesbaden, the Universitätsbibliothek Mainz, and most recently the Bridwell Library at Perkins School of Theology. Thanks to my many colleagues at the various schools where I taught prior to joining the faculty at Perkins School of Theology. I appreciate their support in encouraging me to teach a course on rape and also the opportunity to integrate aspects of my research into my regular courses on gender and the Bible. I also would like to thank the faculty at Starr King School for the Ministry for giving me the opportunity to be part of their intellectual community as a visiting scholar in 2007–2008.

I am grateful for various opportunities to present my research at scholarly conferences and meetings. I thank the participants of the conference "The Rhetorics of Identity: Place, Race, Sex and the Person" for their willingness to engage my ideas on "Reconstructing Rape for the Olden Days: The Challenge of Biblical Rape Laws in Biblical Studies." The conference was sponsored by the Centre for Rhetorics & Hermeneutics and the New Testament Rhetoric Project, and it took place at the University of Redlands in Redlands, California, in January 2005. Thanks also to the Critical Biblical Studies Colloquium of the Boston area for the opportunity to present materials on "Rape Legislation in the Hebrew Bible and Ancient Near East" at Andover Newton Theological Seminary on April 7, 2006. I thank the Society of Biblical Literature for the opportunity to present my research on biblical and ancient Near Eastern rape legislation at the Annual Meeting in San Antonio, Texas, in November 2004, and to read a paper on "Rachel's 'Battle of God'? Women's Competition and Enslavement in Gen. 29:31—30:24" (which became part of chapter 3), in Nashville, Tennessee, in November 2001.

Heartfelt thanks to the following colleagues and friends who supported me in various ways during the time of this project: Gabrielle Lettini, Rebecca Ann Parker, Elisabeth Schüssler Fiorenza, Beverly W. Harrison, Rich Weis, Ed Greenstein, Athalya Brenner, Archie Lee, Nancy Tan, Esther Fuchs, Sze-kar Wan, Evelyn Parker, Marjorie Procter-Smith, Jeanne Stevenson-Moessner, Ruben Habito, Ted Campbell, Robert Hunt, Jörg Rieger, Isabel Docampo, Susanne Johnson, Pat Davis, Jaime Clark-Soles, Richard Nelson, Roy Heller, Abe Smith, Jessica Boon, Valerie Karras, Karen Baker-Fletcher, John Holbert, Bill Lawrence, Marie Fortune, Roland Boer, Marie Plasse,

ACKNOWLEDGMENTS xv

Janet Parker, Katharina von Kellenbach, Lisa Hock, Marc Ellis, Annemarie Kidder, Cheryl Anderson, Dora Mbuwayesango, Carleen Mandolfo, Todd Penner, Caroline Vander Stichele, the late Tikva Frymer-Kensky, Jane Webster, Yeong Mee Lee, Kristin De Troyer, Gale Yee, Toni Craven, Phyllis Trible, Angela Bauer, Erhard Gerstenberger, Luise Schottroff, Irmtraud Fischer, Angela Standhartinger, Christl Maier, Marie-Theres Wacker, Silvia Schroer, Greg Mobley, Gabriele Schröder, Kathinka Kaden, Diemut Cramer, Renate Rose, Monika Jakobs, and members of the ESWTR and NAESWTR.

I thank the many and various students who have attended my courses since 2001, all of whom have heard me talk about rape in the Hebrew Bible. Some wrote papers on a biblical rape text, and many provided me with valuable feedback in their responses. Rape is a "hot-potato" topic for many institutions of higher learning, which turns the teaching of this issue into a *Drahtseilakt* (literally, a tightrope walk). Who knows how many victim-survivors (and perhaps even rapists!) sit in the room? I always said that statistically it was very likely that several people in our classroom have intimate knowledge about the topic at hand and we would need to remember this fact. More than one student has come to me after class and told me that she survived rape or incest. Sexual violence "lives" in our world everywhere. I pray particularly that these students are doing well in life.

A special thanks to my research assistant, Sara K. Ray, for her final editorial help in spring 2009 and to my longtime editor, Chris Herlinger, a journalist who also helped steer me toward new insights on the issue of rape and war in Africa. And without my first and perceptive-intuitive manuscript reader, Lorraine Keating, valuable insight, passion for the subject matter, and critical rethinking would be much harder to sustain. I am most grateful to all.

I also would like to acknowledge that three chapters of this book have been previously published in earlier and shortened versions. Parts of chapter 3 were published as "Gender, Class, and Androcentric Compliance in the Rapes of Enslaved Women," in *lectio difficilior: European Electronic Journal for Feminist Exegesis* 1 (2004).[7] Parts of chapter 5 were published as "Back Then It Was Legal: The Epistemological Imbalance in Readings of Biblical and Ancient Near

Eastern Rape Legislation," in *Journal of Religion and Abuse* 7, no. 3 (December 2005): 5–35, and also in *The Bible and Critical Theory* 1, no. 4 (December 2005).[8] A section of chapter 8 can be found in the fourth chapter of my book *Introducing the Women's Hebrew Bible*, Introductions in Feminist Theology 13 (London/New York: T&T Clark, 2007).

A full bibliography for *Sacred Witness* is available at www.fortresspress.com/Scholz.

INTRODUCTION
A PROMISE FOR A BLESSING

The Sacred Scriptures of Christianity and Judaism play a marginal role in the social, political, economic, and religious affairs of everyday life in Western societies. Social institutions such as public schools or transportation facilities function without reference to biblical texts. In the United States, politicians are sworn into office by placing one hand on the Bible, but they do not follow the law codes in the book of Exodus or Leviticus. The capitalist formation of Western economies also progresses without considering biblical recommendations about the distribution of wealth. Christian and Jewish institutions are the only groups that regularly refer to biblical literature, but their approaches vary, and only some religious groups—mostly fundamentalist Christians—want to apply their literal readings to the public structures of society. Bible reading is usually relegated to the private realm of religious life and serves personal, devotional, and confessional purposes. Overall, then, biblical literature has little influence in contemporary society.

This book suggests that the intellectual marginalization of biblical literature is regrettable, because the Hebrew Bible has much to contribute to the historical, sociological, political, and religious understanding of rape. One does not need to adhere to a Christian fundamentalist approach to gain from reading the ancient texts, some of which even portray the divinity as a perpetrator of rape. No easy and simplistic answers are at hand: complexity of thought in reading highly ambiguous texts is needed because ambiguity teaches sensitivity, insight, and respect toward the multifaceted issues we face in a world in which sexual violence prevails. What is required is a willingness to wrestle with biblical "rape texts" and the history of their interpretation.

This suggestion may come as a surprise. Not many people know that the Hebrew Bible contains a wealth of rape texts. Even if they do, they do not relate them to contemporary discussions on rape. In Genesis 19, Lot's daughters are threatened with rape when their father offers them to the mob outside the house. In Genesis 34, Dinah is raped by Shechem, and in 2 Samuel 13, Amnon rapes Tamar, his half-sister. In Ezekiel 23, God condemns Aholah and Aholibah to sexual violations by their former lovers. Rape laws appear in the book of Deuteronomy, and the stories of enslaved women who are forced into sexual intercourse are detailed in Genesis and the books of Samuel. No single lesson emerges from this plethora of narratives and poems, but they demonstrate that the topic is of social, political, and theological importance, despite neglect in Christian and Jewish histories of interpretation. The present study invites readers, whether they identify as secular or religious, to engage biblical literature and to learn how to read it in conversation with contemporary debates on rape.

Engaging the Hebrew Bible in this way is not easy, nor is it done frequently. It demands that readers hold on to the ancient body of literature with the goal of gaining insight from it. Placing ourselves in a long reading tradition, we assert our hermeneutical positions as readers within contemporary cultures where rape and sexual violence are tragically prevalent. Like Jacob, whose engagement with the demon is chronicled in Gen 32:24-32, we wrestle with the demon and demand a blessing. Some argue that Jacob wrestled not merely with a demon but with God. When Jacob does not submit, the demon (or is it the divinity?) injures Jacob's hip socket. Still Jacob does not let go of the demon, who requests: "Let me go, for dawn is breaking," to which Jacob replies: "I will not let you go, unless you bless me" (Gen 32:27). Thereupon Jacob receives a blessing in the form of a changed name: "Israel, for you have striven with God and with humans, and have prevailed" (Gen 32:28). As Jacob receives a blessing from the life-threatening force, so perhaps today's readers will gain a blessing from wrestling with biblical rape texts. Many meanings emerge because biblical stories and poems contain many possible meanings that depend on *who* is doing the wrestling.

The following pages and chapters present a wealth of possibilities as they have emerged over decades and centuries in the multigenerational reading process. They are juxtaposed with contemporary descriptions about various forms of rape because the goal is not only intellectual or theoretical but also practical. This study aims to contribute to the urgent task of ending rape wherever and whenever it continues to occur.

Rape Prose and Poetry in the Hebrew Bible

Rape texts are common, if not ubiquitous, throughout biblical prose and poetry. Among them are the stories of Hagar and Sarah (Genesis 16; 21), Bilhah, Zilpah, Leah, and Rachel (Genesis 29–30), Sarah and Rebekah (Genesis 12; 20; 26), Lot's daughters (Genesis 19), Dinah (Genesis 34), Ms. Potiphar (Genesis 39), Delilah (Judges 13–16), the concubine and the daughters of Shiloh (Judges 19–21), Bathsheba (2 Samuel 13), and Abigail (1 Kings 1). Other rape texts are part of the legal codes (for example, Deuteronomy 22) and the prophetic literature (for example, Jer 13:22; 20:7; Ezek 16:6-8, 36-42). Several passages are well known; others are rarely mentioned. For instance, the tale of Sarah and Abraham in Genesis 12 (parallels in chapters 20; 26) is famous, though not usually understood as a story about a rape threat. For fear of death, Abraham introduces his wife to the Egyptian pharaoh as his sister. In the first version of the story (chapter 12), the king learns about the deceit only after terrible plagues hit his house. In the second version (chapter 20), another ruler, King Abimelech, has a dream that reveals to him the relationship between Sarah and Abraham. In the third version (chapter 26), King Abimelech accidentally looks out of the window when wife and husband, in this case Rebekah and Isaac, "caress" each other.

Another story—the narrative about Samson and Delilah (Judges 16)—is renowned, but rarely presented as a tale about a male rape threat. It is a famous story that made it even into a French opera, *Samson et Dalila*, composed by Camille Saint-Saens and first produced in 1877. There Samson is a tragic hero who falls in love with Delilah.

The opera tackles the question whether "she really love[s] him"[1] and conveniently ignores an ambiguity in 16:5, where the Philistines advise Delilah: "Coax him, and find out what makes his strength so great, and how we may overpower [ענה, *'innâ*; possibly "to rape"] him, so that we may bind him in order to subdue [ענה, *'innâ*] him; and we will each give you eleven hundred pieces of silver" (Judg 16:5). What does it mean that they want to "subdue" him (see also Judg 16:6, 19)? As we will see later, the linguistic ambiguity makes it possible to identify this text as a rape threat. Then there are rape texts that are largely unknown, such as poems about divine rape (for example, Jer 13:22, 26; Nah 3:4-7) or laws on rape in war (for example, Deut 21:10-14); they remain in the shadows of cultural creativity and scholarly discourse.

It was not until the late 1970s that feminist scholars focused attention on these disturbing texts in the Hebrew Bible and highlighted the fates of the unnamed concubine and the women of Shiloh (Judges 19–21) as horrific tales about gang rape. Yet these interpreters also disagreed on the meaning of other rape stories. Among them is Genesis 34, which features prominently in feminist scholarship and is portrayed in a novel, *The Red Tent*, by Anita Diamant, as a love story rather than a rape story.[2] Diamant's novel tells the story of the "patriarchs" in Genesis from the women's perspective, from inside their tents, and makes Dinah's fate central to the events. In this version, Dinah loves Shechem but her brothers do not want to include strangers in the family.

The narratives about Sarah and Hagar also have posed challenges for feminist interpreters. Struggling against an androcentric history of interpretation that identifies Abraham and his son Isaac as main characters, feminist readers have successfully turned Sarah and Hagar into prominent figures, portrayed Hagar as the first biblical character who names God (Gen 16:13), and stressed that Sarah—and not Abraham—determines the future of the family. Yet their emphasis on Hagar and Sarah often misses that Hagar's story is a rape narrative. Feminist interpreters rose from an androcentric history of interpretation and focused attention on some rape texts while overlooking others.

This book, remedying this uneven situation, benefits from forty years of solid feminist studies on the Hebrew Bible and offers a comprehensive analysis of many, if not most, biblical rape texts. These texts are read within various historical-cultural contexts, as defined by contemporary feminist perspectives on rape, and they are presented as rape literature emerging from a long androcentric history of interpretation. The book is grounded in a feminist hermeneutic that honors the perspectives of raped victim-survivors. It turns the ancient literatures into sacred texts about rape.

Biblical Historicity of Rape

A word is needed, though, about the biblical historicity of rape because many modern readers assume that the Hebrew Bible is based on actual historical events. Since the seventeenth century C.E., scholars have examined the historicity of biblical texts, placed them into ancient Near Eastern and Hellenistic literary and archaeological contexts, and brought historical questions to the forefront of the Western mind. Consequently, today's readers are quick to relegate biblical texts to the distant past, assuming that the texts describe customs, habits, and events from "way back then." The historical emphasis results from the empiricist-scientific outlook of Western epistemology, which equates history with truth and considers a document to be "true" only when the described events can be shown to have occurred. Both the Christian fundamentalist position and the secular approach, insisting on the historicity of biblical literature, presuppose this modern worldview. They differ only insofar as the secular approach does not find "historical truth" in biblical texts and classifies them as fiction, as "not true." Yet neither view challenges modern epistemological assumptions, and both share the same basic premise that biblical literature is significant only as a document of history.[3]

The modern need to define biblical literature as historical literature also prevails when the topic is rape. Many modern readers wonder: Did biblical rape stories *really* happen? If they did, do they not contain androcentric views about gender and rape that we do not share anymore because "way back then women were the property of men"? This belief situates biblical meaning in a distant past, even though we do not know enough about the historical circumstances of biblical authors to hypothesize about the original meaning of the Hebrew Bible. Moreover, many androcentric interpreters do not discuss the topic of rape and relegate biblical rape texts to discussions about Israelite family life and marriage customs.

For instance, Johannes Pedersen's classic and often-cited study entitled *Israel: Its Life and Culture* does not refer to rape in biblical times, although his work contains an extensive section on "forbidden degrees of relationship."[4] Pedersen's work mentions several rape texts in sections on "appropriate" or "inappropriate" marriage arrangements[5] and prohibitions against incest. There he refers to Abraham and Sarah's scheme of introducing themselves as siblings to the king (Gen 20:12). He also discusses Tamar's proposal of marrying her brother (2 Sam 13:13). The potential for rape or the depiction of rape remain unacknowledged in Pedersen's treatise even when he writes about the story of Tamar and Amnon: "The story of Amnon who ravished [*sic*] his half-sister Tamar presupposes that he [Amnon] might make her [Tamar] as his wife, if his father's consent were obtained (2 Sam. 13:13)." Pedersen states that Amnon "ravished" Tamar, but he does not outline the sociohistorical ramifications of the fact that marriage after "ravishment" constitutes a "pronounced one-sidedness which places the center of gravity in the man only."[6] To Pedersen, this story could have led to marriage, and this fact shapes his interpretation. Thus, rape is not mentioned even once in sections ranging from marriage to war.[7]

Nor has the historical development of rape in biblical times received much attention from feminist scholars. The omission reflects the fact that Israelite historiography in general is fraught with problems, but it is particularly problematic when it concerns Israelite women. We do not know, for instance, if women enjoyed equal status with men in the family-oriented and self-governed tribes of premonarchic Israel, as Carol Meyers maintains.[8] Some scholars, among them the so-called minimalists, cast serious doubt on such historical reconstructions and move the reliable stages of Israelite historiography into the sixth century B.C.E. or even into the Hellenistic period.[9] Historiographical problems seem insurmountable when the topic is rape. To what extent do biblical rape narratives relate to actual women's or men's experiences, and how, for instance, should the story about Tamar and Amnon be read when the goal is the establishment of Israelite rape history? The precarious historiographical nature of biblical rape literature makes it difficult indeed to write about the history of rape in ancient Israel, and so it seems unlikely that a comprehensive history of rape in ancient Syria-Palestine-Israel will be penned any time soon.

Reader's Responses to Biblical Rape Poetry and Prose

When readers recognize that the Hebrew Bible contains numerous stories and passages about rape, they are often puzzled. They would not have expected the Sacred Scriptures of Judaism and Christianity to contain such texts. Consequently, their responses are often mixed because they wonder what to make of biblical literature giving rape more than a nominal recognition. The observation often leads to two responses. One response appreciates that the Hebrew Bible includes rape texts, whereas the other response is negative. People who respond appreciatively maintain that the presence of rape in biblical literature proves the seriousness of the topic. Not only do the rape texts demonstrate that rape has long been part of human experience, but the very fact that these texts exist proves the significance of the issue. The Bible deals with it, and so should we. Biblical rape literature is seen also as a pedagogical tool that strengthens our ability to confront sexual violence. Biblical rape texts *describe* human interaction as sexually violent but they do not *prescribe* it. These texts become important avenues by which to examine hermeneutical assumptions, to discover the history of interpretation, and to ponder marginalized perspectives such as those of raped victim-survivors. In short, to adherents of the appreciative response, biblical rape texts serve as learning opportunities about epistemologies and genealogies of rape discourse as it evolved in the Christian and Jewish traditions.

The other response articulates serious objections to the presence of rape texts in the biblical canon. It emphasizes that rape is a human problem that should not be related to religious teachings. People of this position often believe that the presence of rape texts makes it, in fact, difficult to read the Hebrew Bible as a spiritually meaningful book because its androcentric attitudes and customs eradicate the perspectives of the raped victim-survivors. To people of this persuasion, particularly when they call themselves Christian, the underlying problem consists in dealing with the Hebrew Bible. Do biblical rape texts not illustrate that this is a book of violence and that the rape texts can teach us little because of their persistent androcentric viewpoints? The difficulties are many, and books of other religious traditions sometimes seem more attractive than the Hebrew Bible because they do not seem to contain any rape texts.

Indeed, the Hebrew Bible stands out among sacred writings for including rape prose and poetry. Rape is absent from the Qur'an, although Islamic societies certainly know of the issue.[10] Hindu sacred texts contain some references to rape, such as the characterization of Lord Krishna as "a bold woman-snatcher," and the Upanishads contain a passage that excuses the rape of a woman who is unwilling to consent to sexual intercourse.[11] The stories about Draupad in the Mahābhārata also mention several sexual assaults that the daughter of Drupada survives.[12] A Buddhist story tells of a nun struggling with male sexual force.[13] None of these texts, however, plays a prominent role in the religious imagination. So how does one explain that the Hebrew Bible contains so many references to rape? Does it reflect biblical literature's unique character? Perhaps—but it is also possible to think that it is only a question of time until Muslim, Hindu, or Buddhist feminist scholars emphasize rape in their sacred texts as well. After all, not long ago biblical scholars did not regard biblical texts as rape literature either.

The last claim is not entirely accurate. Some Christian theologians of old considered rape to be a Christian theological issue. This is the case with Augustine (354–430 C.E.), who made rape a theological problem when he argued against his Christian and Roman contemporaries. They required a woman to commit suicide after rape so that she would keep her honor. Among them is Jerome, a Christian theologian (347–420 C.E.) who advised a woman to commit suicide after her "chastity is jeopardized."[14] Augustine proposed a theological alternative that turned, however, into a precarious theological argument.

He maintained that rape represented an opportunity for a woman to repent for her sins before God. For Augustine, rape was God-sent, and thus he opposed a woman's suicide after rape because suicide would not give her the spiritual benefits of the God-sent rape. The benefits, as Augustine saw it, were that the rape would coach a woman to move away from future sinning. In Augustine's view, then, rape was a form of "prophylactic punishment."[15] This argumentation is obviously problematic, not only because Augustine views God as the bringer of rape but also because he does not condemn the rapist, he holds the woman responsible, and he thus contributes to the stigmatization of raped women as sinners.

Despite these inherent problems, some feminist theologians and ethicists find value in Augustine's approach, among them Mary Pellauer. She points out that Augustine's position recognizes rape as a theological issue, saying that feminist theologians should emulate this strategy. Like Augustine, they ought to maintain the theological and biblical significance of rape, and, like Augustine, they should place their argumentation within the contemporary rape discourse. Since Augustine affirmed that rape belongs to Christian theological discourse, feminist theologians need to analyze biblical rape literature as part of feminist thought on rape and to provide theo-biblical opportunities for pondering, examining, and evaluating the ongoing presence of rape in today's world.

Feminist Discourse on Rape from Brownmiller to Postmodern Feminist Theory

Since the 1970s, feminists have investigated rape as an issue of theoretical significance and have created awareness about the prevalence of rape in human history and society. They have critiqued the prevalence of rape as a form of oppression that men have perpetrated against women over the millennia. Susan Brownmiller's *Against Our Will: Men, Women and Rape* started the discussion in the United States.[16] She postulated that since prehistoric times, men's physical nature has turned them into potential and actual rapists and a threat to women of all cultures and histories. Brownmiller's work is a classic in Western feminist discourse, not only because it was the first on the subject but also because it created a storm of opposition. Some feminists objected to the biological reasoning. Catharine MacKinnon, for instance, maintained that "biology is not destiny" and analyzed rape as an expression of power "in its gendered form." She defined rape as part of the continuum of sexuality, "the dynamic of control by which male dominance . . . eroticizes and thus defines man and woman, gender identity and sexual pleasure."[17] Other feminists challenged Brownmiller's universalizing and timeless depiction of rape and urged that rape not be defined exclusively as a form of gender oppression but that it be connected with racism and classism.[18]

Grounded in this expanded notion of rape, feminist theorists began examining rape in relation to other social categories. One of them, Susan Griffin, categorized rape as an expression of a power structure that not only "victimizes women" but also engages in "raping Black people and the very earth we live upon."[19] Rape relates to all forms of violent oppression in the world that reinforce the hierarchical structures of human interaction, including gender relations. Another feminist thinker, Angela Davis, stated similarly that "[a]ny attempt to treat it [rape] as an isolated phenomenon is bound to flounder."[20] In her view, rape has to be analyzed within a framework of racism, classism, and the economic system of capitalism.

Increasingly, therefore, feminists became suspicious of biological explanations and analyzed rape as a social construct. They published countless studies in the 1970s and 1980s which identified many different forms of rape, such as stranger rape, acquaintance rape, marital rape, date rape, or gang rape. They founded rape crisis centers, particularly in the United States, where the public recognition of rape increased dramatically. Psychological research exposed public assumptions about rape and discriminatory attitudes toward rape victim-survivors. Feminist historians wrote about rape in past and present societies, and international discourse emerged as a powerful means of criticizing the prevalence of rape in Western and non-Western countries.[21]

The proliferation of rape studies, however, did not expand much beyond the 1980s. The conservative backlash to the feminist movement in Western societies stereotyped and also marginalized the feminist movement in general and rape studies in particular. Consequently, feminist theoretical debates on rape decreased. Postmodern feminist theorists were also reluctant to examine rape. To them, gender notions are "in process, a becoming, a constructing that cannot rightfully be said to originate or to end."[22] Rape, as an enduring phenomenon in gender interactions, posed practical and epistemological challenges, and so postmodern feminists neglected rape as an issue.

Some postmodern feminists, however, articulated theoretical positions on rape. For instance, Sharon Marcus defined rape as a "gendered grammar of violence," in which men are the agents of violence and women the subjects of fear. She stressed the postmodern conviction that all reality is constructed by language, and so rape-prone societies are "subject to change" if rape is understood as a "linguistic fact: to ask how the violence or rape is enabled by narratives, complexes and institutions which derive their strength not from outright, immutable, unbeatable force but rather from their power to structure our lives as imposing cultural scripts."[23] In other words, she and other postmodern feminists asserted that Western culture, as it is manifested in art, literature, and music, has been complicit in producing rape, and this cultural complicity has to be exposed and its power dismantled. They opposed the idea that rape is a biological necessity and moved the understanding of rape far beyond Brownmiller's initial position, which claimed: "In terms of human anatomy the possibility of forcible intercourse incontrovertibly exists."[24] Postmodern feminists have rejected such biological essentialism because it does not sufficiently address the different kinds of past and present rape rhetorics.

In the 1990s, other scholarly voices, advancing cross-cultural and anthropological perspectives, emerged as a challenge to feminist rape discourse. Among them is that of Nigerian anthropologist O. Oyewumi, who criticized Western feminist discourse—postmodern or not—for the universal acceptance of gender as a social category. Oyewumi observed that Western feminists apply categories such as "woman" and "man" to studies of non-Western cultures even when gender does not characterize the social dynamics of these cultures. This is also the case when Western feminists studied pre-colonial

Yoruba society, and projected their notions of gender onto a differently located society. Oyewumi explained:

> The potential value of Western feminist social constructionism remains, therefore, largely unfulfilled, because feminism, like most other Western theoretical frameworks for interpreting the social world, cannot get away from the prism of biology that necessarily perceives social hierarchies as natural. Consequently, in cross-cultural gender studies, theorists impose Western categories on non-Western cultures and then project such categories as natural.[25]

Oyewumi showed in her work that Western notions of gender prevent Western feminist anthropologists from understanding the non-Western societies they investigate. They assume a Western "bio-logic" and apply it to non-Western cultures. In contrast, Oyewumi stressed that all gender categories are particular and contextual, emerging from specific historical and social locations. She maintained that one set of gender definitions, as it developed in the West, should not be imposed on other societies.

The cross-cultural challenge to Western feminist thought has also been part of the anthropological work of Christine Helliwell. She aimed to demonstrate that rape does not exist in every culture. For this purpose, she studied the Gerai people, "a Dayak community of some seven hundred people in the Indonesian province of Kalimantan Barat (West Borneo)." She discovered that the Gerai people were horrified about the very idea of rape[26] because, according to Helliwell, they find forced sex "unthinkable." It would destroy the spiritual and communal balance between individual and community.[27] Helliwell also explained that the Gerai gender ideology of "biological sameness" makes rape impossible in this society. The Gerai people assume that women and men's sexual organs share the same biological structure and form: women's organs are inside and men's outside. This biological sameness of women and men is the basis for women getting pregnant, and it also makes them convinced that some men menstruate like women. In addition, the idea of biological sameness promotes the notion of women's and men's *social* sameness, which assumes that both genders have the same goal in life: to produce bountiful rice harvests every year and to raise several healthy children to maturity. According to Helliwell, this striking principle in the Gerai approach to life, "the identity between men and women at the expense of radical difference," explains why this society is rape-free.

Helliwell then made an unusual comparison between the Gerai people and Western feminism. Whereas the Gerai people emphasize sameness and live in a rape-free society, Western feminists assume a notion of gender that differentiates between femininity and masculinity. This idea about gender differentiation is problematic, Helliwell suggested, because it perpetuates assumptions about women and men that foster rape. In fact, Helliwell even argued that the feminist acceptance of the Western view of "men's genitalia and sexuality as inherently brutalizing and penetrative and women's genitalia and sexuality as inherently vulnerable and subject to brutalization"[28] supports the very practice of rape that feminism seeks to end. In other words, Helliwell holds feminist theorists responsible for the prevalence of rape in Western societies.

This is a serious charge that requires closer scrutiny, which exposes three problems in Helliwell's position. First, Helliwell does not address the practical gender inequality among the Gerai people when she explains that the Gerai people do not apply the idea of gender sameness to *all* aspects of their society and sometimes differentiate between women and men. For instance, Helliwell observes that they attribute a "higher" position to men than to women in public decision-making processes, in which women have less authority than men. Hence, Gerai women often remain silent and defer to men in legal disputes and community functions.[29] The women seem not to question this unequal arrangement, although men also seem not to use their privileged position to dominate the women. But perhaps this tolerance of practiced inequality in the public realm indicates that the Gerai people have not yet had their "feminist revolution." Another Gerai practice seems indicative of this possibility. Gerai female and male work assignments follow gender-specific roles, but Helliwell does not consider what might happen if Gerai women refused being "responsible for rice selection and storage."[30] Would Gerai men accept changed role assignments? At least in light of Western gender dynamics, a positive response from the men seems unlikely.

Second, even if the principle of gender sameness prevents the occurrence of rape in Gerai society, Helliwell's advice that Western feminists relinquish "some of our most ingrained presumptions concerning differences between men and women"[31] is suspect, and predictably some feminists oppose it. Among them is the Native American and feminist writer Paula Gunn Allen, who rejects the very idea of gender sameness because, in her view, gender sameness prevents women from realizing a "sense of self as women and as individuals" within the "patriarchal social contract." Allen recommends an "uncompromising commitment to multiplicity, to the concept of difference."[32] In contrast to Helliwell, Allen sees a way out of "rape culture" only if we follow a "feminine" model, as suggested by Italian feminists or as traditionally practiced by the Laguan Pueblo. This model emphasizes difference between women and men with the goal of building a rape-free society. Allen explains:

> If we are willing to make our membership in our common womanity the centerpiece of our lives, if we are willing to face the judgment not only of other women but of Femininity's multiplicitous dimensions; if we take women as our models and female deities as our gods; if we are willing to make the principles of the ineffable Feminine our *modus vivendi* and our femininity our blazing signature while taking on the causes that are of urgent concern to women worldwide; if we will accept multiplicity, diversity, difference, and celebrate them . . . [violence against women will end.][33]

Third, Helliwell's position is problematic because of the different scale of the Gerai society and Western societies. Gerai society is so small that it does not seem convincing to take Gerai culture as a model for millions of Western people. Can a small community of seven hundred people seriously serve as a standard for Western societies? It is certainly appropriate to value the Gerai community as a rare case of a rape-free society, but the political, economic, and religious history and the social conditions of the Gerai people are so different from the West that a transfer of Gerai gender sameness seems awkward at the very least, if not improbable.

Still, it needs to be acknowledged that Helliwell does not disagree with the Western feminist agenda that rape is an important issue. In fact, Helliwell's study encourages the effort to understand the prevalence of rape without unduly generalizing about women or men whether they are of Gerai or Western origins. Similar to postmodern and other cross-cultural works, then, Oyewumi's and Helliwell's studies raise an important question: How can contemporary Western feminists talk about rape without disregarding women's diverse experiences? Linda Nicholson, a postmodern feminist, gives an answer that perhaps works best. She urges: "It is time that we [Westerners] explicitly acknowledge that our claims about women are not based on some given reality but emerge out of our own places within history and culture; they are political acts that reflect the contexts we emerge out of and the futures we would like to see."[34] Feminist discourse has to locate itself within the particularities of history and culture and to acknowledge its political nature. It needs to recognize, as feminist theorists assert, that rape is "culturally produced at *every level*."[35]

The issue of particularity and universality is not easily resolved. Many feminists, especially when they daily face the consequences of rape, view sexual violence as a universal phenomenon. The Women's Human Rights movement insists that human rights are women's rights, and so Julie Peters and Andrea Wolper, editors of *Women Rights— Human Rights: International Feminist Perspectives*, ask, "Does the right to preserve cultural and religious practices take precedence over human rights norms? If so, is the very concept of international (universal) rights inappropriate in a multicultural world in which values and practices differ from place to place?"[36] They maintain the need for universal norms when they suggest that "women worldwide can formulate norms" and simultaneously "allow for cultural multiplicity."[37] For Peters and Wolper, conversations among women organizers of different nationalities prove the urgency for international laws that prohibit violence against women everywhere.

Other feminist scholars propose that the problem be addressed on the level of international law. Rhonda Copelon, a professor at the City University of New York School of Law, supports international norms because of the persistence of rape in Western and non-Western wars during the twentieth century—wars that continue into the twenty-first century. In all of these wars, male soldiers raped women.[38] Even today, the practice of rape is pervasive in many places—in times of war and peace—and feminist work has shown that quick solutions are unavailable and international norms are much needed. In short, biological and societal explanations have proven to be unjustifiably general, and universalizing tendencies in Western feminist discourse often ignore particularities of time and place in women's experiences of rape. Perhaps one of the results of the discussion is that rape has to be theorized in the tension between particularity and universality and must be recognized as a considerable problem. That the Hebrew Bible includes numerous references to rape turns this body of literature into a promising resource for society and religion today.

Several Influential Feminist Studies on Rape in the Hebrew Bible

Feminist scholars discovered the prevalence of biblical rape texts and began publishing scholarly treatises on this topic from the 1970s onward. Some publications have enjoyed lasting impact, while others are significant mainly for their methodological sophistication or their success in communicating with audiences beyond academia. The following four pioneering publications illustrate the emerging discourse on rape in biblical studies; others will appear throughout the ensuing chapters of this book.

Phyllis Trible, *Texts of Terror*

The first scholarly publication that included several biblical rape texts from a feminist perspective is Phyllis Trible's *Texts of Terror: Literary-*

Feminist Readings of Biblical Narratives.[39] It includes the rape stories of Hagar (Genesis 16; 21), Tamar (2 Samuel 13), and the unnamed woman (Judges 19). Trible also discusses the tale about the murder of Jephthah's daughter (Judges 11), a horrific story but not about rape and thus not included here.

Other scholars appreciate that she broke the silence about these narratives. Jon D. Levenson, for instance, notes: "Phyllis Trible's . . . keen ear and her fine sense of narrative technique help her to shed a revealing light on . . . stories that . . . deserve more attention than they have received."[40] Trible uses rhetorical criticism to highlight the terror present in the narratives. About the rape of Hagar, an Egyptian slave woman, she writes: "All we who are heirs of Sarah and Abraham, by flesh and spirit, must answer for the terror in Hagar's story. To neglect the theological challenge she presents is to falsify faith." About Tamar, who is raped by her half-brother, Trible observes: "A woman of sorrows and acquainted with grief." About the gang-raped and unnamed woman, she laments: "The betrayal, rape, torture, murder, and dismemberment of an unnamed woman is a story we want to forget but are commanded to speak. . . . To take to heart this ancient story, then, is to confess its present reality. The story is alive, and all is not well."[41] The book reveals the extent of androcentric bias throughout the centuries that has marginalized these stories so completely in the Christian and Jewish imagination.

Renita J. Weems, *Battered Love*

Another important contribution to the burgeoning field of rape in sacred texts is Renita J. Weems's *Battered Love: Marriage, Sex, and Violence in the Hebrew Prophets*, published in 1995.[42] In four chapters, Weems examines prophetic texts that contain the so-called marriage metaphor. One chapter focuses on the marriage metaphors as speech about violence against women in Hosea, Jeremiah, and Ezekiel, and it also explores the literary context of such metaphoric speech in biblical prophecy. In another chapter, Weems hypothesizes about the social and historical context of marriage metaphors within ancient Israelite society, and in the third chapter she inquires what the metaphors reveal about God. A fourth and final chapter correlates prophetic rape texts with contemporary sensibilities and discusses how prophetic literature can be read as a spiritual and religious resource when the topic focuses on sexual violence against women.

Weems uses a pastoral tone as she guides readers through the plethora of terrifying biblical poetry. She shows that the prophets Hosea, Jeremiah, and Ezekiel employ the marriage metaphor to criticize ancient Israelite political, economic, and societal practices. Portraying Israel as a wife and God as a husband, the metaphor presents God as a punisher of the adulterous wife. The metaphors are composed from the husband's perspective and present him as justifiably threatening his wife with rape. Notions of hierarchy, power, and retribution characterize the metaphor, which, according to Weems, goes "terribly awry."[43] Weems also insists that readers need to distinguish between metaphor and God, and she warns not to adhere too quickly to the metaphor. Weems does not want readers to merge this image of God with the deity because the theo-political consequences would be horrendous. The metaphor depicts God only *like* a husband and not *as* a husband. If readers were to follow the metaphor that presents God *as* a husband and in this case as a *violent* and *raping* husband, they would accept, perhaps even promote, the justification of sexual violence. Yet Weems does not want readers to fall prey to these metaphors. She wants them to include women's experiences as alternative expressions for meaningful God-talk.

J. Cheryl Exum, *Fragmented Women*

Another important book that covers three biblical rape narratives appeared in 1993, *Fragmented Women: Feminist (Sub)versions of Biblical Narratives*, by feminist literary critic J. Cheryl Exum.[44] One of the chapters is entitled "Samson's Women." Among them is Delilah, who, according to Exum, "violated" Samson (Judges 16). Another chapter interprets the stories of "the endangered ancestress," also called "the wife-sister stories" (Genesis 12; 20; 26), and still another chapter reads the stories of Bathsheba and David (2 Samuel 11) and the nameless woman (Judges 19) as rape narratives. Other chapters elaborate on matriarchal figures in Genesis such as Sarah, Rebekah, Rachel, and Leah, but rape is not central in Exum's analysis. Exum also briefly mentions Dinah's story:

> Genesis 34. Dinah, "*the daughter of Leah*," is raped by Shechem when she goes out to visit the women of the land. The Shechemites make a treaty with Jacob, but two of Jacob's sons avenge the rape by killing the men of Shechem and plundering the city. (p. 102)

This short comment on Dinah is the sole mention of this narrative in Exum's study. Still, it is a telling and important mention, as Exum does not shy away from discussing rape as an issue in biblical literature and interpretation, especially when she writes:

> I am not dealing with real violence against women, but rather with violence against women as it takes place in biblical narrative. I take this violence seriously, though I do not take it literally, for like pornography—though not so blatantly—these literary rapes perpetuate ways of looking at women that encourage objectification and violence. . . . But like actual cases of rape, literary rape is difficult to prove. . . . Proving it depends upon taking the woman's word for it. And taking the woman's word for it is crucial for recovering women's experience in patriarchal literature.[45]

Jonathan Kirsch, *The Harlot by the Side of the Road*

Finally, the journalist and fiction writer Jonathan Kirsch published a book in 1997 that emphasizes the significance of rape in the Hebrew Bible. In *The Harlot by the Side of the Road: Forbidden Tales of the Bible*,[46] Kirsch focuses on three rape stories: the story of Lot's daughters (Genesis 19), Dinah (Genesis 34), and Tamar (2 Samuel 13). His goal is to familiarize readers with lesser-known Bible stories that are filled with violence, sex, and murder, and consequently are not often mentioned in synagogues and churches. In Kirsch's view, this situation should change, because "the Bible describes and even seems to encourage a range of human conduct that goes far beyond what is permitted in the Ten Commandments."[47] He opposes Jewish and Christian efforts of "cleaning up the Bible,"[48] and presents the "forbidden texts," including rape stories, to excavate "the traces of much older spiritual traditions that have been ignored or suppressed by all three faiths."[49] In these traces, Kirsch explains, appear daring, powerful, and resourceful women who "outshine even the venerable patriarchs and prophets."[50] These women are "intriguing remnants of forbidden spirituality" that included goddess worship and fertility rituals. Kirsch finds a "humane and compassionate message at the heart of the Bible,"[51] which he conveys to his readers in a journalistic tone.

Sometimes biblical scholars dispute whether the above-mentioned stories should be classified as rape texts.[52] Still, many agree that rape has become a prominent topic in biblical studies, since monographs and journal articles give ample witness to the undeniable presence of rape in biblical prose and poetry. This book brings the various scholarly discussions and biblical texts together and examines them as part of the long and diverse history of interpretation.

Toward a "Hermeneutics of Meaning"

Once readers recognize the difficulties involved in historiographical readings of the Hebrew Bible, they wonder how else to read this ancient body of literature. To such readers, the historiographical difficulties raise important hermeneutical questions about the purpose of the Hebrew Bible. How and why should it still be read and what are the benefits of reading it? Since not all interpretations are equally valid, the question is how to assess the merits of different interpretations. When interpreters come to see that they too are part of the meaning-making process, not distant and value-neutral observers, they learn to appreciate that authorial meaning is ultimately unknowable. Instead, text and readers are intrinsically linked.[53]

The hermeneutical insight that text and readers are intimately connected is significant, because Western society functions largely without the Hebrew Bible, attributing at best symbolic meaning to this body of literature. Moreover, many people do not even care for it. The late theologian and writer Dorothee Soelle was aware of this situation when she made an intriguing suggestion. She called for a "hermeneutics of hunger" and questioned the need for a "hermeneutics of suspicion."[54] She recognized that a hermeneutics of suspicion has enabled feminist theologians to criticize churches and synagogues for omitting, excluding, and marginalizing women from religious thought and practice. The hermeneutics of suspicion equipped feminist scholars to investigate biblical literature and the history of interpretation and to seek alternative biblical meanings.

Yet this deconstructive approach should not be the last step, Soelle asserted, and hence she wanted the hermeneutical project to move to the next level. She recognized that the hermeneutics of suspicion does not take into account the needs of the next generation, which lives outside institutionalized religion. People of this generation do not struggle with religious traditions, do not know its oppressive history anymore, and mostly live disconnected from religious institutions. To this generation, the purpose of and need for a hermeneutics of suspicion are unclear because religious doctrines have not thoroughly shaped their religious imagination and experience since childhood. Religion has played only a limited role in this generation's individual and collective lives. According to Soelle, then, this generation does not feel the urge to criticize Christian or Jewish traditions. The need to be liberated from religion is minimal, and instead people struggle to identify a spiritual home. Hence, Soelle suggested developing a "hermeneutics of hunger" that nurtures the spiritual hunger of this secularized Western generation.

Interestingly, religious activists of other religious traditions have proposed similar hermeneutical strategies for reading sacred texts. Already decades ago, Mohandas K. Gandhi wrote about his first encounter with the *Bhagavad Gita*: "Even in 1888–1889, when I first became acquainted with the Gita, I felt that it was not a historical work, but that under the guise of physical warfare it described the duel that perpetually went on in the hearts of mankind [*sic*], and that physical warfare was brought in merely to make the description of the internal duel more alluring."[55] Gandhi recognized that the sacred text of his religion refers to spiritual struggles apart from historical meaning. Perhaps the interpretation of biblical literature in Western societies of today would benefit from a hermeneutics that both deconstructs and constructs biblical meaning beyond the literalist-historical sense. If so, it might be worthwhile to supplement a hermeneutics of suspicion with Soelle's "hermeneutics of hunger" and what I want to call here a "hermeneutics of meaning." It might indeed help a secularized generation of Western people to gain a deepened understanding of the sociopolitical, religious, and cultural meanings of biblical rape texts in today's world, where rape occurs daily.

But I want to avoid misunderstandings. This hermeneutics of meaning is based on a feminist-critical hermeneutics that is grounded in a postmodern epistemology. It assumes that all interpretation is perspectival, particular, and sociopolitically located, never objective, universal, and value-neutral. My hermeneutical operations posit a strategic positivism, perhaps even a strategic essentialism, to combat scientific-empiricist epistemology, but the seemingly positivistic elements are strategic. My hermeneutical operations must be understood within a dominantly positivistic and modern paradigm. It is a problem of language that requires alternative interpretations to be articulated within the dominant language game currently available. If I want my work on biblical rape to be understood, I have no alternative but to present it within the rules of that game. Otherwise, few if any would accept the alternatives, which would be ignored or, worse, not even published. This is an old hermeneutical dilemma that the ancient Greeks already recognized.[56] In this sense, Todd Penner and Lilian Cates got it right when they explained, "Modern historical-critical scholarship, whether it seeks sources, literary and rhetorical structures, or the recovery of the repressed voice of the Other overrun by patriarchal ideology, frequently succumbs to a fundamental assertion of so many forms of analysis: the text's meaning is determinate and its ethic manifest."[57] This problem pertains also to postmodern scholarship.

The dilemma, then, is how to articulate alternatives. An "operative poetic-ethical framework that strains against the structure of textual determinacy"[58] seems a viable option because Penner and Cates's proposal to find pleasure in the textual indeterminacy does not go anywhere in our global rape culture. Their wish of "allowing the text of pleasure to operate on its own terms"[59] comes perhaps from an ultimate location of colonizing superiority and disembodiment. Thus, my hermeneutical stance assumes that as long as the materialistic conditions grounded in sociopolitical and theo-cultural structures of oppression and discrimination facilitate and tolerate rape on a global scale, androcentric patterns of sexual violence need to be deconstructed within the intersections of racism, classism, and other social categories. Under such materialistic conditions any classification of biblical rape texts as "blissful" is dangerous, leaving unchallenged rape-prone attitudes and allowing a pervasive silence about the pain of rape victim-survivors both inside and outside religious institutions and ideologies. Therefore, any seemingly essentialist positivistic rhetoric of this book is only a rhetorical strategy that counteracts, deconstructs, and reevaluates modern empiricist methodologies, hermeneutical assumptions, and the practice of objectifying and universalizing ethics of rape-prone stances. My goal is to provide readings of biblical rape texts that endorse a hermeneutics of meaning and present the Hebrew Bible as a "sacred witness" to rape in the lives of women, children, and men.

The Content of This Book

The chapters of this book examine rape stories and poems thematically. Each chapter deals with several rape texts and aligns them with a particular form of rape. So, for instance, one chapter deals with narratives on acquaintance rape, another with marital rape, and yet another with rape in war. The thematic rather than text-based organization of the book focuses the attention on the various kinds of rape and relates biblical literature to terminology familiar to contemporary readers. Since many readers know little about the Hebrew Bible, the thematic arrangement should help them to relate specific forms of rape with particular biblical texts and to remember the content of the stories and poems. For instance, few know the details of Genesis 34, but many know of acquaintance rape. Similarly, not everybody knows the stories in Judges 19–21, but most have heard of instances of rape in times of war and of peace. People have heard about marital and gang rape, and perhaps even about male-on-male rape, but they probably do not know biblical texts that relate to these topics. In short, the thematic approach assumes modest knowledge about the Hebrew Bible and begins with contemporary categories of rape.

It is important to acknowledge that the thematic approach is not based on a literalist correlation between biblical narratives and contemporary rape categories. The process of classifying a biblical text as "acquaintance rape" or "marital rape" requires imaginative work, as well as a solid knowledge of both the categories of rape and biblical literature. Sometimes the correlation seems immediately acceptable. For instance, the story of the concubine in Judges 19 is obviously about gang rape. In other cases, the categories are more difficult to establish because a text under consideration is not widely viewed as a rape story, as in the case of David and Bathsheba (2 Samuel 11). Other readers with other hermeneutical interests have argued for different interpretations, and this study alludes to many of them, but the focus will always be on rape.

The ambiguities of correlating contemporary categories of rape with biblical texts lead to another important point. Biblical Hebrew does not have a technical term for "rape," a linguistic situation that Hebrew shares with other languages. In Biblical Hebrew, the verb most frequently translated as "to rape" is the verb ענה, *'innâ*, but this verb may also refer to other forms of violence and oppression. For instance, in Exod 3:7, the word describes the oppression endured by the enslaved Israelites under Egyptian rulership ("I have observed the misery [ענה, *'nh*] of my people").[60] Erhard S. Gerstenberger explains that the verb describes "unjust situations," "the creation of a miserable situation," and "physical or psychological violence."[61] Others insist that the verb refers to consensual sexual intercourse. Consequently, scholars debate whether the verb should be translated as a reference to rape.[62] Sometimes the discussion about this term is heated and participants forget that, as inherently ambiguous literature, the Hebrew Bible demands an evaluative stance from readers. Interpreters generation after generation have faced the arduous task of deciding among apparently irresolvable multiple meanings of a biblical text. The very fact that Biblical Hebrew does not offer a specific term for rape makes the interpretive task a continuous challenge. This book aims to help this generation of readers in developing relevant biblical meaning for our time.

Yet all interpretations stand in a long tradition with, it is hoped, a long future ahead of them. Many hermeneutical goals have led, lead, and will lead to an even wider range of biblical meanings. This book aims to enhance contemporary understanding of rape, and so it reads the ancient texts alongside feminist perspectives on rape. It advances a literary-cultural approach and searches for meanings in biblical rape stories and poems as they seem appropriate in today's rape culture. The nature of Sacred Scripture allows—and in fact calls for—open-ended discourse. Textual multiplicity should therefore be understood as enrichment and not as distraction or contradiction to the interpretative endeavor. After all, the ongoing hermeneutical process ensures that biblical rape texts remain an indispensable resource, a sacred witness, in the enduring task of reflecting, seeking, and understanding the sociopolitical, religious, and cultural meanings of biblical literature.

1

BREAKING THE SILENCE
THE LEGACY OF ACQUAINTANCE RAPE

The Emerging Discourse of Acquaintance Rape

Acquaintance rape is a form of sexual violence that Western countries have come to recognize only since the 1980s. Feminist scholars and activists have played a major role in this development. Among them is Susan Estrich, whose book *Real Rape* examines the legal status of acquaintance rape in the United States.[1] Estrich, a professor of law, begins the book with her own story. In 1974, she, a white woman, was raped by a black man. The police officers believed her immediately when she reported that she had not known her rapist. Many years later, Estrich realized that "her" rape fit a popular cliché: rapists are strangers, often black, who attack white women on the street. Estrich's study shows that even today American laws favor situations of stranger or "real" rape in contrast to "simple" or acquaintance rape. The legal bias is similar to public opinion, she says. "Many women continue to believe that men can force you to have sex against your will and that it isn't rape so long as they know you and don't beat you nearly to death in the process. Many men continue to act as if they have that right."[2] In other words, acquaintance rape is still an underrated problem. Books such as Estrich's have brought attention to the prevalence of acquaintance rape in the Western world.

Another publication stresses that acquaintance rape is an actual *crime*. Robin Warshaw's *I Never Called It Rape* describes women who were raped by male acquaintances, and she also refers to her own experience of rape. She reports that in the early 1970s, she was raped by a man whom she knew. The man had coerced her into sexual intercourse, and she had succumbed to his threats. He raped her although she "never called it rape."[3] For many years, Warshaw did not regard

the event as rape and named it so only much later when she realized
that she was not the only woman who had undergone this experience.
As the women in Warshaw's book demonstrate, many female survivors
of sexual violence do not call it rape when a male acquaintance attacks
them. One of the interviewed women is Paula. She remembers the
evening when a male friend raped her:

> I thought how nice it would be to spend a platonic evening with
> a sympathetic ear. The first couple of hours were just that—good
> conversation, a wonderful meal, and a bottle of wine. He lived
> in a nice apartment with expensive furniture. After we finished
> eating, I felt ready to go. He pleaded with me to stay a bit lon-
> ger. . . . I remember saying, "No, no, no," and crying profusely.
> I remember feeling like it was never going to stop. . . . I was in
> denial and disbelief up to that point, but when it was over with,
> I was very much in shock and really quite unable to maneuver
> around much. . . . I remember somehow getting in my car, some-
> how driving home.[4]

Paula liked the man who had invited her into his apartment, and
the attack came unexpectedly. He forced her to have sex with him
against her will, and she remembers the confusion when she finally left
his apartment. Other women, too, remember such situations. Christine
Kim recalls how she reacted when her boyfriend raped her:

> I didn't tell anyone for two years that I was raped. I couldn't
> because not only did I not really know myself, but I felt ashamed
> and weak and stupid for what I felt was a foolish act on my part.
> I didn't want other people's pity or their disbelief. It was a secret
> that I kept inside me. I thought that it would go away if I forgot
> it, if I tried not to think about it. I didn't want anyone to know—
> not my family, not my friends, not anyone. If I told them, I would
> have to admit that it had actually happened.[5]

Christine was raped by her boyfriend but suppressed the memory. Like many women in her situation, she tried to forget what had

happened. It took feminist courage to name these situations as rape and to bring them into the open. When this was done, overwhelming data began to emerge. Sociologist James D. Brewer showed that seventy-six percent of victim-survivors know their attackers, leading him to say: "Wade out of the ankle-deep statistics and what you find is that we as a nation have a much bigger problem with acquaintance or nonstranger rape than we believed in the past."[6]

Despite these numbers, prejudices about women who are raped by a male acquaintance still prevail. Many women continue to be silent about such an experience because acquaintance rape is often not recognized as a sexually violent act. Many people believe that acquaintance rape is not rape because rapist and victim-survivor know each other and the couple may have had sexual relations prior to or even after the rape. This murky situation makes people unable to differentiate between acquaintance rape and consensual sex. Acquaintance rape also challenges deeply ingrained notions about rapists. People often believe that rapists are crazy, wild maniacs who attack women on the streets in the middle of the night. It seems difficult to accept that most rapists are ordinary men. They are brothers, sons, husbands, boyfriends, cousins, or fathers known and liked by family, friends, and coworkers. It is thus easier for people to blame a woman for her so-called provocative behavior, her lack of resistance, or her seductive outfits than to face the hostile aggression of ordinary men toward women in their lives.

Many people also distrust women who have had an active sex life prior to the rape. These people are inclined to blame the victim if she agreed to sexual intimacy before the rape, and they wonder why she went with him voluntarily. It is still expected that a woman sets the limits during sexual courting, and that she, not her male sexual partner, is responsible for upholding restrictions at all times. Many people still believe that the woman should have resisted more and been clearer that she wanted to stop. To those who think this way, the presence of sexual intercourse proves that the woman was "willing" and, as a result, is "untrustworthy."

Moreover, people do not recognize that violence is present when an acquaintance rapist relentlessly pressures a woman. Often he merely uses threats and other forms of severe pressure; frequently he manipulates her into "consent" with alcohol or drugs, or tricks her into his apartment. People ignore the fact that the woman may have had little experience, does not dare to resist, or feels that he will not stop or listen to her. Unfortunately, many people do not see threats, alcohol, or psychological pressure as problems and instead blame the woman. They disregard that she acquiesces only temporarily, perhaps exhausted by the pressure.

Finally, people are often confused about acquaintance rape because the woman herself is often unclear about the nature of the sexual intercourse. She knows him; perhaps he is a friend of a friend, a date, or, even her boyfriend. Afraid of being disbelieved, she decides not to tell anybody and to forget the moment when she lost control. Usually she continues her life without proper support, and others will never know that she survived a rape by a man whom they all know. Acquaintance rape is thus a form of rape that is not easily recognized even by the participants themselves, much less by outsiders.

Acquaintance Rape in the Hebrew Bible

Biblical Hebrew does not have a term for "acquaintance rape." After all, the term is fairly new even in English. Some scholars find it anachronistic to describe biblical texts with terminology of our time, especially when it involves such charged terms as "acquaintance rape." While the application of modern terminology emerges from contemporary sensibilities, there is no other way of reading biblical rape texts. Though some interpreters say otherwise, we always read from a particular social location, with particular interpretive interests, and within a particular conceptual framework. The scholarly community acknowledges the contextual character of the meaning-making process. Yet when this notion is applied to specific texts and issues, many people—lay and scholarly—often become nervous, worrying that the biblical meaning is lost or skewed, or that "anything goes." Far from it. A basic hermeneutical insight remains that a reader's interpretive interests shape biblical meanings.

When the perspective turns to acquaintance rape, the Hebrew Bible becomes a resource—containing four stories of threatened and completed acquaintance rape. They are the narratives about Dinah (Genesis 34) and Tamar (2 Samuel 13), a brief reference to Abishag the Shunammite (1 Kgs 1:1-4), and the story of Susanna (Daniel 13). The four stories illustrate important characteristics of this form of sexual violence: Dinah, Tamar, Abishag, and Susanna are attacked or threatened by men whom they know. Neither Shechem nor Tamar's half-brother Amnon, neither King David nor the two elders are strangers attacking random women. They live in the neighborhood or even in the same home. Moreover, two of the women do not speak a single word. Neither Dinah nor Abishag is reported to speak during the attack. They do not share their distress with others, nor do they explicitly consent. Dinah's silence has allowed interpreters to imagine that she consented. While the opposite is more likely, it is rarely mentioned in the commentary literature. Abishag is forced to be a servant of the king and has to acquiesce to her fate because he is the king. In contrast to Dinah and Abishag, Tamar and Susanna resist vehemently, both verbally and physically. Only the story of Tamar is widely known as a rape story, perhaps because this woman's articulate resistance demonstrates even to the most androcentric interpreters that she does not agree to intercourse with her brother. She even proposes marriage as a way out of the pressured situation. The same cannot be said about Susanna. Despite her outspoken resistance, many interpreters believe she was threatened with seduction, and they stress her piety and virtue. Focusing on the legal procedures and Daniel's accomplishment, they often mention the attack in a hushed voice.

These stories display prominent characteristics of acquaintance rape, but interpreters rarely name the issue at hand. Perhaps this neglect relates to the fact that none of the women is physically injured. Moreover, some of the women seemingly gain social status, such as Abishag, who lives with the king in the palace. If a woman is threatened with physical harm, she is still blamed for placing herself into a dangerous situation, as in the case of Susanna. Consciously or unconsciously, countless interpreters do not find the situations of these women precarious and overlook the rape. It remains buried, submerged, silenced.

Is it simply a dispute over terminology that defines stories on heterosexual intercourse as stories on acquaintance rape? Perhaps, but the issue is ultimately much more serious. When we begin to read the narratives with terminology meaningful to us today, they inform our understanding about a prevalent contemporary problem. The narratives can then turn into resources that help us develop a deepened understanding about rape and the sociopolitical, historical, and cultural responses to this problem. For centuries, biblical imagery has provided a basis to locate oneself in society. By defining these texts as stories of acquaintance rape, we are encouraged to develop this skill and to read these stories in relation to our world, pondering questions such as these: How do we define sexual consent? When do we identify a man as a rapist? What are our standards for "real" rape, and where do these standards come from? When we begin to interpret biblical texts with such questions in mind, the Hebrew Bible is no longer a dusty and ancient book of the past but a resource for understanding past and present culture.

Seduction, Love, and Marriage? The Rape of Dinah

When Dinah, the daughter of Leah and Jacob, goes out to visit women in her neighborhood, she is raped by Shechem, the prince of the land. Desiring her after the rape, Shechem abducts Dinah and asks his father, Hamor, to assist him with his plan to marry her. In the meantime, Dinah's father, Jacob, and her brothers hear about the rape. The brothers react strongly. When Shechem and Hamor negotiate the marriage, the brothers request that all the Canaanite males in town be circumcised. While the men lie in pain after the circumcision, Dinah's brothers attack the city and kill all the males, including Shechem and Hamor, and they abduct the women and children of the city. When Jacob hears about these actions, he condemns his sons. They ask in return if their sister should be treated like a prostitute, and with this question the story ends.

The story of Dinah (Genesis 34) is one of the most contested rape stories in the Hebrew Bible. During its extensive history of interpretation, Jewish and Christian interpreters mainly ignored Dinah. They focused on the men, investigated the literary-historical composition or tribal connotations, searched for anthropological comparisons, and viewed the first verses—the report of the rape—as a description of Shechem's seductive behavior.[7] In many interpretations, the fraternal killing is the criminal moment, and in more recent years scholars have argued explicitly against the possibility that Shechem rapes Dinah. They maintain that Shechem's love and marriage proposal do not match the "scientifically documented behavior of a rapist"[8] and that therefore he should not be reduced to one. For instance, Tikva Frymer-Kensky claims, "Shechem never intended any harm"[9] but simply ignored the custom of his day, which required him to get legal consent from Dinah's parents before the intercourse. Frymer-Kensky explains that Dinah's opinion would not have counted because in ancient Israel, unmarried women and girls did not have the right of consent. In her view, therefore, rape is not the point for the ancient storytellers, but "the question of honor and self-defense in high drama."[10]

Another scholar, Lyn M. Bechtel, endorses this position with support from anthropological studies.[11] She reasons that individuals of ancient Israelite society lived and worked to serve the good of the larger group. In such a society, sexual intercourse perpetuated the values of the family or the clan and became shameful only when it lacked family or community approval. This is the problem in Genesis 34, because Dinah and Shechem have sexual intercourse as "two unbonded people."[12] The issue is not whether rape occurred but whether this group-oriented society considered the sexual intercourse to be "shameful." Since Shechem tried to repair the social bond, proposing marriage and offering many goods, his "overall action . . . is one of honor" and "there is no indication that Dinah is raped. The description of Shechem's behavior and attitude does not fit that of a rapist."[13] Consequently, rape is not the issue in the narrative, Bechtel asserts, but whether or not outsiders are allowed to join the group. Many other scholarly interpretations have emerged, but none considers Genesis 34 as a story about acquaintance rape.[14]

There are, however, three rhetorical strategies that support reading Genesis 34 as a rape story. One strategy emphasizes two

literary features that center on Dinah. One such feature is the speech
of Dinah's brothers that is located in the very middle of seven
speeches:

1. Son Shechem's Speech (v. 4)
2. Father Hamor's Speech (vv. 8-10)
3. Son Shechem's Speech (vv. 11-12)
4. Sons of Jacob's Speech (vv. 14-17)
5. Son Shechem, father Hamor's Speech (vv. 21-23)
6. Father Jacob's Speech (v. 30)
7. Sons of Jacob's Speech (v. 31)

By form, the brothers' speech is the central oration of the seven.
By content, this speech centers on Dinah because it begins and ends
with references to her. In fact, Dinah's trouble is the reason for the
fraternal discourse, so the central placement of the brothers' speech
and their advocacy on behalf of their sister keep the woman central
in the narrative. She and the rape are the reason for all the events of
Genesis 34.

Another literary feature of the first rhetorical strategy underlines
the centrality of Dinah. Although the woman never speaks, the narrative mentions her persistently. In vv. 1-3, every sentence refers to
her, once as the subject (v. 1) and eight times as the object (v. 2a; vv.
2b-3). Thereafter, she appears numerous times: Shechem calls her
"his young woman" (v. 4). She is Dinah, his "daughter" (v. 5) and the
"daughter of Jacob" (vv. 7, 19; cf. v. 3). Hamor mentions her as "your
[plural] daughter" and "her" (v. 8); Jacob is "her father" (v. 11). The
brothers are "her" brothers (v. 11). She is a "young woman" (v. 12),
"Dinah, their sister" (vv. 13, 27); "our sister" (vv. 14, 31) and "our
daughter" (v. 17). Her brothers are "the brothers of Dinah" (v. 25),
and she is simply "Dinah" (v. 26). Every character refers to Dinah
in almost every verse, although only the narrator uses her name. In
short, Dinah is the focus throughout the narrative although she never
speaks. As part of the first rhetorical strategy, the two literary features
make Dinah the center of the story. Her fate is crucial to this story of
acquaintance rape.

A second strategy suggests that rape is at the heart of Genesis 34. The story begins with the rape scene in vv. 2b-3, in which Shechem is always the grammatical subject and Dinah the object. The whole unit stresses his position of power over Dinah. The first three verbs report the rape, the last three its immediate ramification, as the following analysis demonstrates.

The Rape (v. 2)
And he took her,
and he laid her,
and he raped her.

The Immediate Ramifications (v. 3)
And he stayed with/kept Dinah, the daughter of Jacob,
and he lusted after the young woman,
and he tried to quiet the young woman.

The three sentences of v. 2 express a single action, that of rape, and simultaneously the progressive severity of the violence. Whereas the first verb means "to take," the second verb presents an interesting twist. In Hebrew, the verb "to sleep" is connected not with the expected preposition "with" but with an object marker, a characteristic feature of Biblical Hebrew that is untranslatable into English. The object marker underlines that Dinah is the *object* of the activity. In other words, Shechem does not lie "with" Dinah as if she willingly consented to the activity. Rather, he is the *subject* and she the *object* whose consent is irrelevant. Thus, the best translation of the verb is, "Shechem laid her." The meaning of the third verb, "to rape," is also contested, and so some scholars claim that the verb does not mean "to rape" but only "to have sex."[15] An examination of classical dictionaries confirms that such a translation misses the point and that the verb signifies an act of violence. The dictionaries present the verb's meaning as "to humble, mishandle, afflict," or even "to weaken a woman, through rape."[16] The verb describes a form of violent interaction including rape. "He raped her" is the appropriate translation.

Often scholarly interpretations avoid this translation of v. 2 because of the next verse. They claim that v. 3 describes Shechem's love for Dinah. It is important, however, to read slowly and carefully. Shechem rapes her first and then supposedly claims "love." But how is this possible? It seems highly unlikely that a man rapes a woman and then immediately loves her. But even if he makes such a claim, what kind of love follows after rape? Many readers are ready to imagine that Shechem's "passion" for Dinah takes over and leads, perhaps mistakenly, to too much force. This is a standard prejudice in acquaintance rape that disregards the severity of the violating act. An alternative translation interprets v. 3 in light of v. 2 and rejects the notion that v. 3 expresses Shechem's deeply felt care for Dinah.

So let us examine the meaning of v. 3. The first verb is often translated as "to love," but it might, in fact, be better interpreted as an expression of spatial closeness. For example, Ruth 1:14 states that Ruth and Naomi stayed together while the other daughter-in-law went to her home country. The translation of the RSV is: "But Ruth clung to her," and the *Jerusalem Bible* translates the verse even more clearly as a reference to spatial relation: "Ruth stayed with Naomi." The same verb appears also in Ruth 2:23, which, according to the RSV, means: "So she kept close to the young women of Boaz." In Ps 101:3, the verb describes the spatial distance between the lover and the hater of God. According to A. A. Anderson, the verb denotes "to keep close to someone,"[17] and consequently Anderson translates Ps 101:3: "It shall not cleave to me" or "he shall not remain close to me."[18] Lastly, the verb appears in Num 36:7, 9. The NRSV translates Num 36:7 as, "For all Israelites shall retain the inheritance of their ancestral tribes," and Num 36:9 as, "For each of the tribes of the Israelites shall retain its own inheritance." Even Wilhelm Gesenius, the renowned grammarian of biblical Hebrew, translates this verb as "to keep something (possession)."[19] In other words, the verb signifies physical and spatial but not emotional closeness, sometimes in the sense of possessing a thing. Consequently, the translation of the verb as "to love" is entirely inadequate. A better translation emphasizes spatial closeness: "Shechem stayed with Dinah" or "Shechem kept Dinah," in the sense of not allowing her to leave.

In the context of rape, the meaning of the second verb has also nothing to do with love. This verb is better understood as a reference to Shechem's desire to treat Dinah as he pleases. Two observations support such a translation: First, as G. Wallis explains: "The terminological context for to love/love is very wide in the language of the Old Testament." Since "love and action are two sides of the same coin," Wallis emphasizes that concrete action fills the meaning of "love."[20] When this insight is applied to Gen. 34:3, it becomes clear that Shechem wants to have sex with Dinah, even against her will, and so the rape is the concrete action that gives meaning to v. 3. Accordingly, love is *not* the meaning, but rather control, force, and violation. Second, according to Phyllis Trible's interpretation of 2 Samuel 13, where the same verb appears, love does not describe Amnon's feelings for Tamar, but rather the "ambiguous word 'to desire', to let the plot disclose the precise meaning."[21] This insight works for the verb in Gen 34:3. In v. 2, the plot discloses what Shechem actually *does* to Dinah. Consequently, the meaning of the verb in v. 3 refers not to mutual intimacy or loving tenderness but to violent "desire" that makes Dinah the object of Shechem's action. As Amnon lusts after Tamar before he rapes her, so Shechem rapes Dinah before he is lusting for more. The second verb of v. 3 does not describe romantic love; rather, it is an expression for Shechem's unrelenting objectification of Dinah. He continues to exert his will for sex over Dinah, and so this part of v. 3 is better read: "And he lusted after the young woman."

The third verb in v. 3 has also contributed to wide confusion about Shechem's feelings for Dinah. The verb appears in a phrase that literally means "to speak to someone's heart." Many interpreters translate the phrase as "he spoke tenderly to her" (NRSV). Yet Georg Fischer notes that the phrase always appears[22] when "the situation is wrong, difficult, or danger is in the air."[23] He argues that the verb has to be translated in the sense of "to try to talk against a negative opinion" or "to change a person's mind."[24] Someone speaks to the "heart" of a fearful person in the effort to resolve a frightening situation in a larger context of fear, anxiety, sin, or offense; someone tries to "talk against a prevailing (negative) opinion." When this meaning is applied to v. 3, the phrase depicts Shechem's attempt to change

Dinah's negative opinion about him and to calm her after the rape. The appropriate translation is: "He tried to quiet down the young woman." In short, vv. 2-3 describe Shechem's disregard for Dinah. Shechem dominates Dinah and turns her from subject to object. Not speaking, Dinah is present only in silence and submission. Verse 3 depicts the continuation of Shechem's domination as he attempts to hide his violent deed.

Related to these textual observations is a third rhetorical strategy that turns Genesis 34 into a story about acquaintance rape. Feminist scholars have shown that acquaintance rapists often try to appear "normal" after the rape and pretend that nothing bad really happened. Although they might threaten and overpower the woman, they are less likely to resort to murder or physical beating than stranger rapists. The problem of acquaintance rapists is that they view women as objects with whom they can do as they please. Such a rapist knows that he has taken advantage of a woman and might attempt to contact her again after the rape, pretending to be friends.[25] Shechem can be viewed as such a "sexual gratification rapist," who considers Dinah an "opportunity" when he sees her walking by. Perhaps he met Dinah earlier when her family moved to the new area and Shechem's father, Hamor, allowed the strangers to live there. Read accordingly, Genesis 34 describes a classic situation of acquaintance rape, but one with rare consequences. After all, Dinah's brothers kill the rapist and all the town's male inhabitants. Some interpreters stress that the brothers violate the Shechemite women when they force them out of their city, and so the brothers participate in male aggression and the oppression of women. Genesis 34 is indeed a complicated story, but it centers on Dinah and the acquaintance rape.

Stupid or Cupid? The Incestuous Rape of Tamar

In 2 Samuel 13, another narrative of acquaintance rape—this one incestuous—Amnon, the firstborn son of King David, lusts after Tamar. He is the son of David and she is David's daughter, but they have different mothers. One day, Amnon's friend Jonadab notices a change in Amnon, who, upon Jonadab's perceptive inquiry, explains that he "loves" Tamar. The two men devise a plot to trick Tamar into visiting Amnon. He pretends to be ill and asks his father to call Tamar to bring food. David complies. When Tamar arrives, Amnon sends everybody away so that the sister finds herself suddenly alone with her older half-brother. When he tries to pull her to his bed, she resists and tells him to wait and marry her first. Amnon, however, does not listen and proceeds to rape her. Afterwards, he begins to hate her and sends her away despite her intense plea. Tamar runs to her full brother, Absalom, who tells her to stay silent. Tamar, however, tears her clothing and wails loudly. When Tamar's father hears about the rape, he is angry but does not punish his son "because he loved him, for he was his firstborn" (13:21). After two years, Absalom takes revenge. Absalom tricks his half-brother into visiting far away from the palace, and then he kills Amnon. Tamar, so the story goes, never marries and for the rest of her life remains "a desolate woman in her brother Absalom's house" (13:20).

If there is a quintessential rape story in the Hebrew Bible, it is the story of Tamar. Scholars regularly recognize the sexual violence perpetrated by Amnon on his half-sister and call 2 Samuel 13 one of the "most-shocking" and "most sordid" biblical stories.[26] Many interpreters make a point of rejecting the brutality with which Amnon subdues his sister. For instance, Bruce C. Birch states, "The story reports in graphic detail Amnon's plot to get Tamar alone, his violent rape of her, and his callous discarding of her afterward."[27] Others signal that Amnon's love was "hardly more than lust" because they recognize the incompatibility of love and rape.[28] Fokkelien van Dijk-Hemmes, a noted feminist interpreter, affirms: "The rapist is guilty. In the reception of the text, so far as I can ascertain, this has never been disputed."[29]

Yet Pamela Tamarkin Reis does exactly that. In her view, Amnon is not guilty of rape because it is really Tamar who initiates and invites the "sexual intimacy . . . by her easy virtue, persistent ambition, and implacable stupidity."[30] Indeed, for Reis, Tamar is a willing partner in an incestuous relationship with her half-brother. Accordingly, the story does not depict incestuous acquaintance rape but consensual incest, if, according to Reis's stipulation, one emphasizes three features. First, one has to recognize Amnon's ambivalent feelings toward Tamar in the early part of the story. For example, his slip of tongue in v. 2 indicates that Amnon seeks both permission and prohibition to meet his half-sister. Amnon is not certain whether he should see her, but David, his father, ignores the hint and orders Tamar to bake a cake and bring it to her brother. In contrast, Tamar is immediately willing to do so. She prepares the cake in the shape of hearts which, to Reis, demonstrates her interest in Amnon.

Second, Reis underscores that Tamar does not leave the room with everybody else although she could have left (v. 9). In fact, Tamar not only remains alone with Amnon but, upon his invitation, volunteers to come close to his bed. This gesture makes Tamar complicit "in the coming denouement," Reis believes. When Amnon says, "Come," he gives Tamar an opportunity to respond negatively because the command implies mutuality. Yet Tamar accepts Amnon's invitation, approaches his bed, and is glad "to flirt, to arouse Amnon's desire with libidinous confections, and to be alone with him after the servants depart." This proves to Reis that Tamar consents to sexual relations and is to blame for the rape.

Third, Reis posits that Tamar resists only when she realizes how far Amnon wants to go. Initially, Tamar does not reject Amnon's offer but urges him to marry her first. When Tamar's suggestion falls on deaf ears, she "surrenders to him." It changes his love to hate. Amnon hates Tamar because she is not as "pure" as he thought, which Reis affirms. Tamar flirts with her half-brother and "submits to intercourse without attempting to call out." For Reis, this view explains "why a savaged woman is so determined to remain in the presence of her attacker." Tamar could have left but chooses to stay because she is interested in Amnon. In general, then, Reis rejects the "rape verdict" because of "the tell-tale verdict, Tamar's willingness to be alone with a man, and her failure to call out." Moreover, Tamar's acquiescence to Amnon's "immoral entreaty" reflects David's "own prohibited carnality." In this reading, Tamar, not Amnon, is held responsible, as her behavior mirrors her father's misconduct. Like him, Tamar is an active and willing participant in immoral behavior, Reis contends.

Reis's interpretation deserves this lengthy summary for one reason. Her claim that Tamar is a willing participant in the sexual encounter reinforces standard prejudices about acquaintance rape, and so her reading unintentionally confirms that 2 Samuel 13 is a story about acquaintance rape. For Reis, Tamar and Amnon know and like each other, which makes Tamar responsible for the sexual intercourse. Reis emphasizes that Tamar consents to prepare food and to visit her brother; her willingness indicates her consent. Typical for many situations of acquaintance rape, Tamar agrees to some form of intimacy, but her agreement does not include sexual intercourse. Hence, Tamar should not be held responsible for the sexual encounter, and Reis's blaming of Tamar reinforces androcentric stereotypes. It diminishes Tamar's right to say no at any moment in the sexual encounter regardless of her closeness to Amnon. Reis also ignores that Amnon needs to respect Tamar's vocal opposition and to let her go at any point.

Reis thus reinforces the classic androcentric pattern that blames a woman for the rape. This interpretation is particularly pernicious because it seems to support Tamar's agency. Reis characterizes Tamar as consenting to sexual relations with her half-brother and as in charge of her desire when she allegedly invites incestuous sex. Here is a woman, Reis explains, who, as popular parlance would term it, "wants it." As a result, Reis holds Tamar responsible when the situation becomes difficult for her. An obvious rape story turns into a story of consensual sex, and the woman's agency is turned against her as she is accused of misleading the man. In short, Reis uses the very concept of "woman's agency," a feminist idea, to hold Tamar accountable for the rape. As the agent of her desire, Tamar is charged with having invited the rape.

Despite this androcentric argumentation, Reis makes an important observation about the nature of this acquaintance rape. She highlights its incestuous nature, stressing that Tamar and Amnon knew each other as half-siblings. This observation helps in making the case for acquaintance rape in 2 Samuel 13. Tamar does not expect Amnon's advances to turn into rape because she has known him for years and trusts him. Even Tamar's initial affection for Amnon makes sense in the context of acquaintance rape. She likes Amnon and can even imagine marrying him. She is not worried about staying alone with him and is neither stupid nor "cupid," but trusting and unsuspecting of her half-brother. In contrast, Amnon exploits the situation and is the guilty party.

While Reis's interpretation, if read against the grain, illustrates that 2 Samuel 13 is a story about acquaintance rape, the narrative does not portray Amnon as a typical acquaintance rapist. In this reading, Amnon does not try to make up but reportedly hates Tamar after the rape. His change of mind from so-called love to hate catches the attention of many commentators. For example, Walter Brueggeman believes that Amnon's hate indicates awareness of his deed.[31] Other interpreters argue that his hate shows that "[h]e was through with her."[32] To many, Amnon's hate proves that his so-called love is only "lust." Amnon gets rid of Tamar because she reminds him of his lack of control. One of the few interpreters who sympathizes with Amnon is Reis. She suggests that his hate is rooted in "a sort of heightened post-coital *tristesse* or prejudice" after he recognizes "their mutual guilt in the crime of incest." Reis understands that Amnon feels resentful for "Tamar's apparent insensibility to the transgression."

Yet could it be that the reference to Amnon's hate illustrates a negative attitude toward women in general and the raped woman in particular?[33] For acquaintance rapists, women are objects to be used according to their needs and desires. Love is not the issue because well-being and care for the beloved person do not inform the action. Viewed in this way, Amnon is selfish and deceiving, trying to get what he wants. In this sense, the description of Amnon's feelings of hate reflect an internal attitude of men who rape women they know. Thus, Tamar should not be blamed for Amnon's hate. It is Amnon *alone* who is responsible for raping a woman who trusts and likes him while he objectifies and violates her. Amnon is the culprit of the rape, and the story imagines sadly that Tamar never recovered from the assault.

Vital Warmth? The Failed Rape of Abishag the Shunammite

Yet another fragmentary story fits the category of acquaintance rape, although issues of power and class contribute to the sexual exploitation it portrays. The story of the young woman Abishag the Shunammite is only four verses long (1 Kgs 1:1-4). In this brief account, King David is old and bedridden when court personnel search for a young woman to warm him and to sleep at his "bosom." The personnel choose beautiful Abishag the Shunammite, who is eventually brought to the king. "The young woman was very beautiful. She became the king's *sōkenet* (סכנת) and she served him. Yet the king did not know her" (v. 4). It is obvious that this short story does not portray acquaintance rape as classically defined by contemporary feminist research. David does not meet Abishag on a date and subsequently take her to his palace. Instead, he is old and bedridden, and his court personnel bring her to him. He is the king and she his servant, and as such they meet. She is made to lie in his bed, but he does not have sex with her. He is old or sick but still Abishag has to sleep in the king's bed. Arguably, he is not a stranger but a powerful man whom she knows as his subject. Possibly, therefore, the story depicts a failed rape of a man who cannot take advantage of his position of power over a woman who is expected to "warm" him back to life.

The question, of course, is why Abishag moves into the king's palace since it is hard to believe that she goes voluntarily or happily. Does her family or her parents sell her to the royal personnel who search all of Israel for a young woman? Does she accept money for her services in order to support her perhaps impoverished family? Does she hope to live in luxury at the palace and to leave poverty behind? The gap between v. 3 and v. 4 leaves considerable room for interpretative conjecture. What seems certain is that Abishag winds up in the palace serving the ailing king. Whether her family's economic status or royal authority make her consent, Abishag has little choice. Circumstances force her to acquiesce, and that is, after all, a typical characteristic of acquaintance rape.

It is not surprising that this brief story has received only modest treatment in the exegetical literature. Even commentators who discuss every verse and chapter consider the circumstances in vv. 1-4 to be "trivial" and undeserving of detailed explanation.[34] To many, Abishag is only an "agent," less than a minor character, a prop lacking interpretative significance.[35] Some commentators express puzzlement about

Abishag's role as the king's servant. She is characterized as *sōkenet* (סכנת) of the king, a term of unclear meaning that appears only once in the entire biblical canon. In 1914, A. B. Ehrlich wrote that the meaning of this feminine participle is unknown, but this has not stopped commentators from speculating. Suggested renderings range from "nurse" or "attendant" to "a high position at court." The latter translation is based on ancient Near Eastern texts that contain the male noun of *sōkenet* (Hebrew *sōkēn* (סכן); Ugaritic *sakkinu*; Akkadian *šakēnu*) with the meaning of "governor" or "high official." To some interpreters, therefore, the noun *sōkenet* (סכנת) describes Abishag's superior position at the royal court, and indicates that she supersedes Queen Bathsheba in all royal rights and duties.[36] Others reject this possibility because "her duties were confined to nursing the failing king."[37] In the end, the term *sōkenet* (סכנת) remains ambiguous, especially in light of phrases such as "to keep him warm," "to lie in his bosom," and "to know her." Even if Abishag's status increases as David's *sōkenet* (סכנת), her job forces her to be "his bedfellow;"[38] but "the decrepit state of David's age"[39] removes the potential for acquaintance rape.

Rapish Desire? The Resisted Rape of Susanna

Finally, the story of Susanna, as told in the book of Daniel the Septuagint, reports an attempted acquaintance rape. This chapter is part of the Catholic canon but is not included in the Protestant and Jewish canons. Nevertheless, the story has enjoyed a rich history of transmission and interpretation. The version of Theodotion, a Jewish translator of the second century C.E., has become the standard basis for vernacular translations of the story on Susanna. The following summary relies on it.

Susanna, who is the daughter of pious parents and the wife of a wealthy man named Joakim, decides to take a bath as refreshment on a hot summer day. She does not know that two men who serve as judges and frequently visit her powerful husband have begun to be sexually interested in her. Initially unbeknownst to each other, the two men "divert their eyes from heaven" and instead watch the woman whenever they visit the house of Susanna and Joakim. During one of their many attempts to spy on her, they discover each other. They confess their interest in Susanna and plot to attack her the next time she is alone.

Since Susanna is a wealthy woman, she has two female servants who prepare the bath in the garden. When the bath is ready, the women leave. The two judges are hiding all the while and, once Susanna is alone, they jump in front of her. They demand to have sex with her, otherwise threatening to announce that she has committed adultery with a young man. She, however, responds: "I am hemmed in on all sides. For if I do this thing, it is my death, and if I do not do it, I will not escape your hands. I must choose not to do it and fall into your hands rather than sin before God" (13:22-23). Then she cries out. When the people arrive, the judges accuse her of adultery and Susanna is sentenced to death. Sending only a prayer to God for help, she does not defend herself nor is she invited to do so. Yet God hears her prayer and sends Daniel, a young man, to question the procedure of the trial. He interrogates the judges separately and manages to uncover discrepancies in their reports. Exposed as false witnesses, the men are condemned to death. Susanna is released and praised for her virtue and innocence.

Besides the version of Theodotion recounted above, there are a number of other extant versions of the story. Another Greek version, called the "Old Greek," probably predates Theodotion.[40] There is also a Samaritan parallel in Arabic entitled "The Story of the Daughter of Amram."[41] The story appears in the Babylonian Talmud, and another Jewish version is contained in the fifteenth-century book called *Sefer Yuhassin*, written by Abraham ben Samuel Zacuto. A variation called "The Pious Israelite Woman and the Two Evil Elders" is part of the famous collection of Arabic stories in "The Thousand and One Nights."[42] Other, less well-known translations are in Syriac, and Origen's "Letter to Africanus" refers to the Susanna story.[43] All of these texts offer fascinating renditions of the basic story line, but the Samaritan version in Arabic exhibits the most dramatic modifications.

In the Samaritan version, Susanna has no name and is mentioned only as the "daughter of Amram," a high priest. Amram's daughter (in other versions called Susanna) is beautiful and "a mistress of wisdom and knowledge, walking in the way of righteousness and all the manner of her deeds were good."[44] Unlike the woman in the Greek versions, who is portrayed as the wife of a wealthy man, she is a single woman with a most remarkable interest; she wants to study Bible. The story reports: "That young woman from her early infancy wished to study the Torah and to keep the Law, and to read in it. And she wrote one with her own hand. And there was no one in her time who could be compared unto her." A Bible expert, Amram's daughter is the only woman mentioned in apocryphal literature who is acknowledged and respected for such expertise, and there is no negative or judgmental comment about her status as a Bible student and teacher. The Samaritan version presents this woman as equal to men, which is indeed a remarkable characteristic. After the extraordinary revelation about the young woman's work, the Samaritan version reports that Amram's daughter wants to become a hermit (nazirite) on the mountain. Her father gives permission for one year and builds her a house in the area where two other hermits live. When the two men hear that the daughter of Amram has joined them on the mountain, they ask her to teach them Torah. "So she came out and went up to her roof and she took with her the Scroll of the Law written by her own hand." At the teaching session, the two hermits "become wanton" for her, forgetting God and their monastic vows. They disclose to each other "the secret of their thought as to her beautiful looks, and they agreed that they would ask her to show them the Scroll of the Law so as to look into it." When Amram's daughter arrives with her Torah scroll the next time, they tell her "the secret thing." And the story continues:

> And the young woman started reproving them with strong reproof, and reminded them of all what God commanded, but they did not hearken unto her. And when she saw their violence she said unto them, "Ye wish to do this evil deed." And they said, "Yes we wish to do it and if it will not be with thy good will, it will be against thy will." And she said, "I listen and I will do, but leave me until I will get into my house, and I will change my garments and anoint myself and put on other garments better than these, and then you may do with me as is pleasing in your sight." And

she revealed unto them that it was her desire more than theirs to do this thing. And it came to pass when they saw it was her will to do this thing, then their joy grew great, and they said unto her, "Pass on and change thy garments and anoint thyself and come unto us." And then she passed on to her house, and she locked the door, and she set herself down behind it and she opened the Scroll of the Law, and she disheveled her head. And she lifted up her hands to heaven and she said, "O God, thou who hast forbidden the committing of any evil deed, of all abominations, and of all wickedness. And I am of the seed of Pinehas, the man of zeal, and I have no redeemer who is to redeem me of these two men, and no saviour who is to save me from the evil deed of these two men, who desire to do the evil deed before thee, O God. My hope is in thee, and I have no one besides thee, O God. And for thy help I hope that thou wilt save me from the hand of thy enemies and thou wilt not grant them power over me and remove their wickedness from me. . . ." And the young woman fell upon her face and prayed and cried all through the length of the night.

The two men pretend to want to learn from Amram's daughter and then try to attack her sexually. She, however, tricks them into believing she will comply and requests to go home and prepare herself. She escapes to her home, where she locks the door and starts praying to God, asking for help. Amram's daughter does not want to consent to the two men who want her; it entails rape ("against your will"). When she does not return as promised the men decide to go to her house. Fortunately, according to the narrative, God hears the daughter's prayers and prevents the men from finding her house. They become blinded like the people of Sodom (Gen 19:11) and stumble around. Finally, they realize that they have been tricked and decide "to blame her before she could blame them." They go to the village and report that Amram's daughter has been lying with "a stranger." The people believe them with great dismay and decide to kill the young woman—an appropriate punishment for her alleged transgression. Luckily, the angels step forward in the form of Samaritan children,

who question the legal procedure and expose the lie of the two nazir-
ites. At this point, Amram's daughter comes down from the mountain.
When her father asks her, "she told him the whole truth of the thing."
The two men confess their guilt and receive the death penalty.

What a different account of Susanna's tale! Amram's daughter is
not taking a bath, as in Theodotion's version, but is a Bible teacher
and a nazirite. Her fate is both similar and dissimilar to Susanna's. Like
Susanna, she is threatened by two men, resists them, is sentenced to
die for her supposed transgression, and is rescued by divine intervention. Yet, unlike Susanna, Amram's daughter is attacked by two fellow
nazirites and manages to make them believe that she will comply with
their demands. This is a story of acquaintance rape in which a woman
pursues her professional interests but runs into difficulties with her
colleagues. In the narrative God protects her twice. The first time
God confuses the lecherous men in a manner similar to the men of
Sodom and Gomorrah who threaten Lot. The second time God sends
children to come to her aid. Yet, like Theodotion and several other
versions, the Samaritan story too reports only a verbal threat of rape.
Neither the two elders nor the two hermits take action.[45]

The omission of an explicit rape attack characterizes numerous
artistic adaptations of the story, which made Susanna an enormously
popular figure in Western culture. For centuries, painters captured the
moment of Susanna entering the bath.[46] Focused on the naked woman,
their works gained fame and added to the story's widespread popularity. Some artists produced several paintings of the same scene, such as
seventeenth-century painter Rembrandt van Rijn (1606–1669). His
paintings *Susanna at the Bath* (1634) and *Susanna Surprised by the
Elders* (1645) are among his most revered creations.[47] Musicians, too,
were inspired by the story and composed musical plays, oratorios,
and even operas. One of them is Carlisle Floyd's opera *Susannah*,
which premiered at Florida State University in 1955. A year later it
was performed at the City Opera, and more than forty years later at the
Metropolitan Opera in New York City (April 1999). Cast as a southern
American version of the biblical tale, the opera turns Susanna into a
young woman living in Tennessee, where she experiences provincial-
ism, small-mindedness, and the ill effects of gossip.[48]

In most, if not in all, of these and other art productions, the attempted rape scene disappears, and voluptuous flesh and the virtue of the heroine are central. In the case of Floyd's opera, the male elders of the biblical story turn into women and men of a small southern town. While the people harass Susanna, the town's preacher becomes interested in her, spends a night with her, and thereupon defends her against prejudicial charges. Neither this nor other artistic interpretations explore the dynamics of a rape attack. Floyd's opera changes the attack into a one-night stand, while many paintings focus on the bathing scene. The image of a bathing young woman has left many readers sympathetic to the elders, as two scholarly remarks demonstrate: "Perhaps he [the reader!] has also felt something of the elders' desire in the detailed description of their voyeurism," or "The bathing scene not only excites the elders, thereby enabling them to attempt their dastardly deed, but it can also fire the imagination of some readers. Of such considerations are good stories made!"[49]

In contrast to these Western cultural approaches, the Old Greek version of the Susanna narrative is surprisingly blunt about the attempted rape. In this version, the rape appears to be carried out when the story states: "And they [the two men] said to each other, 'Let us go to her.' They made an agreement, went to her, and tried to coerce her" (v. 19). The Greek verb that is translated as "to coerce" expresses violence and force, which the two men applied to Susanna to force her to submit.[50] Interestingly, commentators such as John J. Collins dismiss this description in favor of Theodotion's version because "the OG [Old Greek] account of the attempted seduction [sic] (they 'tried to coerce her') is extremely terse and reads like an abbreviation. Theodotion has the elders make the situation explicit and threaten Susanna with reprisal."[51] Collins prefers Theodotion because it is more "explicit" than the Old Greek text. In the Theodotion version, the elders talk about their desire to "seduce" Susanna, but the Old Greek version describes a much more severe attack. In the Old Greek version, the elders are not only talkers but attackers; they try to rape Susanna. Collins does not recognize this difference and characterizes the rape attack in the Old Greek version as "the attempted seduction."

Collins's description of the rape attack in the Old Greek version as an attempted seduction is problematic. He also does not recognize that the expanded text of Theodotion obfuscates the rape scene with a plethora of words placed in the mouths of the elders, but even this version alludes to the possibility of rape (vv. 19-21): "When the maids went out, the two elders arose and rushed upon her and said, 'Look, the gates of the garden are shut and no one can see us. We desire you, so consent to us and be with us. But if not, we will testify against you that there was a young man with you, and on this account you sent away the maids.'" In Theodotion's version, the men threaten Susanna verbally with rape, whereas in the Old Greek version they attack her directly and then threaten her when they fail to slip away in secret. Thus, the Old Greek version should be considered the *lectio difficilior*, for it includes the actual rape attack. The other versions build upon it and try to modify the rape, reducing it to a verbal threat only.[52]

Even with this hypothesis, all versions leave little doubt that "rapish desire"[53] is unacceptable. Whatever the request of the elders actually is—whether they attack Susanna, threaten her verbally, or ask her to marry one of them—the elders are punished with death for their attempts to give false witness. The turn of events has inspired scholars to examine the legal procedures described in the story,[54] but they often fail to recognize the centrality of the rape. When they erase the rape from the story line, the narrative turns into a moralizing tale that domesticates women into the presumed safety of married life. Only when readers recognize that Susanna is raped or threatened with rape does her effort to avoid the attack make sense. Susanna's story then has a liberating effect: encouraging women to fiercely, forcefully, and uncompromisingly resist violent advances from men in their communities and lives. Then the story becomes a resistance tale that reminds readers, female and male, of the prevalence of acquaintance rapes even in biblical literature.

On Speaking and Resisting: Concluding Comments

Despite a number of interpretative contestations, the identified narratives about Dinah, Tamar, Abishag, and Susanna confirm the persistent silence concerning acquaintance rape. Was it love? Did she not volunteer? Was it seduction or a harmless opportunity for old men? The commentary literature indicates the ongoing confusion about sexual violence when the attacker and the one attacked know each other, when a woman is not *physically* harmed during or after the act of sexual violation, or when a rapist enjoys communal recognition. The interpretations also illustrate the ongoing confusion about sexual consent, what makes a man a rapist, and what the standards for "real" rape actually are. When we read the biblical passages with contemporary terminology in mind, we read them with the eyes of our world, with our sensibilities and concerns. No longer are biblical texts confined to the dusty past; they become contested territory, a resource for understanding past and present society and religion. Read accordingly, the stories of Dinah, Tamar, Abishag, and Susanna turn into testimonies reminding us of the seriousness and prevalence of acquaintance rape both then and now.

2

SUBJUGATED
BY GENDER AND CLASS
THE RAPE OF ENSLAVED WOMEN

Stories of Rape and Slavery in Nineteenth-Century America

Nineteenth-century female slaves of African descent described the pain and suffering that their bodies and souls experienced from repeated sexual violations at the hands of their masters. One of them, Harriet A. Jacobs, characterized rape as one of the "trials of girlhood" in her memoir on being enslaved in America:

> I was compelled to live under the same roof with him—where I saw a man forty years my senior daily violating the most sacred commandments of nature. He told me I was his property; that I must be subject to his will in all things. My soul revolted against the mean tyranny. But where could I turn for protection? No matter whether the slave girl be as black as ebony or as fair as her mistress. In either case, there is no shadow of law to protect her from insult, from violence, or even from death; all these are inflicted by fiends who bear the shape of men.[1]

Jacobs did not receive support from other enslaved people on the plantation. Everybody knew "the guilty practices under that roof," but nobody asked her about it, and the slave owner was, of course, never held accountable. In her sorrow, Jacobs exclaimed: "O, what days and nights of fear and sorrow that man caused me!" Her master and rapist built a small house to have constant and private access to her, but she swore never to enter it. Jacobs was adamant in trying to resist her master and made a drastic decision. She wrote:

> I vowed before my Maker that I would never enter it [the small house]. I had rather toil on the plantation from dawn till dark;

I had rather live and die in jail, than drag on, from day to day, through such a living death. I was determined that the master, whom I so hated and loathed, who had blighted the prospects of my youth, and made my life a desert, should not, after my long struggle with him, succeed at last in trampling his victim under his feet. I would do any thing, everything, for the sake of defeating him. What *could* I do? I thought and thought, till I became desperate, and made a plunge into the abyss.[2]

She described unambiguously how much she hated her master's daily sexual attacks, but she was powerless. Eventually she found a way to resist his relentless advances. To scare him off from placing her into "the lonely cottage," she "made a headlong plunge" and began a sexual relationship with "a white unmarried gentleman" who had become interested in her. When her grandmother found out about this relationship, she was incensed because she did not know the reason for her granddaughter's action. She ordered her to leave and never again to visit her house, but when the grandmother heard the whole story later, she took pity on her granddaughter. Jacobs remembered that "[s]he laid her old hand gently on my head, and murmured, 'Poor child! Poor child!'"[3]

Enslaved women in America lived with the constant reality of rape because they were the property of their white male masters. Laws accommodated the status quo, which classified the progeny of such unions as children of the mothers only. Black women were called seducers, "Jezebels," as if they tempted the rapists into the encounter. Sympathetic observers recorded a different reality, and one of them described the fate of the enslaved women with these words:

Oh, how often I've seen the poor girls sob and cry, when there's been such goings on! Maybe you think, because they're slaves, they ain't got no feeling and no shame? A woman's being a slave, don't stop her having genteel ideas; that is, according to their way, and as far as they can. They know they must submit to their masters; besides, their masters maybe, dress'em up and make'em little presents, and give'em more privileges, while the whim lasts; but that an't like having a parcel of low, dirty, swearing, drunk patter-rollers let loose among'em, like so many hogs. This breaks down their spirits dreadfully, and makes 'em wish they was dead.[4]

Enslaved women had little choice but to submit. Nevertheless, some fiercely resisted the sexual exploitation and shared resistance strategies with each other. One, Jermain Loguen, attacked a would-be rapist with a stick and a knife to chase him away from her mother. Two other women who were approached by an overseer wrestled him to the ground together and ran away. Enslaved women took recourse to poison when they served as cooks and nurses. They feigned illness and when they did not succeed in time, they resorted to birth control and abortion.[5] They did not easily give up their rights over their bodies and tried hard to keep some form of perceived control over their bodies and their lives.

The Rape of Enslaved Women in the Hebrew Bible

The Hebrew Bible contains several passages that deal with the rape of enslaved women, some better known than others, although biblical scholars do not usually characterize them as rape texts. Perhaps the best known story is about Sarah and Hagar (Gen 16:1-16; 21:9-21). The enslaved Egyptian woman Hagar, mistreated by Sarah and forced to submit to sexual intercourse with Abraham, has attracted the attention of feminist scholars such as Phyllis Trible and Elsa Tamez, and womanist theologians such as Delores S. Williams and Renita J. Weems. All of them sympathize with Hagar but for different reasons. Trible uplifts Hagar as the first person in the Bible who names God. Tamez values Hagar as a slave woman of African descent who receives God's word of liberation. Williams empathizes with Hagar because she has provided hope to generations of African American women and helped them to trust their survival skills. Weems praises Hagar because her story teaches contemporary women, white and black, the pervasiveness of interlocking forms of oppression, such as sexism, racism, and classism. To all of them, the

Hagar-Sarah story is an important biblical exemplar for feminist and womanist analysis.[6]

A less well-known narrative centers on Bilhah and Zilpah, who are enslaved by Leah and Rachel. In a dramatic story (Gen 29:31—30:24), the matriarchs compete for children and their husband's love, and in the process force their slaves into sexual intercourse with Jacob. Interestingly, the narrative has not gained much scholarly attention, whether from androcentric or from feminist scholars. Gerhard von Rad, whose work has influenced generations of biblical interpreters, maintained that this story does not present "the great words of God." It appears in a larger literary context of a "great" narrative, but, to von Rad, a story about women competing for male babies is theologically irrelevant. He does not find "a religious framework" in this tale, and the authors "who told of Abraham's call and the renewal of the promise to Jacob" succumbed to "long descriptions of an event upon which they do not comment theologically."[7] Following this assessment, many traditional commentators have said little about Genesis 29–30 and often refer to it as a tedious list about "The Birth and Naming of Jacob's Sons: Genesis 29:31—30:24" or "The Birth of Jacob's Children (29:31—30:43)";[8] sometimes a mother's name is included, for example, "Jacob's Four Sons by Leah (29:31-35)" and "Jacob's Children by Bilhah (30:1-8).[9] If the narrative is recognized, it is for the sons who become important as the representatives of the twelve tribes of Israel. The women, free or enslaved, remain largely unnoticed. In line with this androcentric characterization, few feminist and womanist interpreters concentrate on Genesis 29–30; and when they do, motherhood, and not the rape of enslaved women, plays the central role.[10]

Of course, there are additional stories about enslaved women who are raped. A short fragment in Genesis 35 mentions an incident in the life of Bilhah, Rachel's one-time slave. A son of Leah takes advantage of his social and gender status and sexually violates Bilhah (vv. 16-19). Couched in ambiguous language, the fragmentary tale has received scant attention from androcentric interpreters and none from feminist commentators. Yet placed in hermeneutical relations with three other passages about enslaved women (2 Sam 3:6-11; 2 Samuel 15–19;

1 Kgs 2:13-25), this story too illustrates the disastrous consequences of gender and class hierarchies for enslaved women. Men fight over the bodies of variously disempowered women whose voices are absent from the narratives. Sometimes class-privileged women join forces with androcentric structures, expectations, and hierarchies. When the women are enslaved and gendered, they are objects in the androcentric and classist plots of the male protagonists. These are not happy narratives. They demonstrate powerfully the combined destructiveness of gender and class oppression in the lives of enslaved female characters in biblical literature.

The Story of Hagar

Enslaved, raped, but seen by God, Hagar has been a cherished biblical character in African American communities. Womanist theologian Delores S. Williams elaborates on Hagar's place in the African American sociocultural and religious imagination:

> The African-American community has taken Hagar's story unto itself. Hagar has "spoken" to generation after generation of black women because her story has been validated as true by suffering black people. She and Ishmael together, as family, model many black American families in which a lone woman/mother struggles to hold the family together in spite of the poverty to which ruling class economics consign it. Hagar, like many black women, goes into the wide world to make a living for herself and her child, with only God by her side.[11]

Hagar exemplifies that survival is possible even under the harshest conditions. When the divine messenger sends the woman back to the house of the enslaver (Gen 16:9), God does not liberate Hagar. She would not survive with her child in the desert, and so God shows the mother how to "make a way out of no way."[12]

The other woman, Sarah, has been a model for many Jewish and white Christian women. She takes destiny into her hands because she sees God as preventing her from bearing children. In the narrative, she demands that her husband impregnate her slave-maid so that "perhaps I shall be built up from her" (Gen 16:2). Scholars have long pointed out that the Nuzi tablets, ancient Near Eastern texts discovered in the early twentieth century, mention this practice. An infertile woman gives a slave-maid to her husband and so provides him with offspring. Whether scholars describe such activity as routine among upper-class citizens or as a common practice among all citizens, they do not identify this ancient Near Eastern custom as "rape"[13] and often advise readers to "lay aside our cultural biases long enough" so that we can appreciate the way of life from a different time.[14]

Yet even if Sarah's decision is reminiscent of an ancient Near Eastern custom, the practice is rarely evaluated from the perspective of the enslaved woman. If it is, this form of surrogacy comes close to what we today call rape. An enslaved woman is forced into sexual intercourse. Her consent is irrelevant because as a slave she has to do what her owners ask of her. Should we assume that an enslaved woman in the ancient Near East did not feel violated to the core of her being when she had to submit sexually to the husband of her owner? Both Genesis 16 and Genesis 29–30 mention this practice, but neither narrative depicts the enslaved woman's reaction to the rape. Hagar responds to Sarah only after she becomes pregnant, and, according to the narrative, she despises her owner: "But when Hagar saw that she had conceived, her mistress was slight in her eyes" (Gen 16:4). The narrative turns the enslaved woman's response against the other woman, and so Abraham is off the hook.

There are various ways of interpreting this response of Hagar. When her response is located within a paradigm of combined gender and class oppression, it reflects a struggle within the social hierarchies of patriarchy. Hagar emerges, then, as a complex character who has internalized sexist oppression by which women are valued as child-producers; fertility makes them valuable to patriarchal society. Hagar appears to have accepted these conditions and assumes correctly that her pregnancy places her above Sarah. She triumphs over her mistress. The question is whether Hagar's response represents a realistic description of an enslaved woman who was raped by her owner's husband or whether v. 4 should be read as part of an androcentric strategy that legitimates the rape by stressing her newfound agency as the result of the pregnancy. After all, ultimately the husband benefits most from the arrangement, and the narrative might be read as a linguistic justification of male and class privileges. Abraham enjoys sexual access to two women and gets a son (Gen 16:15-16), whereas the women compete against each other with harmful strategies, each trying to eliminate the other. In the story, Abraham is a player in the background who also relinquishes his responsibility when Sarah complains to him about the tension between her and her slave. His only response: "Since your slave is in your hand, do to her the good in your eyes." When the husband withdraws, the woman in charge exerts her class privilege over the enslaved woman. Does the narrative attempt to blame the wife for a practice from which the husband benefits? In response to Hagar's contempt, Sarah "afflicted" (piel 'innâ; עִנָּה) her slave (Gen 16:6).

The unresolved question is what Sarah does to Hagar, because the Hebrew verb 'innâ (עִנָּה) has many shades of meaning. Generally, it refers to the physical oppression of slaves or people in general. The Egyptian taskmasters oppress ('innâ, עִנָּה piel) the enslaved Israelites (Exod 1:11-12). In the so-called Dynastic Oracle, God tells the prophet Nathan that the people of Israel will not experience oppression ('innâ, עִנָּה piel) during King David's reign (2 Sam 7:10). The verb also connotes rape, such as in the stories of Tamar and Amnon (2 Sam 13:14) and the unnamed concubine (Judg 19:25). Can Sarah "rape" Hagar? Phyllis Trible rejects the idea. To her, the verb depicts the intensification of the oppressive system in which Sarah and Hagar live.[15] To other interpreters, Hagar's violation and torture can be specified as the sexual violation of her physical integrity. Hagar was raped.[16] Yet another meaning is possible which recognizes an androcentric strategy that makes Sarah the subject of the verb "to rape" and characterizes Abraham as compliant with her will. The question is, Who is ultimately responsible for the rape, Abraham, Sarah, or both? Or is it God because God does not give fertility to Sarah (Gen 16:2)? The story does not provide a clear answer but challenges readers to wrestle with the brutality of Hagar's predicament, shaped by both gender and class oppression.

The story continues with Hagar. After Hagar escapes from the house of her owners, she reaches an oasis in the desert, where she encounters a divine messenger. The presence of water signals her relative safety; she will not die of thirst. Strikingly, the messenger of God asks her the obvious question: "Hagar, slave of Sarah, from where have you come and where are you going?" (Gen 16:8). Answering only the first part of the question, Hagar replies: "I am fleeing from my mistress Sarah" 16:8). In the desert, alone, pregnant, and brutalized, Hagar knows from whom she runs. But the messenger does not sympathize with Hagar's condition and only tells her what to do next. "Return to your mistress, and suffer affliction ['innâ, ענה piel] under her hand" (16:9). What tormenting advice! The divine messenger orders the raped and pregnant slave to return to the master and to endure further maltreatment, "rape."

Interpreters have often glossed over the difficulty of this verse. Trible links the messenger's statement to the two following promises: Hagar will have countless descendants (v. 10), and she will give birth to a child, a son (vv. 11-12).[17] Katheryn Pfisterer Darr, too, evades the glaring problem and characterizes the divine promise as "indeed a panacea for her pain." Darr wonders briefly whether this is God's way of sanctioning "abuse" but then suggests that the messenger tries to comfort Hagar.[18] Weems goes further and blames the slave for her own misery. With a "pathetic sense of herself," Hagar accepts her status as a slave and Sarah as the "mistress." Thus, for Weems, "the angel had no other choice but to send the runaway slave back to the reality in which she had defined herself."[19]

Sometimes, however, interpreters engage head-on the theological problem that the messenger's command poses. Delores S. Williams, for example, questions why God sends the slave back to the slave owner and wonders about divine prudence: "Did God not know about Sarai's brutal treatment of Hagar?" The divinity appears to side with the oppressor, and so Williams asserts, "The angel of Yahweh is, in this passage, no liberator God."[20] The personal encounter with God does not release Hagar from the oppressive structure but makes her submit until her masters chase her away (Gen 21:10-14). The God of this narrative does not support the raped and enslaved woman but instead encourages Hagar to accept an oppressive life in the present with the promise of a large progeny in the future. The God of this story endorses a doctrine that tolerates conditions of oppression for a promise of future bliss. After hearing the divine advice, Hagar responds by naming the divinity: "You are a God of seeing" (Gen 16:13). Is this name meant to be ironic? After all, God has only "seen" Hagar's status as a slave, and after evaluating her condition the divinity sends her back. Does the name suggest that the God of this story is not "a God of deliverance," but only "a God of seeing"?

The theological ambiguity is reinforced by linguistic obscurity. Hagar's response is grammatically unclear, and interpreters try to resolve this problem in various ways. Some explain that Hagar speaks gibberish. For instance, Trible translates v. 13: "Have I even here seen after the one who sees me?" (Gen 16:13). Others believe that perhaps Hagar reflects on her newly attained insight when she speaks in v. 13, which Nahum Sarna translates: "Have I not gone on seeing after He saw me!" Or perhaps v. 13 is Hagar's expression of awe for having survived an encounter with God, as suggested by Gerhard von Rad: "Have I really seen God and remained alive after seeing him?"[21] Whatever the translation of the cryptic Hebrew, the ambivalence of the text relates well to Hagar's complex relationship with God. The unclear meaning of v. 13 illustrates that Hagar does not simply praise God but that, at the center of the encounter, there is a theological problem. God addresses Hagar, even "sees" her, and still orders her to return to her owner. The obscurity of the Hebrew illustrates the problematic theological stance of the narrative in which God is not unequivocally on the enslaved woman's side.

Yet neither is this story's God unequivocally on the side of Sarah, who disappears at the end of Genesis 16 when patriarchal order finds its full expression again. When Hagar returns from the desert, Abraham becomes the father of "his" son: "Hagar bore Abram a son, and Abram gave his son borne by Hagar the name Ishmael" (16:15). Hagar is reduced to her fertile body, which secures the paternal line, and she hands over her son to the father, who names him Ishmael. Genesis 16 emphasizes male lineage, which upholds Abraham's paternal authority, and not Sarah's. Patriarchy is "well in control" in the entire narrative, even when God commands Hagar to return to her mistress (v. 9).[22] Hagar's return does not secure Sarah's or Hagar's future, but only Abraham's. He benefits from the return of the enslaved and pregnant woman who gives birth to "his" son and helps him make his future look bright. God sides with Abraham not only in v. 15 but throughout the entire narrative.

The second part of the Sarah-Hagar story also shows that God favors Abraham (Gen 21:9-21). When Sarah shows displeasure at the thought of Ishmael and Isaac playing together, she instructs her husband: "Cast out this slave woman and her son. For the son of this slave woman will not inherit with my son, Isaac" (v. 10). For the first time in Abraham's interactions with his wife and her slave, the father reacts emotionally when the narrator explains: "This thing was evil in the eyes of Abraham on account of his son" (v. 11). He agonizes over the fate of Ishmael and does not want to send him away, but God changes Abraham's perception of his wife's request (vv. 12, 13) with a linguistic strategy. In the divine speech Ishmael is "the boy" or "the son of the slave woman" (vv. 12, 13) and is not mentioned by name.

Despite the overwhelming support Abraham receives from God in the narrative, God does not forget the enslaved woman and helps Hagar, the mother, in the conversation with Abraham. For instance, God advises Abraham: "Do not feel evil in your eyes on account of the boy" (v. 12), and the verse continues: ". . . and on account of your slave woman" (v. 12). Abraham responds by providing her and her son with bread and water and sending them off.

> So Abraham rose early in the morning,
> and took bread and a skin of water,
> and gave it to Hagar,
> putting it on her shoulder, along with the child,
> and sent her away. (21:14)

In the desert, God shows concern again when the mother despairs over the fate of her son. Sitting "a good way off, about a distance of a bowshot" (21:16a), Hagar watches her son dying. She raises her voice in grief when little Ishmael cries in pain. God responds to the baby's cries (v. 17), helps the mother to find water for the child (v. 19), and ensures that the mother can keep her child alive.

The story ends with a focus on Ishmael. "God was with the boy; and he grew up and lived in the wilderness, and he became an expert with the bow. He lived in the wilderness of Paran; and his mother got a wife for him from the land of Egypt" (vv. 20-21). Hagar's son grows into "an expert of the measuring tool" that once measured the distance between his mother and him when Ishmael almost died as an infant (vv. 15-17). Even when Ishmael is an adult, his mother provides for him. She finds him a wife from her native country (see Gen. 25:12-18). The comment portrays Hagar as sharing the patriarchal and ethnic order. She wants her son to be married to a woman from Egypt. Could there have been a different end to this story, one that does not try to make believe that women, enslaved or free, live through their sons only? Perhaps it is possible to read this ending as an illustration of the difficulties inherent in envisioning a society that does not limit people to their gender, ethnicity, or class. The next biblical story, too, demonstrates the difficulties of such a vision.

The Story of Bilhah and Zilpah

Women play central roles also in Gen 29:31—30:24, in which Leah and Rachel compete with each other for children and husbandly love, and in the process force their slaves, Bilhah and Zilpah, to become pregnant by their husband, Jacob (29:31—30:24). The narrative portrays Leah as "hated" by their husband, but then she gives birth to six sons and one daughter. When her fertility ceases, she adds two more sons borne by her slave, Zilpah. In contrast, the other sister, Rachel, is loved by their husband but infertile. She competes with her sister's fertility and forces her slave, Bilhah, to become pregnant by Jacob. Bilhah gives birth to two sons, and only at the end of the story does Rachel herself give birth to a son. In a later chapter, bearing another son, she dies in childbirth (see Gen 35:16-20). In chapters 29-30, two women are the main actors, and two women are their slaves. Husband Jacob appears at the margins, speaking only once (30:2), while his wives do not stop talking. The story is troubling because, like Sarah, the sisters use enslaved women to secure their progeny.[23]

Although the story is centrally placed in the book of Genesis and describes the origins of the twelve tribes of Israel, it has not enjoyed much attention in the scholarly literature. Whether readers subscribe to traditional, feminist, or womanist perspectives, this tale about two free and two enslaved women does not figure prominently in the Jewish or Christian imagination. Even when interpreters mention Leah and Rachel, they do not usually focus on Bilhah and Zilpah. Perhaps the silence of the enslaved women has made them invisible to interpreters because, unlike Hagar, Bilhah and Zilpah do not protest their treatment, do not run away from the enslavers, and do not name God. Only their sons figure centrally and become equal members of the twelve tribes, unlike Hagar's Ishmael. Bilhah's and Zilpah's oppression means liberation for their sons, who become leaders in the historiographical mythology of ancient Israel.

On Whose Side Is God?

Here, then, lies the theological crux of the story: On whose side is God? The beginning of the narrative suggests that God supports Leah. "When Yahweh saw that Leah was unloved, God opened her womb" (Gen 29:31). Later, God also "remembers Rachel" (30:22), which leads to her long-awaited first pregnancy and the birth of Joseph. Yet no reference is made to Bilhah and Zilpah. For the enslaved women, raped and silenced, God seems absent. Williams observes that biblical narratives depict God as choosing when to side with the oppressed and when to side with the oppressor.[24] In Genesis 29–30, God sides with the slave owners, first with Leah and later with Rachel (29:31; 30:22). This is not an attractive power dynamic for feminist and womanist readers, and so it is not surprising that these chapters have received little exegetical attention.

An exception is a feminist reading by Esther Fuchs.[25] For Fuchs, the literary characteristics of Genesis 29–30 belong to a genre that justifies polygamy when a wife is infertile. The genre is found also in Genesis 16, Fuchs explains, and in both cases it exhibits andro-centric bias that always centers on men and male concerns. The hus-bands, Abraham and Jacob, have sex with Hagar and Leah because these women are "naturally" fertile and share "a rather dubious array of characteristics, such as foreignness, pridefulness, unat-tractiveness."[26] For Fuchs, the stories were composed to justify the men's polygamous behavior. Men need sons, and when their wives cannot become pregnant, the men have to ensure their progeny with other women.

While Fuchs's interpretation needs to be commended for including Genesis 29–30, it is striking that her focus is exclusively concerned with gender. According to her, Leah is exclusively a victim of patriarchy. In the world of the narrative, however, Leah participates actively and benefits directly from her social status as a slave-owning woman. She is a married woman of consider-able social status who holds power over her own slave woman, Zilpah, and who forces her slave to have sex with her husband. When Fuchs compares Leah with Hagar, she neglects to take into account their different class locations. It is not only fertility that defines the women's fate but also their economic status. Hagar is an enslaved woman and has no say in the forced sexual intercourse with Abraham. Thus, her situation is parallel to the circumstances of the enslaved women Zilpah and Bilhah, rather than to the situ-ation of Leah.[27]

Fuchs is not the only interpreter who misses the class distinc-tions in Genesis 29–30. Other interpreters, too, omit this critical aspect and instead focus on God's support of Rachel and Leah, the slave-owning women. Generally, scholars approve of God's support because, to them, the married women seem oppressed. For instance, Hermann Gunkel is relieved that God helps Leah and Rachel: "That Yahweh cares for the despised is a comforting belief: Yahweh helps the poor, the despised, the despairing, the fugitive slave (16.7ff.), the rejected child and his unfortunate mother (21.17ff.), the shamefully sold and slandered (39.2, 21ff.)."[28] For Gunkel, the fact that Leah and Rachel receive God's help while they also hold slaves does not contradict his belief that the situation of the two slaveholding women compares with other marginalized people. That their class status makes their lives more privileged than "the poor, the despised, the despairing, the fugitive slave" does not occur to Gunkel.

Similarly, Gerhard von Rad highlights God's role in Leah's life: "After all the thoroughgoing worldliness of the previous story, God is again the subject of the event. He is the one who blesses and comforts the neglected wife."[29] Like Gunkel, von Rad focuses on the fact that God brings fertility to one of the wives. This is where Leah needs divine help: in motherhood. Meanwhile, von Rad ignores that she forces her slave into sexual intercourse with her husband. This interpretative bias is not limited to androcentric interpretations; even feminist reader Elyse Goldstein ignores the fate of Bilhah and Zilpah when she praises God's support of Leah and Rachel. Goldstein explains: "God rewards Leah with fertility to make up for her troubles with her husband, and the women are now equalized. One gets a man's love; the other gets a child's love. One woman gains status through her husband, the other woman status through her children."[30] Again, only Leah and Rachel feature prominently, whereas the enslaved women receive no consideration.

Many interpreters appreciate God's option for the "despised," whom they identify as the competing sisters. At the same time, they ignore the complex social position of Leah and Rachel, consider Leah's fertility a blessing, and positively evaluate God's seeming support of both sisters. However, the interpreters have little or nothing to say about Bilhah's and Zilpah's situation, though, as Fuchs stresses, ultimately divine care benefits neither Leah nor Rachel. In the narrative, communication between God and the women functions merely as divine justification for the institution of motherhood, and so Genesis 29–30 presents androcentric and class hierarchies as divine order. Once the women, free or enslaved, give birth to sons, they become superfluous in this order and disappear from the story line or die. In short, Genesis 29–30 does not endorse feminist values, except perhaps when it is understood as an illustration of the traps of androcentric and classist ideology for women, whether they are free or enslaved.

Androcentrism Par Excellence

There is little dispute over the fact that Genesis 29–30 represents an androcentric story par excellence. Scholars assert that the narrative depicts Leah and Rachel as embracing androcentric values in their struggle for children and husband. Athalya Brenner contends that the story is a "male-oriented, male-written judgment on female sociability and potential of socialization." For Brenner, Leah and Rachel are like other biblical mothers who eventually give birth to "heroes" and are portrayed as rivals who are mostly concerned with motherhood.[31] Sharon Pace Jeansonne also maintains: "The struggle between Rachel and Leah clearly arises from a context of patriarchal structures and expectations."[32] Similarly, Peter Pitzele recognizes that these chapters "dramatize in the starkest possible terms the worst features of the patriarchal system. Women bear sons for men. Motherhood has been co-opted in the interests of lineage and class. . . . Two sisters are corrupted by a system that prizes sons."[33] Francine Klagsbrun, too, acknowledges the androcentric character of the narrative: "From a feminist point of view, we would say that they [Leah and Rachel] have incorporated patriarchal values, and certainly their stories are presented from a male perspective."[34]

Recognizing the blunt androcentrism of this tale, interpreters nevertheless hesitate to condemn Leah and Rachel or the narrative. Klagsbrun cautions one not to "dismiss these women simply as products of patriarchy," and imagines that perhaps Leah and Rachel follow "a divinely directed destiny." They know that their sons will become founders of a great nation. Klagsbrun believes that "an intimacy with the divine . . . perhaps lay at the heart of their desire for children,"[35] and so in her reading Leah and Rachel are figures full of strength and determination with crucial roles in the destiny of Israel. Although Klagsbrun's position tolerates, perhaps too easily, Leah's and Rachel's co-optation into androcentric and class oppression, her position is important. It explains why some women endorse androcentric hierarchies. Class privilege makes them eager to conform to the patriarchal demand to produce sons, and so they force other women of lower social status into helping them. When Genesis 29–30 is read with class in mind, the narrative illuminates societal forces that make some women accept and support androcentric hierarchies in society even today.

The Story's Literary Structure

A closer look at the literary structure uncovers the particularities of this dynamic. Four literary scenes structure the story. The first scene, 29:31-35, establishes the situation: Leah is unloved but fertile and gives birth to four sons: Reuben, Simeon, Levi, and Judah. Their names receive explanatory comments from the mother. Although the relationships between the sons' names and Leah's explanations are etymologically mostly incorrect,[36] the explanations are significant. All of them refer to God except for the name of Levi (v. 34). After the first birth, Leah acknowledges: "Yahweh saw my misery; now my husband will love me" (v. 32). After the second birth, she remarks: "For Yahweh heard that I was unloved, and so God has given me this one too" (v. 33). After the fourth birth, she exclaims: "Now I shall praise Yahweh!" (v. 35). In other words, Leah correlates her fertility with the divinity, although her goal—to gain the love of her husband—remains unattained. Initially, Leah believes she will gain love for her fertility, but after the fourth son she recognizes that her God-given fertility will not provide her with Jacob's love, and so she praises God without a reference to her husband (v. 35).

The second scene, 30:1-8, reports Rachel's infertility, which leads to Bilhah's rapes. When Rachel realizes that she does not become pregnant, she instructs Jacob: "Give me children, or I shall die!" (v. 1). He, however, is more cautious than his wife: "Am I in the position of God, who has denied you the fruit of the womb?" (v. 2). Jacob does not respond to his wife's sorrow and refuses responsibility for her infertility. He defends himself because infertility is not his problem but ultimately God's. Jacob's brisk response startled the rabbis of the early centuries of the Common Era. In a midrash God intervenes: "Said the Holy One, blessed be He, to Jacob: Is that a way to answer a woman in distress?"[37] Here God disapproves of Jacob's abrupt answer to his wife, and so the rabbis reprimanded Jacob for his lack of sympathy.

Yet in the narrative, Jacob's answer leaves it to his favorite wife to determine what to do next. Rachel takes action. "Here is my slave, Bilhah. Sleep with her, and let her give birth on my knees. Through her, then, I too shall have children" (v. 3). Without another comment from her husband, the deal is done. "Jacob slept with her" (v. 4) before his father-in-law Laban could communicate his demand that his son-in-law not take other women (31:50). When Bilhah becomes pregnant and gives birth to a son, Rachel invokes the divinity for the first time. "God has done me justice. Yes, God has heard my voice, and God has given me a son" (v. 6). Rachel feels she has learned her lesson and believes that the divinity provides offspring through any means available. Forcing another woman to have intercourse with her husband, Rachel takes advantage of her class and later thanks God for the child. This is disturbing theology because Rachel considers gendered class oppression to be God's will. Is God the provider and denier of fertility under such conditions? Rachel's affirmative answer demonstrates her co-optation into androcentric and classist ideology. She wants a son regardless of the cost, and since the process works for her, Rachel forces Bilhah a second time to have intercourse with Jacob (v. 7). After the birth of another son, Rachel invokes God again, exclaiming: "I have wrestled a wrestling of *Elohim* with my sister, and I have won" (v. 8). Rachel believes that her success in fulfilling patriarchal expectations means that God is on her side. This theology is not only disturbing, but even dangerous, because it classifies patriarchy and classism as divinely sanctioned mechanisms of the societal order.

Rachel's exclamation in v. 8 raises many questions. At stake is the noun "God/*Elohim*." Interpreters often reject translating the Hebrew phrase as "a wrestling of *Elohim*" and recommend alternatives. For instance, Nahum M. Sarna proposes: "A fateful contest I waged with my sister." He explains that this translation is based "on the occasional use of *'elohim*, 'God,' as an intensifying or superlative element," although he recognizes that the phrase could be translated as "a contest for God."[38] Many interpreters follow Sarna's grammatical advice and consider the noun "God" in v. 8 as an intensifying adjective.[39] For example, Terence E. Fretheim, has penned a translation that attempts to communicate the effort of Rachel. He translates the sentence as, "With mighty wrestlings I have wrestled with my sister."[40] Likewise, Victor P. Hamilton compares Rachel's experience of wrestling "with Jacob's in Gen. 32:25f and considers God in v. 8 'as an intensifying epithet'." He translates v. 8: "I have been entangled in a desperate contest with my sister."[41] Other interpreters, such as Everett Fox, suggest a translation closer to the Hebrew text: "A struggle of God have I struggled with my sister."[42] It is indeed remarkable that the narrative relates the conflict between Leah and Rachel to the divinity. Does the Hebrew indicate more clearly than many vernacular translations that the women are deeply co-opted into androcentric theology?

The third scene, 30:9-13, switches back to Leah, who, now infertile, resorts to having her slave raped twice. Unlike Rachel (30:1), Leah does not react to her sister's success in getting two sons; she worries about herself. Thus, v. 9 does not state: "When Leah saw that Rachel had two sons," but observes instead: "When Leah saw that she had ceased to bear children." Hated by her husband and co-opted into androcentric values, Leah has learned to establish her social status through fertility. For different reasons, then, Leah resorts to the method earlier employed by Rachel. "Leah took her slave, Zilpah, and gave her to Jacob as a wife [*'iššâ*]" (v. 9). One interpreter, the medieval Jewish commentator Nachmanides (Ramban), points to the unusual nature of Leah's decision: "I do not know what motivated this deed of Leah and why she gave her handmaid to her husband, for she was not barren that she should hope to have children through Zilpah, and it is not natural for women to increase the number of their husbands' wives."[43] It is significant that the terminology of v. 9 relies on the slave owner's perspective. Zilpah, the slave, is not treated like a wife, as Nachmanides observes, but is reduced to the mere physical functions of her body. Sexually violated, she gives birth to a child that she probably did not want and is not able to call her own. Later, Zilpah is raped yet again (30:12), and both times Leah names the child. As in the case of her fourth son, Leah does not invoke the name of God (29:32-35) and refers only to luck and her social recognition: "What good fortune!" and "What blessedness because women will call me blessed!" (30:11, 13). The enslaved woman herself does not speak, since she is a prop giving birth. Even Jacob obeys quietly. Does he actually enjoy having sex with so many women? The text is silent about this possibility but perhaps the silence exposes Genesis 29–30 as an androcentric fantasy that imagines wives inviting the husband to have sex with enslaved women. Whatever the conclusion, the husband is once again off the hook.

The fourth scene, 30:14-24, depicts a negotiation between Leah and Rachel that leads to more children for Leah and, eventually, to a son for Rachel. The severity of the hostility between the sisters finds expression in their only conversation. When Reuben, Leah's eldest son, finds a special fruit and brings it to his mother, Leah exchanges the fruit for a night with Jacob. When Rachel demands the fruit, Leah replies bitterly: "Is it not enough to have taken my husband? You take my son's mandrakes as well?" (v. 14). Embroiled in rivalry over husband and children, Leah vents her feelings of loss. Rachel hears the disappointment in her sister's voice and easily relinquishes the man for the fruit: "Very well, he can sleep with you tonight in return for your son's mandrakes" (v. 15). Without objection, Jacob obeys Leah's order at the end of the day: "You must come to me" (v. 16). In this narrative, the husband does not care with whom he sleeps, going wherever his wives tell him. Is this text a realistic description of slave-owning women or an androcentric fantasy? Jacob must have gone to Leah at least twice more because Leah gives birth to another son (vv. 19-20) and to her only daughter, Dinah (v. 21). After the births of the sons, Leah praises the divinity again. She believes that God has rewarded her (v. 18), having given her a true gift (v. 20). The birth of her daughter, Dinah, does not receive such praise (v. 21), yet another indication of the narrative's androcentric tendencies.

When the scene turns again to Rachel (v. 22), she becomes pregnant herself. The narrative states: "Then God remembered Rachel and heeded her and opened her womb. She conceived and bore a son" (vv. 22-23). The race for fertility has found a preliminary end. Rachel names the son "Joseph" and exclaims: "God has taken away my reproach!" and "May Yahweh add to me another son" (vv. 23, 24). This painful story about the co-optation of two sisters into patriarchal and class structures ends with the request to God for yet another son. Eventually, the belief in God as the provider and denier of fertility kills Rachel (35:16-19). The story of her slave Bilhah, however, continues in another fragmentary narrative.

Another Story of Bilhah and Some Royal Concubines

Bilhah appears again in one verse, in which the destructive relational pattern of Leah and Rachel apparently moves to the next generation.

This, at least, is the sad conclusion based on an incident that involves Reuben and Bilhah, Rachel's slave. The story demonstrates what Reuben has learned: Enslaved women are property to be raped without repercussion. Here is the short description of the event:

> And-it-was when-lived Israel in that land,
> and-went Reuben,
> and-he-laid Bilhah, the-concubine-of his-father,
> and-heard Israel. (Gen 35:22a)[44]

Rarely mentioned in scholarly discussions, this brief report about Bilhah appears after Rachel dies during the birth of her second son. Indirectly, the verse refers to rape. The Hebrew verb, šākab (שכב), is followed not by the preposition ('im, עם) but by the Hebrew object marker, 'ēt (את), as in other rape stories, for instance the rape of Dinah (Gen 34:2) or the rape of Tamar (2 Sam 13:14). The grammatical observation has consequences for the verse's meaning. Reuben does not sleep "with" Bilhah, a translation that feigns consent by Bilhah. Rather, he laid her. He is the subject of the action and she the object. As a concubine and slave, Bilhah is sexually violated, raped.[45]

Two interpreters discuss the verse in some detail, and their work merits closer scrutiny. One is George G. Nicol, who rejects E. A. Speiser's idea that Gen 35:22 is an ethnographic explanation for the decline of the tribe of Reuben in the course of Israelite history. Speiser proposed that "[t]hese scattered hints suggest that the tribe of Reuben once enjoyed a pre-eminent position, only to fall upon evil days."[46] Nicol claims instead that the story remembers how Reuben avenges his mother, the woman whom Jacob never loved. Bilhah was the slave of Rachel, the beloved wife. The son rapes this enslaved woman as a challenge to his father's authority, as other royal sons do when they "take possession" of another man's concubines. Nicol elaborates: "This incident must therefore be considered to have caused deep humiliation to Jacob, who . . . had been usurped in the bed of [Rachel's] slave." For Nicol, Reuben introduces "an element of justice into the narrative" by taking revenge in unexpected ways. Previously, Leah called the birth of Reuben "the reversal of my humiliation" (29:32).

Since Reuben is not able to reverse Jacob's hatred for her into love, he reverses his father's fortune by humiliating his father "at precisely the time when he is emotionally at his weakest and least able to resist."[47] Attacking Bilhah, Reuben tries to destroy his father.

In short, Nicol's reading depicts Gen 35:22 as a struggle for power between two men, the son Reuben and his father Jacob. This is a fragment about men, and so Nicol is not concerned with Bilhah's perspective. Accordingly, he calls Reuben's activity "sexual intercourse," "his offence against his father," or "taking possession of Bilhah." For Nicol, Reuben challenges Jacob's authority by "committing his offence." Nicol even offers the compliment that the story demonstrates "a certain tastefulness in the fact that Genesis 35.22a associates Rachel's slave, and not Rachel herself, with Reuben's action." That the son is a rapist does not matter to this scholar, who praises the "good taste" of the narrator who makes Reuben choose his aunt's slave and not the aunt, Rachel, for the presumed "offense." When men dominate each other for power, rape is rhetorically absent.

This approach to Gen 35:22a is not new or unique. Mordechai Rotenberg refers to the ancient rabbis who applied to this verse what Rothenberg calls "rehabilitative story telling."[48] The rabbis observed that certain narratives display particularly troubling activities of central biblical figures, and Reuben is among them. His "sin" is explicitly described in Gen 35:22 and remembered by Jacob in Gen 49:3-4. In other words, the rabbis were aware of Reuben's problematic behavior and tried to "rehabilitate" him. They wanted Reuben's behavior to be understood as "a righteous deed of honoring his mother Leah," and so they commented on Gen 35:22a: "He stood up against the humiliation of his mother by saying: If my mother's sister was a rival to my mother, shall the bondsmaid of my mother's sister be a rival to my mother? He thus arose and transposed the beds."[49] For the rabbis, the story depicts how Reuben defended his mother. They focus on the son and his mother, but they ignore the woman who faced the violent son. Nor do they explain what precisely "his deed" was and in this sense excuse his "sin."

Although many centuries apart, the interpretations of Nicol and the ancient rabbis are similar. Both stress the male characters and both soften the sexual violence perpetrated by Reuben. Further, they attempt to reinterpret Reuben's rape, ignoring Bilhah's perspective. Perhaps it is not surprising, then, that Gen 35:22 belongs to a list of biblical texts, the so-called forbidden Targumim that "may be read [in Hebrew] but not translated [into the language of the congregation, e.g. English]."[50] They were not to be explained to lay audiences in the synagogue. The Christian strategy has not been that different. Even today, Christian lectionaries exclude Gen 35:22 from the recommended list of sermon texts, and so the verse is rarely if ever read aloud during Christian worship. Even so influential an interpreter as Gerhard von Rad indirectly endorsed this ecclesiastical silence when he stated: "The crime itself is condemned by the narrator, without the necessity for his expressly stating it. The note is so brief and fragmentary that one can form no opinion about what is told in vs. 21f."[51] Other Christian scholars, such as Richard J. Clifford and Roland E. Murphy, avoid specifying the content of v. 22: "The details of this ugly incident are not given; in fact, the text breaks off at this point."[52] To these Christian scholars, Genesis 35:22 is too short, too unclear, and too "ugly" to merit further commentary. They are interested neither in Bilhah nor in the issue of rape, and so Reuben's rape of Bilhah disappears in silence.

Another aspect of the verse deserves mention. Bilhah is here characterized as Jacob's "concubine" (*pilegeš*, פילגש). The terminology is unusual, since Bilhah is Rachel's slave and the majority of biblical references identify her as "a slave of Rachel." In Gen 29:29, Rachel's father, Laban, gives Bilhah as a slave (שפחה, *šiphâ*) to his daughter Rachel when she marries Jacob. In 30:3, 4, 7 and 35:25, Bilhah is called Rachel's slave. In addition, Gen 46:25 refers to Bilhah as a slave of Rachel, given as a wedding gift. Yet in 1 Chr 7:13, Bilhah is neither Rachel's nor Jacob's possession. There she belongs to her sons, who are identified as "the descendants of Bilhah." Bilhah appears in relationship to Jacob only one more time, in Gen 37:2. This verse calls her and Zilpah "the wives [נשים, *nāšîm*; sing. אשה, *'iššâ*] of his [Joseph's] father."

Immersed in androcentric bias, commentators take the term "concubine" for granted and presume that Bilhah turns automatically into

Jacob's concubine after Rachel's death.[53] The switch from "slave" to "concubine" does not bother them because, in their mind, Bilhah has "slept with" Jacob before. Indeed, the difference between an enslaved woman and a concubine is small. Like concubines, enslaved women are accustomed to giving birth to children who will be taken from them.[54] Both concubines and slaves have to submit to the orders of the superior, whether this person is a slave owner, a husband, or a king. Sometimes their tasks are different. A concubine's primary role is to provide children, whereas a slave also fulfills other functions. Furthermore, a concubine gives a man more prestige than a slave. A concubine may also reconcile political power struggles at the royal courts, whereas a slave never interferes into such affairs.[55]

Overall, however, the roles of a concubine and a female slave are similar, so that the term "concubine" in Gen 35:22 does not necessarily indicate a socially higher status than the term "slave." Even as a concubine, Bilhah is owned by Jacob, who has unrestricted sexual access to her body. It is thus inconsequential to Bilhah's position whether she is a concubine or a slave because in either case Bilhah lacks control over her life. She is property, and so Reuben challenges his father's property rights when he rapes Bilhah. Thus, this sad narrative illustrates an important, though depressing, truth about rape in androcentric and class-stratified texts: men rape women, enslaved or free, to mark their territory over against other men. In turn, a raped woman is irrelevant not only in the androcentric story world but also in the world of the interpreters. It is as if she is being violated twice.

The Royal Concubines

Three other passages that address the male struggle over leadership roles include rape or attempted rape of concubines. In these stories, lower-ranking military men, sons, or brothers challenge another man's higher standing. One narrative, 2 Sam 3:6-11, describes the power struggle between King Ishbaal and his commander, Abner. The woman involved is Rizpah, the concubine of Saul, Ishbaal's father. A second story is scattered throughout 2 Samuel 15–19 and illustrates the conflict between King David and his son Absalom. In this story, the son rapes ten unnamed concubines of his royal father and so challenges his authority. A third story appears in 1 Kgs 2:13-25 and exemplifies the power struggle between King Solomon and his older brother Adonijah. Abishag the Shunammite is the object of their dispute. Scholars have identified these passages not as "rape texts" but as depictions of disloyalty or claims to the throne. To many interpreters, the three narratives describe how one man, challenging another and more powerful man, "sleeps with" the latter's wives or concubines. As in other stories in which enslaved women appear, interpreters do not consider the viewpoint of the women, and rape is not an issue of concern to them.

A closer look at the three stories reveals the male self-centeredness. According to the first story (2 Sam 3:6-11), Abner is King Saul's army commander. After Saul's death, Abner stays under the command of Saul's son Ishbaal, who is the king of Israel for two years. Ishbaal's reign excludes the territory of Judah, over which his enemy, David, rules. When the army of David expands successfully beyond the Judean borders into Ishbaal's territory, Abner switches his loyalty (2 Sam 2:8—3:1) and begins supporting David. Abner's sudden allegiance to the Davidic monarchy finds expression in a dialogue between Ishbaal and Abner. When Ishbaal accuses Abner of having "come into" the concubine of his father, Abner is furious. He realizes that Ishbaal reprimands him for his attempt to gain royal authority, but Abner hides his real motives. Abner argues deceitfully that Rizpah, the daughter of Aiah, is just a "woman" and as such not worthy of their dispute. Then Abner turns against Ishbaal: "Here am I, full of faithful love towards the House of Saul your father, his brothers and his friends, not leaving you to the hands of David, and now you find fault with me over a woman!" (3:8). Abner claims innocence and asserts that he did nothing wrong with "a woman." Abner continues the lie when he argues that the king's distrust forces him to withdraw his support: "So may God do to Abner and so may God add to it! For just what Yahweh has sworn to David, that will I accomplish for him, to transfer the kingdom from the house of Saul, and set up the throne of David over Israel and over Judah, from Dan to Beer-sheba" (3:9-10).

The dialogue demonstrates that the concubine is secondary to both Ishbaal and Abner. She is an object through which each of the two men understands the other man's intention. She is irrelevant because Ishbaal and Abner are interested only in themselves. Ishbaal recognizes the difficulty of his situation, but he is a weak king and fails to take immediate action: "Ishbaal dares not say a single word to Abner in reply, as he was afraid of him" (3:11). Ishbaal, the king of Israel, understands that Abner has become his enemy, but he misses the opportunity to get rid of the commander. Lack of decisiveness costs Ishbaal his life; he is killed by David's army (2 Sam 4:1-12). Yet Abner does not live much longer; in 2 Sam 3:22-39, David's supporters kill him.

Is it just a coincidence that the narrated discourse names the concubine quite carefully as "Rizpah, daughter of Aiah" (2 Sam 3:7), whereas the male characters do not use her name even once? To them, she is "my father's concubine" (v. 7) or "the woman" (v. 8). God appears only in the curse of Abner, the rapist, who swears that "God may bring unnamable ills on Abner, and worse ones, too" (3: 9) if he does not support David. Abner does not survive his loyalty to this new king (3:27), and perhaps the murder indicates that the God of this narrative disapproves of Abner, the rapist. If so, the story indirectly supports the raped woman, Rizpah. Yet she disappears from the narrative almost as quickly as she appeared. Only one more time does Rizpah show up—when she mourns her two dead sons (2 Sam 21:8, 10, 11).

In this androcentric story world, concubines and enslaved women are secondary characters far from the centers of power. At best, Rizpah survives in the memory of a sympathetic reader. The short episode illustrates that a power-seeking man rapes a royal concubine and so expresses his disloyalty to his king. Abner's act is not only "an insignificant indiscretion" or "adultery"[56] but part of the male game for power. Whether the concubine consents is insignificant to the androcentric narrative perspective. The concubine is a prop of men and has to submit to them. In this sense 2 Sam 3:6-11 is a rape story that can be read as a lamentation about the fate of enslaved women as objects of men.

The other story about the rape of royal concubines centers on a conflict between King David and Absalom (2 Samuel 15–19). When David realizes that his son has won the solidarity of "the men of Israel," he decides to flee Jerusalem. "So the king set out on foot with his whole household, leaving ten concubines to look after the palace" (15:16). Later, Absalom's army occupies Jerusalem; during the occupation, Absalom's adviser, Ahithophel, recommends to Absalom: "Go in to your father's concubines, the ones he has left to look after the house, and all Israel will hear that you have made yourself odious to your father, and the hands of all who are with you will be strengthened" (16:21). Absalom heeds the advice and rapes the women in a tent placed on a flat roof so that the population is the witness (16:22).

Are the rapes of David's concubines part of the realized prophecy to David, as some commentators claim (without identifying Absalom as a rapist)? In an earlier story, the prophet Nathan warns David: "I will raise up trouble against you from within your own house; and I will take your wives before your eyes, and give them to your neighbor, and he shall lie with (עִם, 'im) your wives in the sight of this very sun" (2 Sam 12:11). Nathan predicts that David will be punished for his rape of Bathsheba and the murder of her husband (2 Sam 11:2-27), but the predicted situation differs from the sexual violation that David's concubines endure from his son, Absalom. The prophecy states that God will initiate the punishment, but in 2 Samuel 16 God does not cause the rape of the ten concubines. If the prophecy were a prediction of the event in chapter 16, the prophecy would create a serious theological problem because it would make God responsible for the concubines' sexual violation.

There is much more that could be focused on God's responsibility, but another pressing question awaits an answer: how to interpret what happened to the concubines. Perhaps predictably, commentators do not specify Abner's activity. Some maintain that Absalom "has taken" the concubines to claim the royal throne.[57] Others suggest that Absalom's action represents a "final humiliation of David" and "strengthen[s] the resolve of Absalom's supporters."[58] When David takes the concubines back upon his return (2 Sam 20:3), interpreters define this action as David's attempt to reassert his royal authority.

Only one interpreter, John Rook, focuses on the fate of the women when he states that, according to 2 Sam 20:3, the concubines "were shut away until the day they died, widows, as it were, of a living man." Rook also explains that in ancient Israel a "widow" (אלמנה, 'almānâ) is a woman who is no longer sexually active and lacks a male guardian. In his view, the king's ten concubines are "like widows" because they no longer have intercourse with men, not even with King David. The story illustrates the effects of male dominance in ancient Israelite society, in which women required male guardianship. Consequently, King David's decision to take care only of the women's economic and legal needs relegates the concubines to the marginalized roles of widows and lowers their status "to the basest level."[59] As Hans Wilhelm Hertzberg suggests, their lives turn into a "human tragedy."[60]

Interpreters sympathize with the concubines because they have to live the rest of their lives without male attention. But the question is, Why would the women want to be with any man, including David who had abandoned them earlier? A marginalized and insecure status is nothing new to the women, who were concubines their entire lives. Most important, they were collectively and publicly raped, so it seems unlikely that they would enjoy male company again. Perhaps they should rather be viewed as being relieved; they are finally left alone. But this possibility is unthinkable to interpreters who ignore that the women were raped. To them, Absalom "illegally claimed" or "royally married" the women,[61] and these commentators obfuscate the sexual violation carried out in public. Only Ken Stone entertains the possibility that Absalom raped the women: "The sexual relations between Absalom and David's concubines, for example, can be considered rape. There is no reason to think that these women would have been willing participants."[62] It is therefore possible to argue that the concubines did not experience their "widowhood" as a "human tragedy." Androcentric assumptions prevent interpreters from characterizing the concubines as finally being freed from heterosexist and classist demands and violence.

The story also illustrates that male competition is fought upon the bodies of the concubines. A son rapes his father's concubines, whereupon the father dismisses the women. Being raped, they depreciate his status. Since their responses are absent from the narrative, Rook observes correctly: "The women are offered no say in what happens to them, and we are not told how they felt or what they might have chosen for themselves had they been consulted."[63] The concubines do not speak, but are their feelings really so unknown, so silenced, so buried? They seem obvious once Absalom's action is identified as rape. The story depicts quite vividly the dire consequences of male domination: androcentrism crushes these enslaved women's bodies and spirits persistently and relentlessly.

Yet another tale illustrates that biblical rape stories have the potential to illustrate the destructiveness of androcentric dominance in enslaved women's lives. In 1 Kgs 2:13-25, Adonijah, the older half-brother of Solomon, seeks to marry Abishag of Shunem, who was previously forced to serve old King David (1 Kgs 1:1-4). When Bathsheba delivers the request to her son, Solomon becomes furious. Immediately, he orders the man killed who challenges his royal authority, and similar to Abner, Solomon swears: "So may God do to me, and more also, for Adonijah has devised this scheme at the risk of his life! Now therefore as Yahweh lives, who has established me and placed me on the throne of my father David, and who has made me a house as he promised, today Adonijah shall be put to death" (1 Kgs 2:23-24). And so it happens (1 Kgs 2:25). Solomon understands his brother's intentions: Adonijah attempts to claim the throne when he suggests marrying the young woman who served his father, the king. The marriage would give him primacy for the crown. Hence, Solomon arranges the murder of his brother to prevent the completion of Adonijah's plan. His death also saves Abishag from being married to a man who is ready to use her solely for his political advancement.

This should not surprise. In all of these stories, men regard women as sex objects at their disposal, and the focus on the men and their behavior exposes androcentrism's destructive consequences. Women, especially when they are slaves or concubines, are acted upon by men, who treat them as symbols of male power. Whether raped or not, the women are quickly forgotten, as the long history of androcentric interpretations demonstrates abundantly. Yet when we identify these texts as rape stories, the women's fate is exposed for what it is: lives either lost or co-opted by androcentrism and classism, as in the cases of Sarah, Rachel, and Leah. The tales do not offer a bright picture, but they offer illumination of tragic dynamics that continue to befall and shape the lives of both women and men even today.

Resistance, Hierarchies of Women, and Androcentrism

At the beginning of this chapter, the words of women enslaved in nineteenth-century America provided the perspective for reading the stories of Hagar, Bilhah, Zilpah, and the various concubines. There are, however, remarkable differences between the stories, and these differences deserve attention. Three differences will be highlighted here. The first relates to the issue of resistance. Nineteenth-century enslaved women, surviving numerous rapes from their slave masters, made many attempts to resist their rapists. In contrast, biblical stories do not portray enslaved women as actively defiant to the various forms of rape to which they are coerced. Not even Hagar, who finds a sense of pride in the pregnancy that resulted from the forced intercourse with Abraham, resists the rape as such. When she becomes pregnant, she conforms to the androcentric standards of her world in which fertility gives women societal recognition. She ends up not resisting Abraham but competing with the slave owner's wife, Sarah. Is this characterization of Abraham an androcentric strategy that aims to divide women? It seems to be. By contrast, nineteenth-century enslaved women displayed a remarkably different attitude when they identified the slave owner as the perpetrator, not his wife, and resisted their attackers as much as possible under the conditions of their enslavement.[64]

A second difference relates to the issue of competition and co-optation of women. Some biblical stories emphasize this problem, but it does not feature prominently in nineteenth-century narratives. Although it is a fair question to ask whether a slave-owning wife would give her slave to her husband for reproductive purposes, the biblical narratives leave little doubt about the impact of class on women. The rape stories of Sarah, Rachel, and Leah demonstrate that male privilege remains in place when women are co-opted into androcentric and classist structures. Under such circumstances, women take advantage of less-privileged women. Often interpreters take for granted such hierarchies, and as a consequence the enslaved women Hagar, Bilhah, and Zilpah are marginalized in androcentric and sometimes even feminist interpretations—leading to the conclusion that the women in these narratives are being violated twice over. At the least, the narratives illustrate the difficulties that many interpreters have in recognizing and dismantling class privilege in the androcentric lives of women in biblical narratives.

Finally, perhaps more than nineteenth-century tales, the biblical stories ask readers to confront androcentric perspectives and interpretations. Is it the biblical text itself that creates the problem of oppression, or can we read the androcentric and class-stratified stories in such a way that we understand experiences of women who live within sociopolitical, economic, and racist hierarchies even today? Since readers create textual meanings, it is up to them to interpret these narratives with alternative meanings. When the interpretations are grounded in a feminist perspective on rape, the stories of Hagar, Bilhah, Zilpah, and the royal concubines turn into brutal rape stories that illustrate the destructive forces of androcentrism and classism in women's and even men's lives.

CONTROLLING WIVES?
MARITAL RAPE FANTASIES

3

Rape in Marriage: A Hidden Phenomenon

Diana E. H. Russell's 1982 landmark book *Rape in Marriage* broke a firmly established taboo.[1] Until then wives did not have legal or social rights to say no to the sexual advances of their husbands in the United States. Once married, wives were at the mercy of their husbands and had to submit because their consent did not matter. Russell interviewed ninety women and asked them about experiences of sexual violence in their marriages. The interviews depict the horror and trauma experienced by wives when their husbands forced them to sexual intercourse. One of them, a forty-eight-year-old divorced woman, recalled her husband's rape this way:

> It was a brutal marriage. He was so patriarchal. He felt he owned me and the children—that I was his property. In the first three weeks of our marriage, he told me to regard him as God and his word as gospel. If I didn't want sex and he did, my wishes didn't matter. Our third child was a result of out-and-out rape.[2]

Her report leaves little room for romantic evasion. The husband's sexual violence toward his wife was grounded in his assumption that he owned his wife and children, and he disregarded his wife's agency thoroughly and completely. He demanded her total submission.

Another woman, who was twenty-four years old when her husband raped her for the first time, fared not much better. This woman's husband also insisted on her complete submission to his will, used excessive physical violence, and did not accept any resistance to his sexual needs. He viewed his wife as sexual property under his total control and domination. This woman describes her predicament with the following words:

He wanted me to have sex with him when I didn't want to. I had no desire. I didn't want him to touch me, so he forced me. He said I was his wife and I had to do it. I wanted to sleep on the couch but he forced me. . . . He said he was going to beat me. . . . He said I was his wife and he had a right to sleep with me when he wanted to.[3]

This wife's succinct description presents a clear power dynamic between husband and wife. The male thinks of his wife as his sexually available prop, as an object that he can physically force to engage in sexual intercourse. Russell's book includes many such "eyewitness" reports told from the perspective of wives who suffered through them. As a result, laws about marital rape slowly began changing in Western countries—though as I argued early in this study, rape continues to be greeted with a deafening silence in many places.

Since Russell's publication, other studies of marital rape have emerged. One of them presents reasons why husbands rape their wives.[4] Among the most prevalent are that (1) men believe they are entitled to have sex; (2) they want to punish their wives; and (3) they use rape as a means of controlling their wives. Raped wives recognize that husbands try to reassert their power and to control them through the rape. One wife observes: "The more control he thought he was losing, the worse it got."[5] Some husbands admit that they rape their wives to establish control. Others explain that they did not like it when a wife visited neighbors and friends, and they tried to curtail their wives' "new independence."[6] In short, studies of marital rape indicate that husbands rape their wives in order to gain control, sometimes very violently. At other times, rape is "just normal,"[7] and if the wife gets pregnant, nobody would suspect that the pregnancy is the result of marital sexual violence.

Marital Rape in the Hebrew Bible

Few biblical texts explicitly address marital rape,[8] but several prose and poetic passages include marital rape fantasies—from the perspective of men. These texts are found in Genesis, Hosea, and 2 Samuel, and this chapter examines these texts in three sections. The first section deals with the so-called wife-sister narratives in Genesis 12; 20; and 26, which feature Abraham and Isaac, their respective wives, Sarah and Rebecca, and a king, either the Egyptian Pharaoh or King Abimelech. The second section examines the poem in Hosea 2, and the final section discusses the well-known story of Bathsheba and David in 2 Samuel 11. The three sets of texts are marital rape fantasies in which a husband imagines his wife with another more powerful man against whom he may win or eventually lose. They present different game plans for a husband who fears the independence of his wife.

The various scenarios interspersed in the biblical canon provide repeated opportunities for such a neurotic husband to play out his deep fear. The wife's voice in these narratives is entirely absent; her perspective is irrelevant to the androcentric neurosis that permeates the texts—narratives that depict struggles with the man trying to regain control over the wife. The result is a series of marital rape fantasies of terrifying proportions. To be sure, these texts are not often read as marital rape fantasies, and sometimes readers grasp for different interpretations and reject reading these passages as stories about rape. Perhaps they hesitate to confront a topic so close to many people's lives. Others want to keep some distance between sacred texts and their experiences in life because they want to keep something holy and separate from the troubles they have experienced in the world. At the same time, a feminist hermeneutic that acknowledges the presence of sexual violence even in married life is honest and gives reason for hope, because it wrestles with a pervasive problem and gives voice to everyday experiences. In the case of marital rape, women may gain a voice to speak out about a taboo that is still rarely addressed. The following analysis of biblical fantasies of marital rape illustrates that a husband's need to control his wife takes many forms, which suggests that sexual violence against women is deep-rooted, with no easy solutions in sight.

Run, Sarah and Rebekah, Run!
A Marital Rape Fantasy

Repetition makes people remember things, and advertisers take advantage of this mnemonic device. They repeat their commercials over and over again. Yet when a story is repeated in the Hebrew Bible, people stop in confusion. Is it not enough to have a story told once? Scholars, too, look for an explanation when they review the thrice-told story in Gen 12:10-20; 20:1-11; and 26:6-11. Although cast and setting vary, the three versions contain the same basic story line. A man, either Abraham or Isaac, leaves his country with his wife, either Sarah or Rebekah. In the foreign land, either Egypt or Gerar, the husband is afraid that another man might want to sleep with his beautiful wife and kill him to get rid of him as the competitor. When the couple encounters the powerful representatives of the other nation, the fearful husband identifies his wife as his sister. She is placed into the harem of the king of the other nation (Pharaoh or King Abimelech) so that he has sexual access to her. At this crucial point the various versions begin to differ. In two narratives, the foreign ruler takes the woman into the harem (12:15; 20:2); in the third, he does not (chap. 26). In all of them the king discovers quickly—through a plague, a dream, or a chance observation—that the presumed sister is the wife of the man. Thereupon, the king returns the woman to her husband, who is compensated with goods and money before the couple leaves.

For historical critics, the hermeneutical problem is not so much the *content* but the *quantity* of these narratives. Critics have established that two different author groups composed the narratives: the Yahwist wrote Genesis 12 and 26 and the Elohist Genesis 20. They also maintain that chapter 12 represents an early stratum that later editors reworked, modified, and expanded into chapters 20 and 26.[9] This theory assumes that the duplication originates from different authors. For example, King Abimelech commits his error twice (chapters 20; 26) because each author group (E and J) composed a version, and both were included in the final redaction. This author-centered theory does not explain why the final redactors did not eliminate the duplications. Content is not central to the search for literary-historical origins, but Abraham's and Isaac's actions have disturbed interpreters and they have tried to explain the husband's decision. Especially in chapters 12 and 20, Abraham so easily and swiftly declares his wife to be his sister that scholars often express concern for the wife's welfare. They categorize the stories accordingly, and so Genesis 12; 20; and 26 are known as the "Endangering of the Ancestress,"[10] a title that expresses the danger in which the "sister-wife" or "wife"[11] found herself.

But what *actually* is the danger? Interpreters are often evasive at this point, although some define the danger as "adultery" and consider the story's vagueness to be an indication of the author's politeness. For instance, Hermann Gunkel explains that we do not know "what took place with Sarah in Pharaoh's harem—it would have seemed altogether too crude to state this in clear language—but we know what usually took place in the harem . . . ," and so "we may imagine . . . ," ". . . the entire ticklish situation."[12] Other interpreters are more explicit than Gunkel and state that the wife[13] is endangered by "adultery" or an "adulterous marriage."[14] The king had or planned to have sex with the married woman, thereby unknowingly threatening divine promises and the future of the husband. Hence, interpreters find "her honor and dignity" and "her life for [her husband's] sake"[15] threatened. Ilona N. Rashkow observes, "Sarah remains degraded as an object and I must share her anguish. . . . I as a reader understand the immorality of adultery, and the crime of female sexual sacrifice, more readily than Abraham."[16] Adultery is the threat that Rashkow classifies as "immoral," and she worries that Sarah's situation is perhaps worse than consensual adultery. What is going on in this narrative?

Several interpreters raise this question and decide that more is at stake than adultery. For instance, Matthias Augustin maintains that the characterization of these tales as "the endangering of the ancestress" conceals the dynamic between the king and the married couple.[17] The royal ruler not only endangers the wife but also takes "possession" of her. His action represents an explicit threat of violence toward the wife because the royal action is aggressive and violent; it relies on authority that disregards the autonomy of the woman. Only when the king's action is viewed accordingly do we understand why God punishes Pharaoh so severely (12:17).

Augustin suggests that the issue in the story is this: the king assumes that a woman can be taken whether or not she is willing, and so the king is willing to violate the created equality of women and men (Gen 1:27). Thus, Augustin argues, God does not punish Pharaoh for the adulterous act itself but for his disregard of the rights of socially

and politically weaker people. After all, the king could claim innocence—he believed a man who deceived him about his marital relationship with Sarah. God cannot punish the king for taking Abraham
(or Isaac) at his word. But God still punishes the king for his abuse of
power, which turns the woman into an object ready for his use. The
king disregards the desperate situation of the couple, who escape a
famine at home and arrive in his territory as strangers. According to
Augustin, this disregard constitutes the king's transgression.

J. Cheryl Exum offers an interpretation that does not focus on
adultery as the main characteristic of chapters 12, 20, and 26. She
assumes a psychoanalytic-literary approach, according to which she
reads the three narratives as an "intra-psychic conflict" of patriarchal
society. For Exum, this conflict consists of a male "neurosis" that fears
female sexuality. The narratives circle around that fear with the aim
of resolving the neurosis; they are a "semiotic cure," cast as a fantasy
that encourages men to imagine situations in which a man other than
the husband desires the wife. Three stories present the semiotic cure
in a three-step program. The first step imagines that the fear comes
true: the other man takes the wife sexually (Gen 12). The second
step presents God as an external authority that prevents the sexual
act after the wife moves into the other man's harem (Gen 20). The
third step describes the other man as having internalized the moral
code (Gen 26), upheld by God in the second step, and so the other
man does not come close to the wife because she remains close to her
husband at all times. Exum describes the three-step process:

> In Genesis 12, the super-ego (the pharaoh) is subject to id
> (Abraham); he takes the woman. In Genesis 20, the super-ego
> (Abimelech) has external moral support (God). He is subject
> to the id (Abraham) in that he takes the woman, but subject to
> external law (God) in that he does not touch her. But morality
> based on external authority is not the best solution for the patri-
> archal neurosis. In the third version (Gen. 26), the moral code
> is internalized; the fascination with the woman's desired and
> feared sexuality no longer poses a threat; the neurosis is cured;
> the cure is believed.[18]

For Exum, then, the three narratives instruct a male audience how to overcome their control issues related to their wives' sexuality. Exum's is a compelling interpretation because it makes all three versions necessary for establishing a coherent meaning of the narratives.

Exum's idea of reading the three narratives as efforts to cure an androcentric neurosis is the basis for yet another interpretation that views the stories as rape-prone fantasies about a husband's right to control his wife. Here the three narratives describe different pathological stages of the neurosis that range from worst-case (Gen 12) to compromise (Gen 20) and resolution (Gen 26). This fantasy is characterized by a husband's fear of losing sexual control over his wife to another man who, in turn, threatens to kill the husband. In the first stage (Gen 12), the neurosis is described to its fullest extent. It depicts the "nightmare" come true in which the husband indeed loses control over his wife's sexuality to another and more powerful man. Typical of the full-blown stage of the androcentric neurosis, the more powerful and wealthy man succeeds in depriving the husband of his wife, while the husband accepts that the more powerful and wealthy man would kill him if he resisted giving up his wife. Still, the neurosis finds solace in the idea that God would severely punish the powerful man who takes his wife.

In the second stage (Gen 20), the neurotic man does not experience the neurosis to the fullest extent because the narrative offers a compromise. The other man, again a powerful man represented by King Abimelech, turns into a less-threatening character because he returns the wife immediately when God informs him in a dream that the woman is another man's wife. The king also acknowledges that he would not have taken the woman if he had known the nature of the couple's relationship. He respects the exclusive rights of the husband over his wife and restores her to the husband, whom he compensates financially.

In the third stage (Gen 26), the narrative fantasizes about resolving the husband's neurosis, and so the other and more powerful man only threatens to take away the wife. No divine intervention is needed for the king to recognize the nature of the couple's relationship. When Abimelech observes the husband "fondling" his wife, he immediately speaks to the husband and learns about the couple's relationship. Both men respect each other's property and the wife remains with the husband as his possession at all times. All three narratives teach men to respect each other's rights as husbands and to stay in control of their wives. They also illustrate that the neurotic fantasies remain profoundly detached from the wife's perspective. She is silent and submissive as the object of male power, whether it is her husband or the other man. These are rape-prone fantasies with which a husband can learn to negotiate his fear about losing control over his wife.

This conclusion finds support from terminological, literary, and hermeneutical clues embedded in the narratives at various points. Terminological clues focus on three verbs that signify sexual coercion (*qārab*, קרב; *nāga'*, נגע; *ṣāhaq*, צחק). In 20:4, the verb *qārab* (קרב) can mean that Abimelech "approached" Rebekah either in a spatial sense or in a sexual way. Victor P. Hamilton chooses the latter, explaining that *qārab* (קרב) means literally "to approach" but "what is intended is not just 'drawing near' but a sexual encounter," similar to other passages (for example, Lev 18:6, 14, 19; Deut 22:14; Isa 8:3).[19] The verb indicates that the "solution" of this rape-prone fantasy entails the sexual coercion of the wife. The violent aspect of these narratives is demonstrated also in the meaning of the verb *nāga'* (נגע), which appears in 20:6 and 26:11 and is usually translated as "to touch (a woman)." M. Delcor explains that the verb "to touch" is "a euphemism for sexual relations" when it describes a man touching a woman.[20] In 20:6, the verb occurs when God addresses King Abimelech in a dream: "I knew that you did this with a blameless heart, and I kept you from sinning against me. That was why I did not let you touch her." In 26:11, the verb is part of Abimelech's speech in which he warns all people: "Anyone who touches this man or his wife shall be put to death."[21] In the former case the woman is the object of the man's touching; in the latter the king himself prohibits the touching of both the husband and the wife.

Yet the meaning of the verb is ambiguous—a fact confirmed in various English translations. The New Translation of the Jewish Publication Society recognizes the sexual nature of the verb only in 26:11 when the verb is translated as "to molest": "Anyone who *molests* this man or his wife shall be put to death" [emphasis added]. Here the translators chose an English verb that describes sexual violation. Yet in 20:6 when only the wife is mentioned, the same translation obfuscates the sexually abusive nature of the verb by simply rendering: "This is why I did not let you *touch* her" [emphasis added].[22] The International Version, too, translates the verb in 20:6 as "to touch" but in 26:11 as "to molest," whereas the Jerusalem Bible, for instance, translates the verb consistently as "to touch." This is peculiar because the basic meaning of the verb *nāgaʿ* (נגע) includes a level of violence and force that is always recognized in the stem's noun, *negaʿ* (נגע). For instance, the noun occurs in Gen 12:17 as a description of the penalty that Pharaoh and his household receive when he places Sarah in his harem. The plural noun, *negāʿîm* (נגעים), which is usually translated as "plagues," means literally "beatings" or "hits,"[23] which indicates the divine forcefulness of the punishment. This basic meaning also shapes the verb in 20:6 and 26:11 and indicates the level of violence that associates the king's touch and his warning with rape-prone activity.

Yet another verb confirms the rape-prone nature of the interaction between husband and wife in the "endangered ancestress" narratives— the verb "to fondle" (*sāhaq*, צחק) in Gen 26:8, according to which "Isaac fondles his wife Rebekah." Interestingly, the same verb appears in Ms. Potiphar's speech when she accuses Joseph of raping her (Gen 39:14, 17). Having undisputed sexual connotations there, the verb implies unwanted sexual advancement that may or may not signify rape, and in 26:8 it is therefore also translated as: "Isaac insulted his wife" and "he was malicious with his wife."[24] In Judg 16:25, this ambiguous verb describes what Samson has to do for the Philistines and is usually translated as "he danced for them"[25] or "he entertained them."[26] The sexual connotation is absent in these translations, perhaps to avoid homoerotic allusions, but some translators also suggest that the verb means "to play, sport, amuse, entertain."[27] The one-sided power dynamic between Isaac and Rebekah allows for a less playful understanding of the verb. Isaac acts upon Rebekah and she submits to her husband's "play." The husband is the grammatical subject and the wife the object. It is possible to argue that Isaac's public fondling carries rape-prone connotations, in which the wife is not a willing partner and the husband's activity entails force. If read accordingly, the verse depicts rape-prone activity by which the husband tries to reassert control over his wife in public.

Besides these terminological clues, a literary clue also endorses the interpretation of Genesis 12, 20, and 26 as stories that engage a husbandly neurosis of losing sexual control over his wife. In these narratives the female character, whether as Sarah or Rebekah, is always the object for the male characters, which suggests the rape-prone nature of the thrice-told story. The woman surrenders to male demands, passively moving from one male character to the other, and her consent is irrelevant.[28] She never speaks and her opinion is insignificant to the androcentric neuroses. The woman is the object of the husband, who is oblivious to her need and cares only about controlling her.

Next to terminological and literary clues about the rape-prone nature of this androcentric neurosis, hermeneutical clues from feminist perspectives strengthen the understanding of these chapters as a neurotic husband's rape-prone fantasies. For instance, Fokkelien van Dijk-Hemmes maintains that Gen 12:10-20 should be read in light of contemporary sex trafficking because Sarah's and Rebekah's fate is similar to contemporary women from impoverished countries who are forced into prostitution. These women's perspectives are usually ignored and, like Sarah and Rebekah, they are made into objects, lack support, and are sexually exploited by the very men whom they initially trust. Like contemporary pimps who cash in by telling the women: "You can't run away," the biblical husband benefits from the transaction with the king. The women stay in anguish, exploited and scared for their lives, similar to Sarah and Rebekah, who do not run away. Van Dijk-Hemmes explains: "Sarai, in her silent loneliness, embodies the fate of all those women who have fallen victim to the traffic in women which, even now, is widely practiced."[29] Both biblical wives and contemporary sex-trafficked women are "the object of men's manipulations," robbed and bereft of their voices and portrayed as passive and silent.

Yet van Dijk-Hemmes also finds significant differences between contemporary sex-trafficked women and the biblical women. In Gen 12:17, God helps Sarah by afflicting the king "because of the *word*

[עַל־דְּבַר] of Sarah." Here God turns into Sarah's covenant partner and rescues her from the ordeal. Yet God does not intervene on behalf of today's trafficked women. Moreover, the threat of sexual violence is not realized in all three biblical stories whereas the conditions of today's sex trafficking nearly always result in rape. What is important in van Dijk-Hemmes's approach, then, is that she recognizes the level of sexual violence in the "endangered ancestress" stories. They reflect rape-prone attitudes that persist in the sex trafficking of women even today.

In conclusion, Genesis 12, 20, and 26 emerge as rape-prone narratives that feature marital rape fantasies in which a husband worries about losing sexual control over his wife when she is handed over to another man who is more powerful than the husband. Exum views these stories as a "talking cure" for the neurotic husband. In line with Exum's idea, the stories can also be viewed as depictions of a chronic and systemic fear that characterizes much of androcentric culture and includes a rape-prone grammar that cannot be cured as long as androcentrism prevails. Read within this grammar, the three stories depict a threefold pattern of the neurotic fear that readers who are suffering from this pathology, can endlessly repeat in their minds. The three stories are not the only ones in the biblical canon that offer fantasies about wives being raped. Another text that illustrates the deeply ingrained androcentric goal of controlling female sexuality, but with a different solution, is a poem in Hosea 2. It describes the interior dialogue of a husband who dreams of acting out his neurosis by imagining the use of sexual violence as punishment for his wife's sexual freedom. He wants to take his wife back and control every aspect of her life. We turn now to this text.

Stripping Her Naked:
Foreplay to Marital Rape in the Book of Hosea

The poem in Hos 2:4-25 (English 2:2-23) describes the interior dialogue of a husband who dreams of acting out his rage over the sexual independence of his wife. He threatens to punish her (vv. 4-17; Eng. vv. 2-15) and later promises to take her back in love (vv. 18-25; Eng.

vv. 16-23). The husband begins with the children and tells them to plead with their mother. This father has a cruel relationship with his children, and he admits that he has no pity on "her" children "because they are children of whoredom" (v. 6). They, too, are only objects directed toward his goal of punishing her. He threatens to "strip her naked and expose her as in the day she was born," and his fantasy is to "make her like a wilderness and turn her into a parched land, and kill her with thirst" (v. 5). After imagining her death, he curses her: "She shall pursue her lovers, but not overtake them; and she shall seek them, but shall not find them" (v. 7). He imagines her with other men but grants her no success, which enables him to keep up the illusion of control. Furthermore, he fantasizes about holding her down and forcing her to expose her genitals in front of her lovers (v. 12). In his pornographic fantasy he does to her whatever he wants, and the punishment takes on cosmic proportions. For instance, he demolishes her gardens and turns them into a jungle in which only wild animals live (v. 14). He also holds back the raw materials necessary for her everyday needs, such as clothing and food (v. 11). In other words, he sees himself as all-powerful in relation to his wife so that no matter where she turns, he prevents her from being independent. In this poem, the husband is a godlike master who punishes his wife for leaving him (v. 15).

As is typical of sexually violent and controlling men, the husband moves from his dream of punishment to a seemingly opposite fantasy. After he imagines dismantling his wife's entire support system, the husband fantasizes about her coming back to his open arms. He also plans on returning her vineyards and offers to make a treaty with wild animals, birds, and creeping things of the earth (v. 20). This creation terminology is reminiscent of Genesis 1, as if to say that a new creation emerges upon her return to him (for example, v. 24). Many interpreters consider this section to be the moment of "reconciliation" between husband and wife. The husband fantasizes about the renewal of his marital vows with his wife (v. 21), dreams of being the creator of peace, and allows everyone to "sleep secure" (v. 20), so that in the end his children too affirm: "You are my God" (v. 25).

Traditionally, biblical scholars have considered this poem evidence of prophetic disapproval of Israel's lack of attachment to God. For these critics, the prophet describes how God, in the role of a husband, bemoans the "adulterous" behavior of Israel, his wife, who runs after other gods, the *bĕʿālîm*. Commentators read "with" the prophet's voice and side with God. The chapter is part of the larger Hosean message that defines God's action as educational and methodical procedures for regaining Israel's loyalty. Interpreters sympathize that God "passionately strives, in various ways, to achieve *one* aim: that Israel turn to him anew."[30] That God, as the husband, initially threatens his wife with severe punishment and later turns caringly toward her seems legitimate to many interpreters because "God suffers under Israel's deceitful love affair."[31] An interpretation that is critical of the image of sexual violence is incompatible with such readings of Hosea 2.[32]

Interpreters divide Hosea 2 into a prologue (vv. 1-3) and a main section (vv. 4-25), which contains various subunits. Dianne Bergant sees three oracles: a judgment oracle (vv. 4-17), a salvation oracle (vv. 18-22), and a concluding salvation oracle (vv. 23-25). Richtsje Abma agrees with these subdivisions, but views vv. 18-25 as a description of a "new future." Marie-Theres Wacker proposes a slightly different structure with the following three strophes: vv. 4-7b, vv. 7c-17, and vv. 18-25, and the middle strophe separates into three short units: vv. 7c-9, vv. 10-15a, vv. 15b-17.[33] Another outline follows the traditional view that divides the text into two strophes, vv. 4-15 and vv. 16-25. The first strophe, vv. 4-15, describes the threats of the husband toward his wife. Here the husband fantasizes about punishing his wife violently; the second strophe, vv. 16-25, elaborates on the husband's fantasy of regaining complete control over his wife. The division between v. 15 and v. 16 is grounded in the grammatical structure of the Hebrew sentence in v. 16a, which introduces a new stage in the marital relationship. The preposition "therefore" (*lākēn*, לכן), the particle *hinneh* (הנה), and the emphatic use of the personal particle "I" (*ʾānōkî*) (אנכי) indicate the break from the previous section. Even the content changes from explicit threats of punishment (v. 15) to establishing control over the wife (v. 16).

A detailed analysis of two elements in Hos 2:16 illustrates the sexual violence of the poem. The first verb of 2:16 (Eng. v. 14; פתה *piel*) hints at the ongoing violence that characterizes the relationship between husband and wife even after the husband regains control over his wife's sexual and financial affairs. The verb that is usually translated as "to seduce" is here in the intensifying stem (*piel*), which may include sexual force. Some scholars suggest that it can mean "to try to persuade." The verb occurs also in Exod 22:15, where it has undisputed sexual overtones,[34] although the legal situation and the young woman's consent are unclear. Another passage in which the same verb occurs also refers to sexual coercion. In Judg 14:15 and 16:5, the male Philistines encourage Delilah to "coax" (NRSV) Samson, to seduce him forcefully, into sexual cooperation. Thus, the terms "seduction" and "persuasion" may be euphemistic expressions for the subtle sexual force that is implied here and in Hos 2:16. To the husband, it matters little whether the wife consents, because he wants to get back his control over her and to be in charge over every aspect of her life, especially her sexuality. Accordingly, v. 16 is best translated as follows: "Therefore, behold, it is I who will enforce sex on her."

The second part of v. 16 offers additional insight into the sexually violent imagery of the poem. The phrase "he spoke to her heart" gives the impression that the husband speaks to his wife in a tender attitude. Yet van Dijk-Hemmes observes that the phrase "to speak to her heart" is "slightly out of place, to say the least" and does not mean, "he'll speak tenderly to her."[35] Other interpreters, too, contend that the phrase does not refer to romantic chatter but is "talk against a prevailing (negative) opinion" or an "attempt to soothe someone" after physical or psychological stress.[36] Accordingly, v. 16b depicts the husband moving from violent punishment to what some call "a pronouncement of salvation," after which the husband has control over his wife and the wife submits to him.

In short, Hos 2:4-25 describes a husband who fantasizes about acting out his fear of losing control over his wife's sexuality. In the first part of this fantasy, the husband threatens his wife with severe physical and psychological punishment, which includes sexual violence. In the second part, he imagines that he has regained control over his wife. In contrast to the thrice-told stories in Genesis, then, the poem in Hosea depicts a husband's response after his wife leaves him. Here the androcentric neurosis imagines the wife not only as an object of male action but as sexually active. The husband's response includes, first, that he punishes her and then promises to take her back, and, second, that he presents himself as always in control and in charge. Naomi Graetz laments such poetry as inherently dangerous: "[T]he prophet's marriage metaphor is problematic. It makes its theological point at the expense of women and contracts rather than expands the potential of partnership."[37]

Feminist interpreters define Hosea 2 as a prime text for imagery of sexual violence in the Hebrew Bible. In their view, it is not a description of an actual event between the prophet and his wife, Gomer, but an important metaphor that also appears elsewhere in the prophetic literature. The metaphor presents God as the husband and Israel as the wife, so that "the voice of God and the husband become virtually indistinguishable."[38] Renita Weems describes succinctly the marital dynamic imagined in the metaphoric poem in Hosea 2:

> The husband was outraged both by his wife's illicit behavior and by the fact that she wrongly ascribed to her lovers what rightly was his alone to boast: the honor of being her provider and benefactor (vv. 7, 12). He accused her outright in v. 5 of acting like a whore (zōnâ). . . . [A]lthough the husband's accusations were vague, his threats were crisp and clear. He threatened to strip his wife naked and to kill her with thirst (vv. 3, 5), barricade her with thorns and a wall . . . and then take back everything he had given her and leave her naked and empty (v. 9). There is no question of the husband's power in the relationship.[39]

Weems describes the extent of the divine husband's rage about his wife's sexual independence. At least in his imagination he is willing to annihilate his wife in order to teach her who is in charge. Weems explains that, when the husband tries to seduce his wife so that she will return to him after the abuse, the poem presents him as "the true victim in the marriage," "a man driven to extreme behavior by his unfaithful wife."[40] For Weems, the prophet is both "a poet and a dema-gogue" because "he captures his audience's imagination by posing to them something of a dilemma: faced with an adulterous wife, what was the logical, conventional, sound thing for an honorable man to do?"[41] The prophet effectively and skillfully presents issues of "power, honor, security, and justice" to his audience by manipulating "stereotypical images of women in assorted sexual dramas" and "exploit[ing] their greatest fears. . . ."[42] The poem follows an abusive pattern that persists today, which proves the ongoing rhetorical power of the metaphor. Weems maintains:

> Language influences our thinking about what is true, real, or possible. Not only does the image of the promiscuous wife have the potential to reinforce violence against women. It also has the potential to exclude whole segments of the population from hearing and responding to the biblical message. . . . With whom do we place our sympathies: the battered wife or the humiliated husband?[43]

Gale A. Yee emphasizes the fear that this poem induces in its eighth-century male and elite audience. In her view, the marriage metaphor is effective because it criticizes the male leaders of ancient Israel through a classic shaming strategy. The audience is asked to sympathize with the husband, who represents God, although in a surprise twist, the poem identifies the audience with the wife, a woman who "whores" with other men. By using the metaphor in this unex-pected way, the prophet criticizes his leaders by depicting their "radi-cal loss of status."[44] The poem tells them that they are like a wife who does not obey her husband as she should, and so the poem reinforces androcentrism. Yee explains: "Feminizing men in a marital relation with a male God reinscribes into the text the ideological and social links among women, subordination, shame, and sin."[45] The poem also exploits the idea that monogamy parallels monolatry, the worship of one god, so that the marital relationship between wife and husband parallels Israel's dependence on God. Yee writes: "He [the prophet] thus utilizes the inequity and exclusivity of ancient Israelite marriage to make his monolatrous point."[46] In her view, then, the poem's gender violence is only part of the surface meaning of the poem because behind it is "a conflict between Hosea and the northern elite." The prophet's marriage polemic intends to shame the male Israelite leaders into political, social, and economic responsibility. Thus, for Yee, the underlying criticism of the prophet focuses on class exploitation rather than on sexual violence. The latter is merely a rhetorical vehicle for the prophet's sociopolitical criticism of eighth-century male Israelite leadership.

In conclusion, the androcentric neurosis in Hos 2:4-25 deals with the husbandly fear come true. The husband can no longer control his wife, who has left him, and so he fantasizes. His fantasy dwells on severe punishment of the wife, which includes massive physical violence that is only a step away from public rape. The husband also dreams of taking her back and having cosmic control over her life. At this point, he imagines, his wife obeys him again and accepts him as "my man" (אישׁי, אישׁי); he is not one of many men anymore (v. 18). Yet, like Genesis 12, 20, and 26, the poem does not offer an escape from the androcentric neurosis but merely presents another game plan for a husband who fears his wife's freedom and independence. Thus, Hosea 2 encourages rape-prone fantasies in which the enraged husband strips his wife naked, punishes her violently in public, and then takes her back as if nothing had happened. These are frightening biblical texts that have been read to excuse a husband's sexual violation of his wife.

The third text that plays with a marital rape fantasy appears in 2 Sam 11:1-27 and invites the husband to imagine himself as the man who sexually takes over a wife. It is yet another game plan for the virulent androcentric neurosis in which a husband tries to control his wife, but this time the story eliminates the husband and turns the other man into the winner, who even marries the woman.

A Woman Bathing: The Fantasy of the Other Man

The third biblical passage does not lead to a happy end for the husband, but it almost results in an escape from the neurotic fear. In Genesis 12; 20; and 26, the husband enters a threefold movement that entangles him in a threat of losing his wife. In Hos 2:4-25, the husband loses his wife, as he fears, but the poem prescribes a response with which he will eventually get his wife back. Yet in 2 Samuel 11, the story of Bathsheba and David, the androcentric neurosis comes to a climax in which the husband not only loses control over his wife but is also killed. The other man gets his wife, impregnates her, and marries her after the husband is dead. In this narrative, the androcentric fear comes true. As in the other marital rape fantasies, the other man is a king, a role that signifies superior power and status. The betrayed husband is Uriah, a foreigner and a soldier of the very king who steals his wife. While Uriah fights the king's war, the king stays comfortably in his palace in Jerusalem, where, during an evening stroll, he sees the wife taking a bath on the roof. The king knows who she is: Bathsheba, the daughter of Eliam and the wife of Uriah the Hittite, and he sends his messengers to bring the woman to him. When she arrives, he sleeps with her (vv. 2-3). Since the power differential between the king and his subject could not possibly be greater, the woman obeys her king's command. Since her consent does not matter, his action equals rape, and afterwards he sends her back home. Time passes and she speaks for the first time only when she realizes that she has become pregnant (v. 5). The information leads to the death of her husband and to her new status as yet another wife in the harem of the powerful king. This is the worst-case fantasy of the androcentric neurosis, because the husband loses control not only over his wife but also over his life. If he wants to survive, he has to learn to identify with the king, yet another game plan for a neurotic husband who fears losing control over his wife. Is it possible that this homeopathic treatment in the form of a marital rape fantasy finally provides a "cure" for the neurosis?

Perhaps, but it might also require that the narrative be read as a marital rape fantasy by a husband suffering from the androcentric delusion of control. Yet, alas, the story of David and Bathsheba has been mostly read as a love story. Visual art, music, and even film have contributed to this view. In paintings of Rembrandt, Cornelis Cornelisz van Haarlem, and Carlo Maratti the woman is displayed as a nude who offers herself to viewers, as if to reinforce the notion that she is a temptress. In the 1951 film *David and Bathsheba*, produced by Darryl F. Zanuck and directed by Henry King, the king and the wife are extensively portrayed as falling in love with each other. In the 1985 film *King David*, produced by Martin Elfand and directed by Bruce Beresford, the king watches Bathsheba bathing, but he has sex with her only after their marriage. In this film, the king helps the woman get rid of an abusive husband while he waits patiently for her.[47] Often, Bathsheba is held responsible for the sexual encounter. Did she not intentionally take a bath on the rooftop to be seen by the king? George Nicol affirms that Bathsheba deliberately chooses this location to attract the king:

> It cannot be doubted that Bathsheba's action in bathing so close to the king's residence was provocative, nor can the possibility that the provocation was deliberate be discounted. Even if it was not deliberate, Bathsheba's bathing in a place so clearly open to the king's palace can hardly indicate less than a contributory negligence on her part.[48]

His is not an isolated position. Even feminist interpreter Lillian R. Klein maintains, "Bathsheba may well have been purifying herself on her roof with the hope of seducing King David into 'seducing' her."[49] Bathsheba seeks to gain the king's attention because, Klein argues, her husband Uriah is infertile. His infertility prevents Bathsheba from societal respectability, which she cannot enjoy without being a mother to a son. She offers herself to the king in the hope of advancing "her standing in the community" as mother and royal wife, according to Klein. In short, many interpreters see Bathsheba as a willing and initiating woman who is in charge of her destiny, a view that lets the king off the hook. Yet some interpreters wonder if Bathsheba was "free to say no,"[50] and some do not answer this question because they believe it "is a moot question . . . whether or not David rapes Bathsheba." They refrain from facing the possibility that the king rapes Bathsheba.[51]

Yet does it not matter that Bathsheba's consent is irrelevant? The power differential between her and the king is obvious. He is the king, whom she has to obey if she does not want to risk her life. She has to go to the palace and do what he wants. Some interpreters argue that she consented, because the phrase "and she came" (v. 4) depicts her arrival as a voluntary act. But he is the king, and she is compelled to obey royal orders. When he dismissed her, "she returned home" (v. 4). She gets in touch with him again only when she notices her pregnancy. Does the passage of time not indicate that love is not the point for the king, who satisfies his physical desire and then forgets the woman? Only pregnancy makes her demand royal responsibility, and so she sends a messenger who is advised to speak only two Hebrew words: "I (am) pregnant" (v. 5).

Read as another game plan that tackles the androcentric neurosis of a husband's need to control his wife, 2 Samuel 11 is assuredly not a love story. The story includes a new turn of events.[52] When the king hears the news, he does not hesitate to order the husband to get into his wife's bed. Yet the loyal husband does not comply and explains: "The ark and Israel and Judah remain in booths; and my lord Joab and the servants of my lord are camping in the open field; shall I then go to my house, to eat and to drink, and to lie with my wife? As you live, and as your soul lives, I will not do such a thing" (2 Sam 11:11). In this marital rape fantasy, the husband does not repeat the circular movement of Genesis 12, 20, and 26 because the narrative aims for another solution. Here the husband refrains from taking back his wife and does not cover up the royal betrayal; as a consequence, he is murdered. Uriah the soldier is sent to the front line of the war, where he dies in battle (v. 17). The king then transfers the wife to the royal palace and takes control over the pregnant widow. He marries her, and she gives birth to their first son (v. 27). Perhaps it is understandable that commentators read a romantic love affair into this worst-case scenario of the androcentric neurosis. After all, the husband is killed and his wife is transferred to the other man.

Thus, in contrast to Genesis 20, where God advises the king to release the wife to her husband, in Samuel 11 God does not save the woman or the husband. Nor does the king give money and gifts to the husband but initiates his death in the battlefield. The perpetrator encounters divine disapproval only when the deed is done: "But what David had done displeased Yahweh" (2 Sam 11:27—12:1-12). Hence, in this marital rape fantasy the husband does not get his wife back; he is murdered, and his wife becomes the possession of the king. The husband receives divine support only posthumously when the king repents and admits his guilt (2 Sam 12:13-14), and the child dies after illness (2 Sam 12:15-18). Still, the wife remains the king's fertile object: "He went to her, and lay with her, and she bore a son, and he named him Solomon" (2 Sam 12:24).

Conclusion: Not a Moot Point

Biblical rape fantasies imagine a wife as having sex with a powerful man who is not her husband; she appears mostly as his object whose consent does not matter. In the Genesis stories, the husbands, Abraham and Isaac, tell their wives, Sarah and Rebekah, what to do. In Hosea 2, the husband brings sexual violence upon his wife and then plans to remarry her. None of these texts uses explicit rape terminology, but the male actors do with the women as they wish. The goal of the fantasy is to get the wife back under husbandly control, even if he has to identify with the other man, as in 2 Samuel 11. Biblical rape fantasies teach husbands to control their wives, at least in their fantasy life, and if necessary, to employ sexual violence. This is a dysfunctional dynamic in which a wife's consent is irrelevant; what matters above all is that the husband subjects her to his will. This classic characteristic of rape, whether fantasized or practiced, needs to be recognized so that its pervasive influence can be brought to an end.

4

REGULATING RAPE
THE CASE OF BIBLICAL
AND ANCIENT NEAR EASTERN LAWS

Rape Laws Then and Now

The legal history of rape is long and varied and includes ancient Near Eastern and biblical laws that recognize rape as a crime—which may surprise some. When people learn about the ancient codes, they typically assume that the laws of old are too limited for the contemporary world. They believe our era is far more sophisticated and advanced than the ancient cultures, and they forget that our laws developed from the earlier laws in complicated ways. It is too simplistic to dismiss the ancient legislation without reviewing it first. Although the ancient laws cannot, of course, be applied to today's cases, they raise intriguing questions that are still important to an understanding of rape in past and present society.

But before we turn our attention to biblical and ancient Near Eastern legislation, a few words are in order about today's rape laws. They are a complex phenomenon shaped by national jurisdiction. Rape laws in the United States are particularly varied because each state has its own legislation.[1] For instance, the New York State Penal Code stipulates in Article 130.35:

> A person is guilty of rape in the first degree when he or she engages in sexual intercourse with another person:
> 1. By forcible compulsion; or
> 2. Who is incapable of consent by reason of being physically helpless; or
> 3. Who is less than eleven years old; or
> 4. Who is less than thirteen years old and the actor is eighteen years old or more.
> Rape in the first degree is a class B felony.[2]

This quotation is part of a longer legal discussion of rape, but one grammatical aspect stands out. The terminology is gender-neutral; both rapist and victim-survivor can be female or male, an assumption made since the legal reforms in the 1970s.[3]

Some American penal codes recognize that a sexual offense occurs in the absence of consent. Lack of consent exists under a number of conditions, such as "forcible compulsion," which elsewhere is defined as physical force, the threat of physical force—expressed or implied—or the threat of kidnapping the victim or a third person. Lack of consent is further defined as involving situations in which a person is physically helpless, of young age, mentally or physically incapacitated, or imprisoned. The New York State rape law also outlines different levels of severity and differentiates among first, second, and third degrees of rape and various degrees of punishment.[4]

Other states have their own rape laws. For instance, Ohio approaches the issue differently but exhibits similar sensibilities toward the issue of consent. In Chapter 2907.02 of Title xxix (Crimes—Procedures) of the Ohio Revised Code, the law specifies rape as follows:

(A) (1) No person shall engage in sexual conduct with another who is not the spouse of the offender or who is the spouse of the offender but is living separate and apart from the offender, when any of the following applies:

(a) For the purpose of preventing resistance, the offender substantially impairs the other person's judgment or control by administering any drug, intoxicant, or controlled substance to the other person surreptitiously or by force, threat of force, or deception.

(b) The other person is less than thirteen years of age, whether or not the offender knows the age of the other person.

(c) The other person's ability to resist or consent is substantially impaired because of a mental or physical condition or because of advanced age, and the offender knows or has reasonable cause to believe that the other person's ability to resist or consent is substantially impaired because of a mental or physical condition or because of advanced age.

(2) No person shall engage in sexual conduct with another when the offender purposely compels the other person to submit by force or threat of force.

(B) Whoever violates this section is guilty of rape, a felony of the first degree....

(C) A victim need not prove physical resistance to the offender in prosecutions under this section.

(D) Evidence of specific instances of the victim's sexual activity, opinion evidence of the victim's sexual activity, and reputation evidence of the victim's sexual activity shall not be admitted. . . .

(G) It is not a defense to a charge under division (A)(2) of this section that the offender and the victim were married or were cohabiting at the time of the commission of the offense.[5]

As this quotation from the Ohio law indicates, contemporary U.S. rape legislation is involved and specific. Emphasis is placed on gender-neutral terminology and the issue of consent. The Ohio law is striking for its first sentence (A.1), which limits the legislation to non-spouses, which a later paragraph (G) invalidates again. The Ohio law recognizes spousal rape in stating that marriage or living together is not a defense against a rape charge. This law also stresses that the rape victim does not need to prove physical resistance (C). As in the New York State law, age and the inability of the victim to resist or consent due to mental or physical conditions are specifically listed.[6]

Contemporary rape laws of other American states and other countries refer similarly to the issue of consent and resistance.[7] There is no doubt that rape legislation developed through a long and tedious process, and today's penal codes owe much to feminist challenges during the latter part of the twentieth century. Feminists had to argue assiduously that rape laws were steeped in patriarchal assumptions protecting the accused and making it difficult for victims to come forward with rape accusations. Still, the feminist success does not mean that androcentric bias is eliminated in contemporary U.S. court houses or in every law code.[8] The history of androcentric bias in rape legislation goes back to biblical and ancient Near Eastern laws, when a male rapist's protection was central, a women's consent disregarded, and gender-neutral terminology unimaginable. It is helpful to remember that many of the ancient laws were probably never upheld. This point is important because even today we are not always sure if rape laws are effective in regulating the crime, or if the general culture shapes the fate of the accused more than our laws do. Hence, contemporary American legal scholars wonder "about the complex connection between legal and cultural change. Which is the chicken, which the egg?"[9] In this sense, then, ancient rape legislation is of contemporary cultural interest because it has contributed to contemporary notions of rape.

The Hebrew Bible and five of the existing ancient Near Eastern law codes address the issue of rape. The biblical laws are located primarily in the book of Deuteronomy. The five ancient Near Eastern law codes are the Codex of Ur-Nammu, the Laws of Eshnunna, the Code of Hammurabi, the Middle Assyrian Laws (MAL), and the Hittite Laws. They cover the geographical territories of the ancient Babylonian, Assyrian, and Hittite kingdoms. Sophie Lafont, a commentator on ancient Near Eastern rape laws, underscores that "the sexual act enacted by physical or moral force is abundantly documented in the legal codes from the Sumerian to the Roman period,"[10] a time frame of more than two thousand years that goes well beyond the parameters of this chapter. Yet Lafont's comment indicates that rape legislation does, indeed, have a long history.

Rape Laws in the Book of Deuteronomy

Though few in number, biblical law codes contain several references to cases of rape. Some of them, widely recognized as rape legislation, are in Deut 22:25-29. Others are more contested and are not usually characterized as rape laws; they appear in Deut 21:10-14 and 22:22-24.

A Case for Marriage? The Law of the Enemy Woman

Many scholars interpret the case of the enemy woman (Deut 21:10-14) as a ruling about marriage during or after war. Accordingly, the law is often classified as a rule about "Marriage with a Woman Captured in War."[11] When the passage is discussed as part of the larger literary unit in chapter 21, exegetes sometimes define the passage more generally as a text on "Issues of Life and Death: Murder, Capital Offenses, and Inheritance,"[12] which regulates the "treatment of a woman taken as a captive in war and subsequently married by her captor, or purchaser."[13] Such definitions are based on an empiricist-positivist epistemology that advances androcentric ideology.

Although commentators do not usually elaborate on their hermeneutical perspectives, except perhaps to say that they rely on historical and literary methodologies, interpretations of the legal materials take on an aura of objectivity and inevitability. Such interpretations claim to present "the" meaning of the law as it was understood in its original context, a position that usually softens the soldierly claim for the "enemy woman" and emphasizes the need for marriage as the law's noble intention. That the marriage is coerced does not become problematic for the commentators. For instance, Duane L. Christensen appreciates the law as advice on abstinence in premarital consensual relationships. He explains that the law stresses "the importance of a husband and wife sharing common spiritual values as the proper basis of a lasting union." He suggests further, "We would do well to follow the example here in deliberately delaying commitment in marriage for a period of time to assure that the decision to marry is not based primarily on physical lust."[14] By asserting that the law of Deut 21:10-14 is morally and spiritually commendable, Christensen not only ignores its particularities—for example, a soldier "desiring" an enemy woman—but also disregards that in such cases the woman has no choice but to convert to the soldier's habits and religion. Christensen's interpretation mutates this rape law into a benign and even desirable ruling on marriage.

Ronald E. Clements also minimizes the coercion in the biblical law: "Even when the marriage was to a woman who had been taken as a captive and turned into a slave, that marriage could never be reduced simply to a master/slave relationship."[15] For Clements, marriage, rather than coercion, is the important lesson, although he does not provide a reason for the claim. He assumes the omniscient stance of an objective, universal, and value-neutral observer who does not disclose his hermeneutical interests. His assumptions remain hidden, and his perspective claims to present objective information, although in the case of Deut 21:10-14 he advances the perspective of the male soldier.

Other interpreters, too, focus on marriage and explain that this law regulates a specific kind of union, in which a male soldier wants to marry an enemy woman after the end of war. This position is perhaps most extensively and comprehensively developed in Carolyn Pressler's study on women in Deuteronomic law.[16] Pressler asserts that Deut 21:10-14 does not regulate a rape situation during war—a position she claims dominated earlier scholarly treatments.[17] In Pressler's view, the law regulates marriage between a male soldier and a foreign captive woman *after* war, providing the legal means for marriage when "normal procedures for contracting marriage are impossible."[18] The law also depicts a ritual necessary for the "former captive"[19] so that the soldier becomes legally qualified to marry her. Pressler stresses that the law regulates only a marriage between a male soldier and a foreign captive woman. It does not prohibit a "man from engaging in sexual relations with the woman without marrying her."[20]

Like other interpreters, Pressler does not disclose her hermeneutical interests. She proceeds as if reading from "nowhere," wanting to read the text as a "window to historical reality"[21] but only illuminating the perspective of the male soldier and the original legislators. Pressler's reading is grounded in the modern fallacies of objective literalism, scientific value-neutrality, and apolitical detachment.

Interestingly, however, Pressler does hint at the possibility that the law is a rape law. Firmly rooted in the reconstruction of authorial intent, she suggests that the law's drafters might have viewed the marriage as an imposition on the woman because it violated the woman "in some way." For Pressler, the original authors used the verb 'innâ (עָנָה) in v. 14 to hint at the violation.[22] In other words, Pressler proposes that the original writers recognized that the woman does not consent to the marital act and indirectly regarded Deut 21:10-14 as a regulation on rape.

Harold C. Washington writes from a more tentatively argued empiricist-positivist framework and clearly defines Deut 21:10-14 as a rape law. In a study on violence in biblical narrative, he maintains that readings are always located "somewhere" even if they presume to read from "nowhere." Accordingly, Washington attempts to connect contemporary lawsuits with biblical constructions of rape law: "My aim . . . is to contribute to the genealogy of this peculiar legal subject who appears in the courts even today—the man who by 'virtue' of his violence confirms his control of a feminine subject. . . . My interest is not in the juristic application of these laws in ancient Israel. . . . Instead I am concerned with the discursive capacity of these laws to construct gender."[23] This is not a historical reconstruction of the legal approach to rape cases in ancient Israel, but a more broadly conceived study of the historical discourse of gender as it emerges from the ancient laws. Washington writes from a "poststructuralist view of gender as a discursive product"[24] and examines the ancient laws as "foundational texts of Western culture . . . [that] authenticate the role of violence in the cultural construction of gender up to the present day."[25]

Washington's interpretation covers several legal texts in the Hebrew Bible, but it includes Deut 21:10-14. According to Washington, this law serves the following purpose: "The primary effect of the law is to assure a man's prerogative to abduct a woman through violence, keep her indefinitely if he wishes, or discard her if she is deemed unsatisfactory. . . ."[26] Unlike other interpreters, Washington recognizes the violence to which the woman is exposed, as outlined in the law. The woman is the object of the soldier's action, and Washington emphasizes the effect of the law on the woman's ability to be in control:

"The fact that the man must wait for a month before penetrating the woman . . . does not make the sexual relationship something other than rape. . . . Only in the most masculinist of readings does the month-long waiting period give a satisfactory veneer of peaceful domesticity to a sequence of defeat, bereavement, and rape."[27] For Washington, the law is about rape, and he criticizes readings for being "masculinist" and charges them with favoring the soldier's perspective.

Yet, despite this strong language and the interpretative focus on gender as a "discursive product," Washington still locates the legal meaning of Deut 21:10-14 primarily within the ancient text. The law is the agent, and so Washington writes: "By authorizing the violent seizure of women, this law takes the male-against-female predation of warfare out of the battlefield and brings it to the home." In Washington's view, the law *itself* creates meaning as if it advanced male violence in the home, ignored the women's perspective, authorized androcentric bias, and was not the basis for a reader's rejection or support of androcentric policy. When Washington addresses the particularities of 21:10-14, he succumbs to an empiricist-scientific epistemology as if readers were not in charge. Still, Washington's analysis is a rare example because it exposes androcentric bias in other interpretations, considers a woman's perspective, and illustrates the potential of multiple meanings in the biblical law. Hence, in contrast to other interpreters, Washington does not promote Deut 21:10-14 as a marriage law. He acknowledges that this legal case is about rape.

The Death Penalty for Adultery? The Legislation in Deut 22:22-29
The debate about the meaning of biblical rape laws is contested also in the legislation found in Deut 22:22-29, although most scholarly interpreters search for authorial intent and hesitate to characterize these laws as rape legislation. They attempt to reconstruct the original intent of the ancient legislators without acknowledging that their reconstructions, in fact, rely on androcentric assumptions. What appears to be the undisputed, fixed, and singular meaning of the laws is actually complicated and dependent on the hermeneutical assumptions being

employed. When the perspective emphasizes rape, Deut 22:22-29 contains four rulings on rape and not on adultery, as many commentators contend. The four cases are v. 22; vv. 23-24; vv. 25-27; and vv. 28-29, and they are part of a larger section on what interpreters variously call "family and sex laws,"[28] "Marital and Sexual Misconduct,"[29] "Miscellaneous Laws, relating chiefly to Civil and Domestic Life,"[30] or "a subset of the general law of adultery preceding them in Deut. 22:22."[31] As these titles indicate, in the history of interpretation these four rulings have rarely, if ever, been regarded as rape legislation.

The first case appears in v. 22. Here, a man and a wife of another man receive the death penalty after they are found "lying" together. The question is if their "lying" is consensual, an ambiguity that the literature does not emphasize. Many interpreters assume that the law addresses consensual sex, and so they characterize it as a rule on adultery. For instance, Jeffrey H. Tigay entitles his interpretation of the law "Adultery with a Married Woman."[32] He relates the law to a ritual procedure described in Num 5:11-31, in which a husband suspects his wife's adultery. Tigay also relates the Deuteronomic law to Lev 20:10, which orders capital punishment for adulterous behavior. Similarly, Tikva Frymer Kensky, following Tigay's lead, characterizes Deut 22:22 as a law against adultery.[33]

The situation is not as simple as it appears, however. The prose in Deut 22:22 is terse and does not provide conclusive information on the precise nature of the relationship between the man and the woman. The law focuses on the punishment and not on the description of the crime; it does not specify if the "lying" is consensual or forced, and it elaborates only on the consequences of the man "lying" with the woman. It is possible to conjecture that the man threatened or forced the woman and that she did not consent, but the focus of the law is on the penalty. It prescribes that both parties are to be put to death. Many interpreters believe that the penalty suggests the consent of the woman. She is guilty too and receives the appropriate penalty as an adulteress. It is also possible, however, to argue that the penalty does not indicate her guilt. Rather, the penalty is based on androcentric jealousy that punishes a woman for any sexual activity outside of marriage and disregards her consent completely.

A comparison with ancient Near Eastern laws in cases of assumed adultery shows that the biblical law is actually quite harsh in prescribing the death penalty for the woman, regardless of her consent. In ancient Near Eastern laws, sex between a man and a married woman does not necessarily entail the death penalty, but these laws prescribe a range of options that are left to the offended husband. He must determine the severity of the penalty. For instance, Middle Assyrian Law (MAL) 15 stipulates:

> 15. If a seignior has caught a(nother) seignior with his wife, when they have prosecuted him (and) convicted him, they shall put both of them to death, with no liability attaching to him. If, upon catching (him), he has brought him either into the presence of the king or into the presence of the judges, when they have prosecuted him (and) convicted him, if the woman's husband puts his wife to death, he shall also put the seignior to death, but if he cuts off his wife's nose, he shall turn the seignior into a eunuch and they shall mutilate his whole face. However, if he let his wife go free, they shall let the seignior go free.[34]

Like the Deuteronomic law, this law focuses only on the moment when a husband finds his wife with another man. In both cases, the emphasis is on the post-discovery phase and the husband determines the form of punishment. The husband may even decide to let the woman go free, which automatically frees the other man. Still, the law also leaves undetermined what the precise nature of the crime is. Is it adultery or was the woman forced by the other man? It is unclear. What matters to the law is that the husband is the offended party who determines the extent of the conviction. In this sense MAL 15 differs from the biblical parallel. The ancient Near Eastern law authorizes the husband to determine the form of the penalty, which ranges from the death penalty for both to cutting off the woman's nose and the other man's testicles, or no penalty at all. The husband is in charge in MAL 15, whereas the Deuteronomic law establishes the penalty independently from the husband.

A similar case appears in §129 of the Code of Hammurabi, which also offers various penalty options that range from drowning to leniency. It, too, emphasizes the post-discovery phase and does not detail whether the woman consented. The scholarly literature classifies this law as one on adultery, although the actual crime is not specified.

> 129. If the wife of a seignior has been caught while lying with another man, they shall bind them and throw them into the water. If the husband of the woman wishes to spare his wife, then the king in turn may spare his subject.[35]

Again, the emphasis is on the penalty options, and the law allows the husband to spare his wife and consequently the other man. In other words, ancient Near Eastern laws do not exclusively prescribe the death penalty for cases that scholars usually categorize as laws on adultery. These laws present several penalty options, whereas Deut 22:22 is more limited and orders much harsher punishment.[36] It is noteworthy that neither the biblical nor the ancient Near Eastern laws identify the transgression as adultery; the question of the woman's consent is left to the readers. It is possible to consider these laws as rape cases in which androcentric jealousy condemns a woman as guilty regardless of her consent.[37] Yet only the ancient Near Eastern laws give an offended husband some leeway in letting his wife off the hook, whereas Deut 22:22 prescribes one option, the death penalty, even if the woman may have been raped. It is a case of androcentric ideology gone awry.

The second case, Deut 22:23-24, supports the interpretation of v. 22 as a rape case, although some scholars read vv. 23-24 as a case of seduction. In vv. 23-24, the law orders the death penalty for both an engaged young woman and a man who has sex with her in town. The law explains that he "met" her in town, and it finds both guilty because nobody heard the woman's cry for help.[38] Many interpreters explain that this law assumes her consent, and so they classify the case as a law on adultery. Tigay, for instance, entitles his interpretation of this and the next unit as "Adultery with an Engaged Virgin (vv. 23-27)."[39] Alexander Rofé elaborates on vv. 23-24 in a section on ancient legislation on adultery,[40] and Duane

L. Christensen talks about "the law of the seduction of a betrothed woman."[41] Nevertheless, some commentators characterize vv. 23-24 as rape legislation[42] because, to them, the law does not exclude the possibility that the woman called for help. It merely states that no one heard her, which could describe a situation of rape in which a man forces a woman to have sex while no one is there to assist her. As in the case of v. 22, the law of vv. 23-24 also stipulates the death penalty for both the woman and the man. Yet again the penalty does not address the issue of the woman's consent. The omission is part of androcentric ideology, which ignores a woman's viewpoint and distrusts her words or actions. Readers who accept this ideology do not look for ambiguity, and they miss the possibility that the woman is innocent.

After the two contested rape laws, a third case (vv. 25-27) depicts an unmistakable situation of rape—even to androcentric interpreters. In vv. 25-27, a woman is raped "in the open country," and the law recognizes her innocence because no one was able to hear her cry for help. Androcentric ideology, trusting outside witnesses rather than a woman's word, does not need to hear anything else. The rapist is declared guilty, and interpreters predictably comply with the legal opinion. Significantly, the laws in vv. 25-27 and in vv. 23-24 hint at sexual violation. The verb "to rape" ('innâ, עָנָה piel) appears in v. 24, and in v. 25 the man "seizes" or "catches" the woman. The verbs convey her unwillingness and his active effort to get her.[43] Similar terminology appears in ancient Near Eastern rape legislation, connoting the force of the attack.[44] Clearly, then, these laws are about rape.

The androcentric perspective, mostly taken for granted in the scholarly literature, is at its worst in the last part of the Deuteronomic rape legislation (vv. 28-29). This fourth case describes the rape of a single young woman and stipulates that her father has to receive financial compensation as a remedy for the rape, a solution that is found also in the Code of Hammurabi §156 and MAL 55. The biblical law orders that the rapist marry the young woman "because he raped ['innâ, עָנָה] her" (v. 29). Here Deuteronomic law is considerably harsher than ancient Near Eastern law, specifically §156 of the Code of Hammurabi, which allows the raped woman to marry whomever she wants. The biblical law is also more restrictive than MAL 55, which gives the father of the raped woman several options, including one in which his daughter can be married off to the rapist. In biblical law codes, only Exod 22:16, a case of pre-marital consensual sex between a young woman and her lover, mentions a father's options. There the father is authorized to order or to refuse a wedding between the two, or to demand financial compensation.[45]

Deut 22:28-29 is unquestionably androcentric in its emphasis on the interests of the father, and interpreters of a modern scientific mind-set accept the androcentric bias without further commentary. Thus, Harold C. Washington remarks correctly: "The laws do not interdict sexual violence; rather they stipulate the terms under which a man may commit rape. . . ."[46] The problem here is that some interpreters follow this stipulation and do not question the *legal* bias that promotes male sexual violence. They perpetuate as objective, value-neutral, and universal a concern that represents only one possible reading, and they do not analyze as rhetorical constructs laws that may never have regulated ancient people's "real" lives.[47] Whether readers discuss these regulations in the context of adultery, seduction, or marriage, their interpretations assume an empiricist-positivist epistemology that drops rape as an explanation for these cases of sexual violence.

"If a Man . . . ": Rape Laws in Ancient Near Eastern Codes

Scholars of ancient Near Eastern rape laws do not show much, if any, appreciation for the notion that all exegetical work is contextualized, particularized, and localized, and that readers are central in the process of "meaning making." They assume objectivity, value neutrality, and universality for their exegetical work, and classify as sex offenses, adultery, or marriage laws what is really legislation on rape. When these laws are read in today's global rape culture, they address issues related

to rape and should be classified as such. Any other terminology obfuscates the serious problem these laws address. Interestingly, older scholarship is sometimes more open to the characterization of these cases
as sexually violent, though the earlier studies also do not consistently
define the laws as rape legislation.[48] For instance, an influential 1966
article by J. J. Finkelstein entitled "Sex Offenses in Sumerian Laws"
differentiates between "coercive" and "consentive" Sumerian laws, and
a chart defines the "coercive" laws as rape laws.[49] In his essay, however, Finkelstein uses only the term "adultery." Indirectly, Finkelstein
provides a rationale for his terminological preference of "adultery"
when he comments on the meaning of a text called "A Trial at Nippur
(3NT403+ T340)." The first line of the Sumerian law reads:

> Lugalmelam, son of Nanna'aramugi seized Ku(?)-
> Ninšubur, slave-girl of
> Kuguzana, brought her into the KI-LAM building, and
> deflowered [sic] her.[50]

The key question here is, What actually happened between the
man called Lugalmelam and the enslaved young woman called Ku(?)-
Ninšubur? Finkelstein allows for the possibility that the woman was
raped but then dismisses it as socially "immaterial" for Mesopotamian
law. In his view, rape, seduction, and consensual sex were interchange-
able offenses against the slave owner. He explains:

> From the juridical point of view it may be worth mentioning
> that the trial does not discuss the question of whether the slave-
> girl was raped or was a willing partner in the offense. This is
> unquestionably to be explained by the fact that in the eyes of
> Mesopotamian law, consent in such cases is immaterial. Hence,
> her sexual violation, whether by rape, seduction, or even by her
> own solicitation, is exclusively considered as a tortuous invasion
> against her owner, for which he may seek redress. . . .[51]

In other words, Finkelstein claims to read from the perspective of the
presumed original writers ("the eyes of Mesopotamian law") when he

characterizes the slave owner as the violated person who "may seek redress." Finkelstein prefers the term "adultery" to "rape" because he claims that to the ancient lawgivers it was irrelevant whether the woman was raped, seduced, or participating in consensual sex. The law focuses on the slave owner, whom it seeks to protect. From this perspective, Finkelstein develops the legal meaning, favoring the male owner or husband and disregarding the woman's perspective, although he does not clearly acknowledge that this is what he does. Thus, Finkelstein mentions the possibility of rape and then dismisses it as an option, claiming that the "intent" of the Mesopotamian law prohibits this choice. Consequently, Finkelstein examines legal cases on "adultery" as perceived by the supposed status quo of ancient society, even though the article's title promises a study of "sex offenses."

Finkelstein's analysis has had considerable influence, and his problematic terminological choices have made their way into other studies. For instance, in an article entitled "Adultery in Ancient Law," Raymond Westbrook refers to Middle Assyrian Law 12 as an illustration of vocabulary that is sometimes used to make a point about the rights of a husband when his adulterous wife is discovered "*in flagranti delicto*."[52] To make his point, Westbrook quotes the law to explain the legality of punishing an adulterous woman. Like Finkelstein, Westbrook does not acknowledge that his attempt to connect MAL 12 and vocabulary of adultery is complicated. After all, this law is a recognized rape law. Perhaps for Westbrook, standing in Finkelstein's tradition, the difference between rape and adultery is negligible because in his view "adultery forms part of a complex of interrelated scholarly problems discussing social offenses such as seduction and rape."[53] Like Finkelstein, Westbrook assumes an empiricist-positivist epistemology that prevents him from disclosing his hermeneutical perspective and makes his study appear to be an "objective" treatment of ancient law. Westbrook can thus assume as fact that adultery and rape are linked while at the same time failing to discuss his rationale for making such a connection, which is obviously androcentric and contributes to prejudices about rape.[54] Perhaps Westbrook's argumentation would be different if Finkelstein had not made a similar case twenty-five years earlier.

Still, some scholars assume a different hermeneutical premise and maintain that ancient Near Eastern law codes address rape as a distinct problem. For these scholars, such laws are part of a long history that is "abundantly documented in the legal codes from the Sumerian to the Roman period."[55] Unfortunately, during the past century, not a single scholarly study has examined ancient Near Eastern rape laws in depth. This is most apparent in the multi-volume *Reallexikon der Assyriologie und Vorderasiatischen Archäologie*, a renowned reference work of ancient Near Eastern materials, which has yet to publish a single entry on rape.[56] We turn now to a discussion of selected laws in the Codex of Ur-Nammu, the Laws of Eshnunna, the Code of Hammurabi, the Middle Assyrian Laws, and the Hittite Laws. In this chapter they are treated as legislation on rape.

The Codex of Ur-Nammu from Sippar

The fragmentary tablet contains two laws on rape in §§6 and 8. According to Fatma Yildiz, the first paragraph reads as follows:

> 6. If a man the wife of a young man in service (*guruš*)
> whose marriage has not yet been consummated,
> using violence deflowers her,
> that male they shall slay.[57]

The particular legal situation remains grammatically unclear in this translation because of its closeness to the Sumerian original. Another, smoother translation rearranges the syntax: "If a man uses violence against the wife of a young man, who has not been deflowered, and deflowers her, this man shall be killed."[58] The ancient law describes a situation that other law codes also mention: a man "uses violence" against a woman who is in the process of getting married but has not yet had sex with her fiancé. The law orders the death penalty for a rapist who attacks a woman of this status. It is important to note that the Sumerian text relies on two verbs to communicate the action of rape, which in English are rendered as "to use violence" and "to deflower." Accordingly, the woman does not consent or volunteer to sexual activity. She is raped. The Codex of Ur-Nammu from Sippar contains a second law, §8, about another situation of sexual violence. There a man rapes an enslaved woman.

> 8. If a slave-girl
> who is a virgin
> a man deflowers
> with violence,
> he shall pay 5 shekels of silver.[59]

In contrast to §6, this law does not prescribe the death penalty. When a man "deflowers with violence" an enslaved young woman, he has to pay only a monetary fee. It is unclear to whom the fee is paid, and usually commentators maintain that the money goes to the slave owner. They also assert that the penalty represents the value of an average enslaved woman, who is of less value to her owner than a married woman is to her husband.[60] Moreover, interpreters explain that the rape of an enslaved woman would not raise paternity issues, whereas the first law is about an engaged virgin. Thus, in §8 the fee is low. Interpreters are silent about the fact that both laws ignore the woman's perspective, whether she is enslaved or free. They focus on the damages accrued to a husband or a slave owner, according to which the rape of a married young woman requires a more severe penalty than the rape of an enslaved woman. Like the laws themselves, then, interpreters endorse an offensive expression of classism.[61] Yet both laws entertain situations of rape—a point that the scholarly literature, tied as it is to modern-scientific epistemology and enmeshed as it is with androcentric bias, has not emphasized. And so, yet again, a recognition of rape is absent.

The Laws of Eshnunna

The Laws of Eshnunna contain two rape cases that are similar to §§6 and 8 of the Codex of Ur-Nammu. They read as follows:

> 26. If a man gives bride-money for a(nother) man's daughter, but another man seizes her forcibly without asking the permission

of her father and her mother and deprives her of her virginity, it is a capital offence and he shall die.

31. If a man deprives another man's slave-girl of her virginity, he shall pay one third of a mina of silver; the slave-girl remains the property of her owner.[62]

In the first case, a man rapes an engaged woman, and in the second case a man rapes an enslaved woman. In the first situation, the man receives the death penalty for the "capital offense," but in the second situation he is merely asked to make a payment. Class discrimination leads to discrimination regarding the extent of the penalty.

The Code of Hammurabi

Several laws of the Code of Hammurabi relate to forced sexual intercourse, but the scholarly literature acknowledges only §130 as a rape law. It reads:

130. If a seignior found the (betrothed) wife of a(nother) seignior, who had no intercourse with a male and was still living in her father's house, and he has lain in her bosom and they have caught him, that seignior shall be put to death, while that woman shall go free.[63]

The law of §130 is similar to §6 of the Codex of Ur-Nammu from Sippar and §26 of the Laws of Eshnunna, but it also adds two pieces of information. First, the woman is still living with her parents, and, second, the law emphasizes that the woman is not to be punished and only the rapist shall receive the death penalty. This is clearly a rape law and recognized as such even by Finkelstein: "This case too is an act of rape."[64]

Sometimes, however, interpreters avoid the term "rape," especially when they speculate about the rationale of ancient Near Eastern marriage laws. For instance, Westbrook finds §130 of the Code of Hammurabi to be similar to §26 of the Laws of Eshnunna. For Westbrook, both laws explain what happens under conditions of an "inchoate marriage,"[65] which is defined by "a lapse of time between conclusion of the marriage contract and the act of marriage."[66] In Westbrook's view, §130 of the Code of Hammurabi is part of a larger rubric of marriage laws; hence, he does not discuss rape there or anywhere else, despite references to this and similar laws.

Westbrook is not alone in the obfuscation of ancient Near Eastern rape legislation. Much of the scholarly literature has not identified rape as an issue. In fact, scholars often treat ancient Near Eastern rape laws as pertaining to marriage and adultery. For instance, Eckart Otto supports the notion that §130 of the Code of Hammurabi describes marital procedures.[67] Walter Kornfeld mentions "the case of a rape of a young engaged girl" in his study of adultery but refrains from further comments.[68] Similarly, Benno Landsberger's translation and commentary mention the relevant rape terminology in German, such as the verbs *vergewaltigen*, and the old-fashioned *notzüchtigen*, and the nouns *Vergewaltiger* and *Notzucht*, but he mentions these laws within the larger context of the subject of virginity.[69] Androcentric bias and modern scientific epistemology merge into a potent combination that eliminates interpretative alternatives and avoids classifying these laws as rape legislation.

Yet, when this potent combination is dismantled and interpretative interests are disclosed, the Code of Hammurabi is shown to contain additional rape laws and, more specifically, laws on incestuous rape: §§154, 155, and 156. The first of these reads as follows:

> 154. If a seignior has had intercourse with his daughter, they shall make that seignior leave the city.

If interpreters mention this law at all, they discuss it as a case of incest and not of rape. Yet it is certainly also relevant as a rape law because it refers to the problematic situation in which a father rapes his daughter.[70] The Code of Hammurabi does not prescribe the death penalty for this crime because, as scholars often explain, the rape does not threaten another man's paternal rights or legal authority. He is the man in charge, but he is, however, required to leave town.

The next law, §155, describes another situation of incest.

155. If a seignior chose a bride for his son and his son had intercourse with her, but later he himself has lain in her bosom and
they have caught him, they shall bind that seignior and throw
him into the water.

In this case, the father has sexual intercourse with the fiancée of his
son. Is it imaginable that the bride consented? The law stipulates that
the father has to be drowned if he is caught in the act of raping his
son's bride. Does this mean that the father would go free if he were not
caught? The law does not consider this possibility and only mentions
what happens if he is caught. As always, the perspective of the young
woman remains conspicuously absent from the law. Does she go free
and marry the rapist's son?
Another incest law focuses on the bride of a father's son.

156. If a seignior chose a bride for his son and his son did not
have intercourse with her, but he himself has lain in her bosom,
he shall pay to her one-half mina of silver and he shall make good
to her whatever she brought from her father's house in order that
the man of her choice may marry her.

This law portrays a situation in which a bride did not yet have sex
with the man whose father rapes her. Accordingly, the father is only
required to pay a fine, and the bride is free to marry whomever she
wishes to marry. This is a surprising offer, since other laws prescribe
a marriage between the woman and the first man who had sex with
her, whether or not the sex was violent.[71] Nor does this case mention
whether the bride consented. It is a potential rape law that grants
decision-making power to a woman.[72]

The Middle Assyrian Laws
The Middle Assyrian Laws describe four such scenarios, all of which
refer to overt situations of a man raping a woman. In §§12, 16, and

23, the woman is married, and in §55 she is young, single, and lives in the parental home.

> 12. If, as a seignior's wife passed along the street, a(nother) sei-gnior has seized her, saying to her, "Let me lie with you," since she would not consent (and) kept defending herself, but he has taken her by force (and) lain with her, whether they found him on the seignior's wife or witnesses have charged him that he lay with the woman, they shall put the seignior to death, with no blame attaching to the woman.[73]

This law depicts an indisputable rape scene. A married woman is attacked by a man in the street. She resists, but he succeeds in raping her. This is the classic rape scenario, and the Akkadian terminology is unambiguous. The phrase *emûqa sabâtu* is usually translated as "to take by force."[74]

The punishment for the rapist is the same as in other ancient Near Eastern laws. He receives the death penalty only if—and this is the androcentric limitation of this particular law—other people wit-ness the crime and incriminate the rapist for it. The charge depends on others because a woman's word does not suffice. Still, the *very existence* of the law demonstrates that rape was seen as a problem, even if this law was never legislatively observed in the Middle Assyr-ian empire.[75]

The law in §16 presents a rape case next to one on adultery. The first case refers to a married woman who invites a man to have sex with her; this is an example of adultery. The second case mentions a man who forces a woman to have sex with him; this is possibly a situation of what we now call acquaintance rape. In the second situation, the husband has the authority to decide the fate of the other man, but it remains unclear if the woman is handed over to her husband's authority or if she is considered innocent. The second case in MAL 16 reads:

> 16. . . . If he [a seignior] has lain with her [another seignior's wife] by force, when they have prosecuted him (and) convicted him, his punishment shall be like that of the seignior's wife.[76]

The hermeneutical problem is, of course, that the law mentions adultery, rape, and the various penalties in one long law. As in other cases, the husband, but not the raped wife, appears as the offended party, which reflects an androcentric bias that Western laws have overcome only in recent decades.

Yet another law (§23) portrays the rape of a married woman. The second part refers to a situation in which a wife is invited to the house of another woman, where she is raped by a man who is already in the house. The wife is declared innocent if she decides to press charges, but the other woman and the rapist receive the death penalty. If, however, the raped woman does not press charges, her husband has the authority to penalize her. In either case, the other woman and the rapist receive the death penalty. The section reads as follows:

> 23. . . . However, if the seignior's wife did not know (the situation), but the woman who brought her into her house brought the man to her under pressure and he has lain with her, if when she left the house she has declared that she was ravished, they shall let the woman go free, since she is guiltless; they shall put the adulterer and procuress to death. However, if the woman has not (so) declared, the seignior shall inflict on his wife such punishment as he sees fit (and) they shall put the adulterer and the procuress to death.[77]

In contrast to the rape laws of MAL 12, 16, and 23, in which the woman is married, MAL 55 refers to the rape of a young, single woman who lives with her parents.

> 55. In the case of a seignior's daughter, a virgin who was living in her father's house, whose [father] had not been asked (for her in marriage), whose hymen had not been opened since she was not married, and no one had a claim against her father's house, if a seignior took the virgin by force and ravished her, either in the midst of the city or in the open country or at night in the street or in a granary or at a city festival, the father of the virgin shall take the wife of the virgin's ravisher and give her to be ravished;

he shall not return her to her husband (but) take her; the father may give his daughter who was ravished to her ravisher in marriage. If he has no wife, the ravisher shall give the (extra) third in silver to her father as the value of a virgin (and) her ravisher shall marry her (and) not cast her off. If the father does not (so) wish, he shall receive the (extra) third for the virgin in silver (and) give his daughter to whom he wishes.[78]

This law is significant for several reasons. It unambiguously refers to the rape of a young, single woman.[79] It also acknowledges that rape may take place anywhere, "in the midst of the city or in the open country or at night in the street or in a granary or at a city festival." In other words, the charge of rape does not depend on the presence of other people.[80] Yet the range of penalties reflects a deeply ingrained androcentric perspective. No matter what the penalty is, the girl's father authorizes it. The father has three basic options. He may seek revenge according to "vicarious punishment"[81] and rape the rapist's wife, afterwards giving his daughter to the rapist in marriage. Alternatively, the father may accept money if the rapist does not have a wife, and he may then give his daughter to the rapist in marriage. Finally, he may choose neither of the prior options, but accept money and give his daughter in marriage to whomever he wishes. In all of these bad options, pernicious, cruel androcentrism rules while women are imagined as afterthoughts—forgotten recipients of male violence and authority.

Interpreters note the stark contrast in the penalty choices here and in the other three rape laws. For instance, Driver and Miles explain that the penalty is more lenient in §55 than in the other cases because the woman is single. "The draftsmen" of these laws "never lost" this distinction because they "always stated definitely at the outset whether the woman is unmarried or married."[82] The interpreters conclude from this consistent distinction that a "sexual offence" with an unmarried woman was "a comparatively trivial offence" in Assyrian law. The problem, however, is that these interpreters do not clearly object to this understanding of the law itself. Steeped in modern scientific epistemology, the interpreters pass off an androcentric explanation as acceptable and perpetuate androcentric views of women and rape. Reading from an empiricist-scientific paradigm, they convey androcentric biases toward women's relations to male power as objective categories, even objective truths.

The Hittite Laws

The Hittite Laws, too, contain several texts on rape. Scholars recognize only one of them and usually classify the others as laws dealing with adultery, incest, and bestiality. The undisputed rape law, §197, is reminiscent of Deut 22:29 and reads:

> 197. If a man seizes a woman in the mountain, it is the man's crime and he will be killed. But if he seizes her in (her) house, it is the woman's crime and the woman shall be killed. If the husband finds them, he may kill them, there shall be no punishment for him.[83]

The law describes two situations.[84] In the first case, a rapist attacks a woman outside an inhabited area, "in the mountain," a location that assumes a woman's unsuccessful opposition to the attack. In the second case, the attack takes place in a house, perhaps even in "her" house. In the first scenario, the rapist receives the death penalty, whereas in the second scenario the death penalty is given only to the woman.[85] If, however, the husband discovers the couple, he has the right to kill both of them. Some commentators maintain that this option is part of a third situation that continues in §198 and is similar to other ancient Near Eastern laws such as MAL 15 or §129 of the Code of Hammurabi.[86] In this case, the husband discovers the couple and has the opportunity to decide the fate of his wife and the other man, either sparing their lives or ordering their death.

It is important to note that the Hittite term "woman" refers to a woman of any status, whether she is young and single, married, widowed, free or enslaved,[87] even when the law includes the option that a woman's husband may kill the attacker and the woman. The terminological inclusiveness indicates that rape is not only a crime when a woman is married or in the process of getting married. According to §197, rape is punished under all circumstances when it takes place outside a town. The other part of the law is more problematic, since it announces punishment for both the woman and the man when the attack occurs in a house. The penalty seems to assume consensual sex, although the man might have forced the woman into the house. Thus, this law too reflects an androcentric worldview that privileges men over women.

Several other Hittite laws are not usually classified as rape laws, but they should be seen as such when rape is defined as "the crime of forcing another person to submit to sex acts, especially sexual intercourse,"[88] and the term "person" is expanded to include other creatures than humans only. The laws mention two cases of incest and four cases of bestiality.[89] Paragraphs 189 and 190 are the incest laws:

> 189. If a man violates his own mother, it is a capital crime. If a man violates his daughter, it is a capital crime. If a man violates his son, it is a capital crime.

> 190. . . . If a man violates his stepmother, there shall be no punishment. (But) if his father is living, it is a capital crime.

The law of §189 describes three cases, two of which are unmistakable cases of incestuous rape. The first case mentions a son raping his mother. The second and third cases refer to a daughter and a son being raped by their father. It is significant that the punishment is not specified, and the law does not make the penalty dependent on the father's so-called property rights. All three cases are called "capital crimes." In the law of §190, a stepson violates his stepmother, which appears to be a crime only when the father is alive. If the father is dead, the son is not punished for raping his stepmother. Enveloped in androcentric bias, this law focuses only on the son or the father and does not consider the position of the stepmother.

The Hittite codes include also four laws on bestiality (§§187, 188, 199, 200), which, according to animal advocates, could be considered rape legislation. Animals are unable to consent, but even if they could, animal rights advocates argue that a human would not know if the creatures were consenting.[90] In fact, Hoffner identifies an eighteenth-century legal decision that declared a female donkey "a victim of [sexual] violence."[91] So perhaps it is within the realm of possibility to discuss the following laws as rape legislation:

> 187. If a man does evil with a head of cattle, it is a capital crime and he shall be killed. They will bring him to the king's court. Whether the king orders him killed, or whether the king spares his life, he must not appeal to the king.

> 188. If a man does evil with a sheep, it is a capital crime and he shall be killed. They will bring him to the king's court. Whether the king orders him killed, or whether the king spares his life, he must not appeal to the king.

> 199. If anyone does evil with a pig, (or) a dog, he shall die. They will bring them to the gate of the palace and the king may order them killed, the king may spare their lives; but he must not appeal to the king. . . .

> 200 (A). If a man does evil with a horse or a mule, there shall be no punishment. He must not appeal to the king nor shall he become a case for the priest. . . .[92]

The four laws illustrate that, strangely, sexual acts with cows, sheep, pigs, and dogs are punished with the death penalty, whereas sexual acts with horses or mules remain penalty free. This distinction leads to two questions. Why did these laws become necessary in the first place, and why do the laws treat the rape of horses and mules differently from other animals? The first question cannot be answered conclusively. Did the laws become necessary because bestiality was such an enormous problem in ancient Near Eastern societies that it required laws to "regulate" such practices? Did the legislators attempt to recognize an owner's property rights? Or are these laws only scribal fantasies? We do not know.

The second question, about the different treatment of horses and mules, has drawn a number of attempted answers. E. Neufeld expressed his surprise about the distinction of such different treatment and suggested that cows, sheep, pigs, and dogs were regarded as sacred in "the cult of animals." Since horses and mules were "latecomers" in the geographical area of the Hittite empire, they were excluded from animal cults and were therefore exempted from the laws.[93] Hoffner refrains from any hypothesis and simply acknowledges his inability to give a reasonable explanation for the distinction.[94] In any case, the laws provide a glimpse into the violent pattern of male sexual fantasy or practice, and as part of rape legislation they are disturbing.

Another point needs to be made here: It is important to note that these incest and bestiality laws share a crucial grammatical characteristic. They use the same Hittite verb, *katta waištai*, to communicate the action performed by the man. Different translations of the verbal phrase provide different meanings. The translation given above is found in the anthology of ancient Near Eastern texts by James B. Pritchard, which offers two translations of the verbs. In the law on incest, the Hittite verb is rendered as "to violate" and in the law on bestiality the same verb is translated as "to do evil." Other translations use the same English term for the Hittite verb. Neufeld translates the verb as "to sin." The bestiality law of §187 thus reads:

If a man sins with a cow, (it is) an abomination, he shall die.

Similarly, the incest law in §189 is translated:

[If a man] sins with his mother, (it is) an abomination. If a [man] sins with a daughter, (it is) an abomination. If a man sins with a son, (it is) an abomination.

Neufeld explains that the verb *katta waištai* means literally "sin together (sexually)"[95] and "denotes indecent exposure or carnal knowledge and is an idiomatic description of sexual intercourse."[96] In other words, the verb depicts the same action in incest and bestiality laws. The translation in Martha Roth's edition of ancient laws is explicit, translating §187 as: "If a man has sexual relations with a cow . . ." and §189 as: "If a man has sexual relations with his own mother. . . ."[97] The verb is the same, and so a reader decides whether the verb implies physical and psychological violation or a moral transgression of normative behavior in Hittite culture. Does the verb connote sexual violence, an "evil" deed, or "sinful" behavior in general? These actions are characterized as *hurkel*, a Hittite noun for a sexual act that, according to Hoffner, does *not* refer to a crime involving "a sexual combination which is condemned by social mores"[98] but more generally is used for a "forbidden sexual combination, incest."[99] In other words, the act is something that is "forbidden." Was the forbidden deed an act of rape? The answer depends on a reader's interpretative outlook.

The difficulty in determining the meaning of these laws relates also to the limited number of existing Hittite laws. Clearly the laws on incest and bestiality describe situations of sexual harm for humans and animals. Whether or not the legislators identified these acts as "rape" is not a question we can answer, nor does the answer matter much, especially since we do not even know if these laws were ever used.[100] What matters is that ancient Near Eastern codes contain an impressive number of rape laws. Whether based in fantasy or reality, they indicate that rape was a social issue in the ancient Near East.

Toward a Conclusion, Not a Settlement

The purpose of this chapter has been to identify and explore biblical and ancient Near Eastern rape legislation and to indicate that these laws have not often been viewed as cases of rape in the recent history of interpretation. Many empiricist-positivist interpreters insist on placing these laws a safe distance away in ancient history, classifying them as laws on seduction, adultery, or marriage. Such interpreters read the legislation from "nowhere," which makes their explanations susceptible to androcentric bias and alienates those readers who are aware of the global rape culture. Usually, these commentators also suggest that hermeneutical work be limited to authorial intent and reproduce historically fixed meaning only, as if this were possible.

We face, then, a serious epistemological imbalance in the study and teaching of biblical law. If the position of empiricist-positivist scholars is that "back then rape was legal" because rape was marital, adulterous, or seductive behavior by men who were legally in charge and able to do as they pleased, it seems pedagogically problematic to teach such history without critical commentary. Yet the pedagogical impetus is entirely absent from research on ancient rape laws, even though the postmodern notion that social location shapes all interpretation largely solves these problems.

What is required is a vibrant and fresh debate on these matters. If this discussion does not take place, the terrain will be left to the increasingly dominant discourse of the Christian right, which insists on the literal meaning of the Bible, a notion that is closely aligned with scientific-objectivist hermeneutics.[101] Ancient rape laws represent a promising opportunity to debate the hermeneutical uncertainties and complexities of sacred texts such as the Hebrew Bible. This approach also enables interpreters to relate the epistemological imbalance in scholarship on ancient rape legislation to the larger arena in which we live, and to communicate the urgent need for dialogue across the hermeneutical, religious, cultural, and political divide in biblical scholarship and elsewhere.[102] Without such discussion and debate, rape itself will remain in the shadows, in a hidden place where those who perpetuate sexual violence want it to remain.

GANG RAPING
ON THE CULTURE OF MISOGYNY
DURING PEACE AND WAR

War Rape, Genocide, and Misogyny
in the Contemporary World

Since the genocidal atrocities in Croatia and Bosnia-Herzegovina (1991–1994), the pervasive problem of rape during war has emerged from the shadows of historical consciousness. When Serbian men systematically gang-raped their Bosnian women neighbors, held them in rape camps, and tried to ethnically destroy the Bosnian people by forced impregnation of Bosnian women, the international public could not ignore the mass raping anymore, as they had during past wars when rape was treated as "extracurricular, as just something men do, as a product rather than a policy of war."[1] Since then the United Nations has treated the sexual violation of women as a human rights violation and has sharply criticized the mass rape of women in armed conflict, as in the countries of the former Yugoslavia, Rwanda, Burundi, the Democratic Republic of Congo, and the Sudan. It was not enough anymore to acknowledge that "rape happens in all war."[2] Rather, wartime rape had to be recognized as a violation of human rights, and so, in 1995, Maria B. Olujic from the University of Zagreb demanded that "war rapes and gender based violence need to be defined as a form of torture and as a war crime."[3] In 1996, the war-crimes tribunal for the former Yugoslavia included sexual violence as "crimes against humanity" and treated rape as a separate category to be prosecuted.[4]

After decades of ongoing resolutions, statements, and calls for international action to address the socio-psychological, economic, political, and international consequences of war rape, the United Nations and non-governmental organizations such as Human Rights Watch and Amnesty International succeeded in bringing international attention to the prevalence of violence against women during war. The manifold demands for legal redress and medical assistance to women affected by mass rape have assumed that war rape is not a private issue but one of public, statewide, and international significance. For instance, Human Rights Watch reported the difficulties of rape victims in Rwanda in gaining justice.[5] The United Nations Economic and Social Council examined contemporary forms of slavery, including systematic rape during wartime, and connected it to sexual slavery and slavery-like practices during armed conflict.[6]

Efforts to stop mass rape during war are ongoing, and they place the issue within broad-ranging agendas. During the eighty-first plenary meeting of December 19, 2006, the UN General Assembly asked member states for the "intensification of efforts to eliminate all forms of violence against women" and specifically urged states "to protect women and girls in situations of armed conflict, post-conflict settings and refugee and internally displaced persons settings."[7] The UN campaign to end violence against women received the full endorsement of UN Secretary General Ban Ki-moon on February 25, 2008—the International Day for the Elimination of Violence against Women. He said, "Violence against women is an issue that cannot wait. . . ."

Although war rape is not explicitly mentioned in those statements, the international horror over the Serbian rape camps in which Bosnian Muslim women were gang-raped and often murdered turned mass rape into an internationally recognized atrocity. Hence, the "Fact Sheet" of the United Nations Campaign To End Violence Against Women acknowledges: "Rape has long been used as a weapon of war. Women as old as grandmothers and as young as toddlers have routinely suffered violent sexual abuse at the hands of military and rebel forces."[8] Similarly, on June 18, 2008, the UN Security Council asserted that "rape was no longer just a by-product of war but a military tactic" that has reached "pandemic proportions."[9] On June 19, 2008, the UN Security Council voted on Resolution 1820, which made war rape a crime. It is a historic resolution in which the Security Council

> *notes* that rape and other forms of sexual violence can constitute a war crime, a crime against humanity, or a constitutive

act with respect to genocide, *stresses the need for* the exclusion of sexual violence crimes from amnesty provisions in the context of conflict resolution processes, and *calls upon* Member States to comply with their obligations for prosecuting persons responsible for such acts, to ensure that all victims of sexual violence, particularly women and girls, have equal protection under the law and equal access to justice, and *stresses* the importance of ending impunity for such acts as part of a comprehensive approach to seeking sustainable peace, justice, truth, and national reconciliation. . . .[10]

Recognizing the severity of mass rape in times of war, scholars argue that war rapes are the result of androcentric gender roles in times of peace. Joshua S. Goldstein maintains that "gendered war roles are nearly universal because men's domination of women is nearly universal."[11] In Goldstein's analysis, war intensifies peacetime gender roles in which men dominate and women's access to combat preparation is limited. In war, such a gender-role system feminizes enemies and defines them as ready to be conquered and subdued, and soldiers execute this mind-set by raping conquered women. Thus, misogyny, prevalent in times of peace and rooted in androcentric insecurity about women, "serves as an important motor of male aggression in war." [12] Such a phenomenon is linked with "military homophobia" and the feminization of the enemy, and so builds on traditional gender roles in times of peace that lead to mass rapes in times of war. An Amnesty International study on the mass rapes in Burundi between 1993 and 2003 supports this conclusion; it finds that "[t]he general discrimination against Burundian women in times of peace was amplified during wartime" when "[r]ape and sexual violence were endemic to the armed conflict in Burundi and were committed by government soldiers, members of armed groups and private individuals."[13] Feminist-legal theorist Catharine A. MacKinnon agrees with this assessment, writing that "men do in war what they do in peace."[14] In her view, pornography, prostitution, and sex trafficking lead to mass rape in war.[15]

Yet MacKinnon goes even further when she distinguishes between war rape and genocidal rape based on the Genocide Convention of 1949. The Convention defines genocide as acts "committed with intent to destroy, in whole or in part, a national, ethnical, racial or religious group, as such."[16] On the basis of this definition, MacKinnon maintains that not all rape in war is genocidal. When war rape occurs without the intent to destroy a people "as such," it is a war crime and a violation of human rights but not genocidal. Rape in war "is not genocidal until it is part of an aim to destroy a people."[17] But she makes a bold connection between genocidal rape and so-called peacetime sexual atrocities against women, suggesting that the key phrase in the genocide definition is "a group as such." In her view, during genocide women of racially, ethnically, nationally, or religiously distinguished groups are treated in ways that women experience "everywhere every day."[18] During peacetime, androcentric structures and practices aim to destroy women as a group. MacKinnon explains:

> All the sexual atrocities that become genocidal in genocides are inflicted on women every day under conditions of sex inequality. Arguably, they are inflicted on them as women. Rape, prostitution, forced pregnancy, forced and precluded abortion, violating sexual spectacles, pornography—all of these are inflicted on women not only within wars and genocides but outside them, because they are women, often because they are women of a specific race, ethnicity, religion, nationality. . . . If this is right, rape in genocide—gender combined with ethnicity, nationality, or religion in genocidal rape—does to women and men on a combined sex and racial, ethnic, national, and religious basis what rape does to women outside genocides on a sex and gender basis every day.[19]

MacKinnon's feminist argument is as follows: She maintains that war rape aims to destroy an entire people through the sexual violation of its women, which makes war rape genocidal. Similarly, during peacetime women "as a group" experience sex inequalities that include rape and other forms of gender persecution. Thus, sexual violation of women during so-called peacetime "destroys women as women,"[20] which makes peacetime violence against women genocidal. In other words, for MacKinnon, wartime sexual violence that aims to destroy an ethnically, religiously, nationally, or racially defined group of women and men resembles peacetime rape of women. She writes:

> Thus men do to women (and some men) through sexual abuse outside of genocides what some men do in genocides when they sexually abuse women (and some men, especially sexually defined groups of men such as gay men) on the basis of their ethnicity, religion, nationality, or race.[21]

Rape is an expression of dominion that systematically and effectively submits groups of people whether they are defined by race, ethnicity, nationality, religion, or gender, and "does in genocide what it does in misogyny."[22] Hence, MacKinnon stresses that rape constitutes a violation of human rights in times of war and peace.

This definition of rape as a destructive force, a human rights violation, in times of war and peace applies also to one of the most horrific narratives in the Hebrew Bible, the rape and murder of the "concubine" and the subsequent mass rape of the young women of Jabesh-gilead and Shiloh in Judges 19–21. When the disturbing stories are read as part of the struggle to eliminate sexual abuse and rape during war and peace, they illustrate that the Hebrew Bible preserves stories about the relentless prevalence of rape in women's and men's lives. It can and perhaps must be read as a witness to the idea that rape is a violation of human rights. The following analysis, grounded in a discussion of biblical text and commentary, links the "peacetime" rape of the concubine in Judges 19 with the wartime rape of the young women and treats Judges 19–21 as a literary unit that links peacetime misogyny with wartime rape.

. . . In Times of Peace

In Judges 19, an unnamed woman, identified as a *pileges* (פילגש—a Hebrew term of unclear social status that is often translated as "concubine" but sometimes also as "secondary wife") runs away from her husband, a Levite. She returns to her father's house. After some unspecified time passes, the man travels to her father's house in an attempt to get her back. He stays and drinks with the father for several days, and eventually he and the woman leave. When night falls, they are invited to stay with an old man in Gibeah, the town of the Benjaminites. During the night, a male town mob wants the Levite to step outside so that they may "know him." The German Luther translation of 1984 indicates the ambiguous meaning of the Hebrew verb, *yāda'* (ידע), by translating it: "daß wir uns über ihn hermachen" ("that we can fall all over him"). This is a demand for rape that occurs also in a parallel story (Gen 19).[23] The men in the house refuse but offer them their two women—the concubine and the host's daughter (v. 24). Eventually the Levite pushes his concubine to the outside. There she is gang-raped by the mob for the duration of the night. At dawn, the men let her go and she manages to reach the doorstep, where she collapses. When the Levite opens the door in the morning, he talks to her but there is no answer. He then puts her on his donkey and returns home, where he cuts her into twelve pieces, "limb by limb," and sends "her throughout all the territory of Israel" (Judg 19:29) with the following message: "Has such a thing ever happened since the day that the Israelites came up from the land of Egypt until this day? Consider it, take counsel, and speak out" (19:30).

In older commentaries, the narrative does not receive detailed treatment because it is often considered part of an "appendix" that extends from chapter 17 to chapter 21.[24] This situation changed only when feminist interpreters exposed the brutality of the unnamed woman's fate clearly und unapologetically. For instance, Phyllis Trible expresses it well when she states: "It depicts the horror of male power, brutality, and triumphalism; of female helplessness, abuse, and annihilation. To hear this story is to inhabit a world of unrelenting terror that refuses to let us pass by on the other side."[25] In fact, Trible sides expressively with the woman, writing: "Our task is to make the journey alongside the concubine: to be her companion in a literary and hermeneutical enterprise."[26]

Other feminist interpreters concur. To them, the story of an unnamed woman in Judges 19 is "one of the most disturbing texts in the Hebrew Bible"[27] and "the most horrible story of the Hebrew Bible."[28] This is a "story of the rejection, gang-rape, murder and dismemberment of a young woman whose body is subsequently used as writing."[29] J. Cheryl Exum calls Judges 19 "perhaps the most gruesome and violent tale in the Bible" in which "the gang rape of the unnamed wife of an unnamed Levite by unnamed members of a mob of ruffians" is recounted.[30] Exum characterizes "the violence against the woman" as "brutally excessive and offensive," emphasizing that this story is a literary creation and not a historical report.[31] Gale A. Yee stresses the interconnectedness of gender and class, explaining that the "cycle of violence" leads from the gang rape of one woman to that of six hundred women.[32] J. H Coetzee, too, correlates Judges 19 with chapters 20–21, presenting a detailed exposé of the interrelatedness of body and voice.[33] She states: "Severe violence against both men and women resulted from violence against a single woman."

Even nonfeminist interpreters have come to agree with this assessment. For example, Andrew Hock-Soon Ng uncovers the sexist discourse in Judges 19 and correlates the biblical story with Gothic horror literature that emerged in Britain at the end of the eighteenth century as a reaction to rationalism. Similar to Gothic literature, which plays with a possible destruction of male dominance only to reassert its social validity, the biblical tale criticizes, exposes, and challenges the patriarchal system that simultaneously keeps assertive women (such as the concubine, who tries to escape the confinements of her husband) in their places.[34] Ng shows that the biblical story should be understood as a "refusal to become appropriated, and its simultaneous conformity to, and resistance against, the *status quo*."[35] According to Ng, the gruesome treatment of the concubine indicts the androcentric system and exposes "the entrenched sinfulness of the *men*"[36] although the narrative affirms androcentric power in the end.

Illuminating literary ambiguity and theo-kyriarchal complexity of this "peace"-time story in Judges 19, the following analysis focuses on grammar, hermeneutical observations, and social location. It prepares the way for the stories about war, mass rape, and murder in chapters 20–21.

Linguistic Ambiguity

Linguistic ambiguities are common here. Already in 19:2, it is unclear why the unnamed woman leaves the Levite man. At stake is the meaning of the Hebrew verb, *zānâ* (זנה). Androcentric commentators often translate this verb as "to play the whore or harlot" and explain that the unnamed woman prostituted herself. Sometimes interpreters reject this translation because they find it unlikely that such a woman would run back to her father's house, because, as Victor Matthews maintains, "[a] woman who had played the harlot would hardly be welcomed back to her father's house."[37] Other interpreters, however, including feminist readers, prefer the modified text of the Septuagint, which is based on a different consonantal spelling of the verb. Instead of *zānâ*, from זנה (ending in the letter *he*), meaning "to fornicate," the Greek translation assumes a different verb with almost identical Hebrew consonants—*zānah*, from זנח (ending in the letter *ḥet*), a verb that depicts the emotional attitude of the woman. The verse then reads: "But the concubine *became angry with him* (*watiznaḥ ʿālāyw*, ותזנח עליו), and she went away from him to her father's house at Bethlehem in Judah, and was there some four months." But even then, it is unclear why the woman became angry, and some feminist interpreters surmise that perhaps the Levite abused her and she could not stand the conditions of her life any longer and ran away.[38]

Interpreter Pamela Tamarkin Reis argues for an entirely different meaning, connecting v. 2 with v. 3. According to Reis, the Levite tries to have the woman take *him* back, which stands in contrast to the dominant view that the man went to take *her* back. This depends on the change in the Masoretic Text of the pronominal suffix attached to the Hebrew verb *šûb* (שוב), "to take back." In the *ketiv* (what is written) of the Hebrew text, the verb has a masculine singular pronominal suffix ("him"), but the *qere* (what is intended to be read) changes it to a feminine singular pronominal suffix ("her"). Reis explains that the Masoretes proposed the modification because they could not accept that "a man whose wife had fornicated needed to sweet-talk her and to convince her to take *him* back."[39] To the Masoretes, the Levite would need to take *her* back, and the changed pronoun is the result of this conviction.

Reis rejects the Masoretic recommendation and relies on the original *ketiv*, which states in v. 3: "He went to convince her to take *him* back." The question is why the concubine would take him back. Reis maintains that in the *ketiv* the Levite emerges as the guilty party, which fits with Reis's interpretation of v. 2. Reis translates v. 2 as "[s]he prostituted herself *for* him,"[40] emphasizing the preposition *'al* (על) in the verbal construction with *zānâ* (זנה). In other words, Reis asserts that "[t]he Levite was prostituting his wife."[41] This interpretation explains why the woman runs away to her father's house. It also explains why the Levite waits several months before he attempts to get her back, and so Reis insists that "there is no illogic in supposing that a father would receive a wronged daughter and a husband would want to recover his meal ticket."[42] One could also imagine that initially the Levite might believe that his concubine will come back voluntarily. He misses her only when, in effect, he runs out of his pimp money—only then does he set out to convince her to take him back.

Another question is why the father is pleased to see the man at his house. Reis believes that the narrative reflects the ill-fated sociopolitical condition of ancient Israel during the time of the judges, as outlined in the entire book of Judges. The father's inadequate response illustrates "Israel's complete abnegation of commitment and compassion down to that last stronghold of attachment and security: the family unit."[43] This is a father who does not help his daughter (*na'ărâ*, נערה), who is of adult age and beyond parental protection. The repetitive phrase "father of the woman," occurring six times in vv. 3-9, underscores that "the woman, no longer under the father's protection, remains unprotected."[44] For Reis, the repetition "hammer[s] the woman's vulnerability and the father's familial relationship into one's consciousness and prompt[s] the reader to contrast the man's bond with his behavior. He is her father, father, father, father, father, father, but he does not act like a father."[45] He is indifferent to her fate, and so the narrative "denigrates" him and not the daughter.[46] Consequently, the concubine is "a woman, pitied and respected by the text, who has been silenced by an intolerable predicament, and whose torment cannot be relieved but will be requited...."[47] In short, linguistic ambiguity demonstrates the gravity of the woman's situation in Judges 19. It places interpretative responsibility on the readers and depends on their sensitivity to the woman's fate, whether they side with the Levite or the concubine.

Hermeneutical Observations

Hermeneutical observations, too, add to the complex meaning of this biblical tale about gang-rape in times of peace. Many interpreters concur that the story raises more questions than it answers. For instance, Ken Stone asks:

> What is the social logic behind the textual variants at the beginning of the story? What do the men of Gibeah intend to communicate to the Levite, and how do he and his host interpret the actions of the men of the city? Why are the women viewed as preferable objects of rape? Why is the offer of two women refused, and the offer of one woman accepted? Exactly what is the offense that the Levite feels ought to be avenged?[48]

Since this narrative is not a "historical" or "accurate" report about actual events, the answers to these questions reveal more about a reader's assumptions regarding gender, androcentrism, and sociopolitical practices than can be known about ancient Israelite life based on Judges 19. As Stone recognizes, "a great deal is left to inference on the part of the reader."[49]

Predictably, interpreters deal differently with the meaning of the story, depending on their hermeneutical interests. Trible charges that chapter 19 should be read "against the narrator, plot, other characters, and the biblical tradition because they have shown her neither compassion nor attention."[50] Such a reading requires the recognition that gang-rape is a contemporary problem, a "present reality."[51] The story does not only address a distant past; Trible hopes that readers "take to heart this ancient story" and acknowledge its relevance in today's world. Accordingly, readers should commit themselves to a "never again" and should "repent"[52] from the ongoing violence against women.

Other interpreters focus on other aspects of the narrative. Michael Carden wants to read Judges 19 "as a text of terror for queer people."

He proposes a "reading perspective that foregrounds homosexuality in the reader's experience rather than as an issue in the narratives," a perspective he calls a "queering approach."[53] His hermeneutic, based on queer studies, turns the narrative into a lesson about compulsory heterosexuality, and so Carden emphasizes that the story "has nothing to do with anal sex or homosexuality."[54] He explains that sexuality in all of its various expressions is constructed in a phallocentric way within a system of compulsory heterosexuality. This was also the case in ancient Mediterranean culture, in which men if they wanted to be "real" men had to be the penetrators. In such a system, even sexual violence reinforces a rapist's heterosexuality—even when a man rapes a man, a dynamic apparent in today's male prison rapes, as Carden observes: "Although Western society has constructed sexuality on grounds of orientation, this phallocentric construction of sexuality still persists, most notably in male prison environments. . . . In other words, in some contexts, Western society also allows sexual activity with other males to be a part of male heterosexuality."[55] Men affirm their male heterosexuality by penetrating others, male or female, because it places them in a superior position. Yet the same is not true for a man who is penetrated, whether voluntarily or forced. His sexuality is cast in doubt. This dynamic explains why in Judges 19 the host refuses to send out his male guest and instead offers his daughter and the concubine. He tries to protect the status of his guest because his guest's violation would question the phallocentric construction of sexuality. Since a woman's status is already low in a phallocentric order, the rape of a woman does not threaten the status quo of phallocentric society.[56]

In Carden's interpretation, then, the narrative presents the host as offering the women, including his own daughter, to the mob in an effort to protect the sexual order upon which ancient society was presumably built. Carden explains: "In this world it is better that women be raped than men because rape of men takes away their heterosexuality."[57] Consequently, the Levite is the "real" target of the mob's violence against his concubine. They attempt to violate him through the concubine and try to make the Levite "queer by the rape of his woman."[58] The phallocentric order engages men in power struggles about who "lies on top" and who penetrates whom, and in this system women are always mere objects in the male heterosexual effort to be the winner against other men. With these hermeneutical assumptions in mind, Carden asserts that Judges 19 "should be more accurately read as an instance of *homophobic* (and xenophobic) violence" than as a story about violence against women.[59] It demonstrates that "misogynists" and "rapists should be regarded as sodomites" who fight over the "requisite" of phallocentrism: compulsory heterosexuality.[60] According-ing to this reading, Judges 19 turns into a tale about homophobia in phallocentric society and is not viewed as a rape narrative, although Carden explains that rape is always also part of a gender-stratified society in which women have little power. Hermeneutical observations create textual meanings in Judges 19 that highlight the relationship among misogyny, rape, and homophobia.

Sensitivity to Social Location

Some interpreters do not focus on grammar or hermeneutical observa-tions but, instead, create textual meanings based on their social loca-tions. Two readings stand out among recent publications on Judges 19. One of them comes from a self-described queer Asian Pacific American and the other from a post-Holocaust German Christian. Both interpre-tations shed light on Judges 19 as a rape story in times of peace. The queer Asian Pacific American reading comes from Patrick S. Cheng, who stresses the correlation between the sexual and geographic mul-tiplicities of the concubine and queer Asian Pacific Americans. He classifies both as "radical outsiders" from mainstream positions in the biblical text and contemporary Western or Eastern societies.[61] Cheng's hermeneutical strategy creates a sympathetic comparison of the bibli-cal and contemporary contexts that has gained popularity also among feminist postcolonial interpreters of the Bible[62] and endows biblical texts with contemporary relevance. Cheng describes the concubine's status as an outsider on two accounts: her sexuality and her geography. The woman's outsider status, based on her sexuality, comes to the fore in the story when she runs away from her husband. At this moment she transgresses the rules of the male-dominated society in which the narrative imagines her. Transgression is punished, and the woman becomes a victim of gang-rape, mutilation, and even murder. As an outsider on the basis of her geography, the concubine moves from the south and to the north, which contributes to the geographical tensions in the story. Similar tensions are part of the lived experiences of queer Asian Pacific Americans. Cheng explains:

> Like the unnamed concubine, queer Asian Pacific Americans are radical outsiders in terms of both our sexualities and our geographies. We remain outsiders, particularly in the theological academy, despite the fact that several important anthologies of queer Asian Pacific American writings have been published in recent years. . . . With respect to our identities as geographical outsiders, we remain on the margins in terms of the small number of Asian Pacific American theologians, biblical scholars, and church historians in the academy.[63]

For Cheng, the outsider status of both the concubine and queer Asian Pacific Americans is grounded in the multiplicity of sexuality and geography. But they also share other commonalities. For instance, Cheng observes that both are called by many different names, which he calls "a multiplicity of naming." The concubine is called concubine, girl, maidservant, and woman. Similarly, queer Asian Pacific Americans call themselves by many different names and other people, too, use various names to describe them.[64] Cheng explains that the multiplicity of names indicates powerlessness because a "lack of a unified signifier" disempowers individuals or groups.[65] "Multiple naming" is a sign of "radical" otherness because the larger group does not know the "other" and therefore does not have a unique category.

Other similarities between the story of the concubine and the lives of queer Asian Pacific Americans consist in the experiences of "multiple silencing," "multiple oppression," and "multiple fragmentation."[66] Cheng wants readers to recognize these multiplicities because they preserve "the complexity and multidimensionality of scriptural texts," and they prevent a singular, "one-dimensional" meaning. He also hopes that the recognition of multiplicities may embolden queer

Asian Pacific Americans to celebrate their diverse life experiences, since they "paradoxically . . . result in the preservation of wholeness and integrity."[67] In Cheng's discussion, then, the concubine becomes a model character for queer Asian Pacific Americans and helps them to celebrate the paradoxical connections among difference, integrity, and wholeness.

A second and differently located position that sheds light on Judges 19 as a rape story in times of peace comes from Katharina von Kellenbach, who writes from a post-Holocaust German Christian position. She correlates the Levite's role in Judges 19 with a memoir of a Holocaust survivor, Calel Perechodnik.[68] Von Kellenbach argues that "[t]he exclusive focus on gender violence . . . neglects and conceals the racialized context of the violence portrayed in the text" (Judg 19).[69] When interpreters avoid a "deeper power analysis" of Hebrew Bible texts, they may perpetuate anti-Jewish stereotypes that create "a caricature of Old Testament culture, Judaism and Jewish men as callous misogynists and hardened male supremacists who renounce women without a second thought."[70] Only a gender analysis that links with other forms of sociopolitical and economic oppression, such as racism and xenophobia, will "combat such anti-Jewish parodies in feminist Christian exegetical texts."[71] For von Kellenbach, it is therefore insufficient to condemn the Levite in the story, because such "feminist outrage" neglects the "real perpetrators, the Benjaminite thugs who are out to brutalize foreigners."[72]

Von Kellenbach determines that her social location requires a focus on the Levite and his "choiceless choice where critical decisions did not reflect options between life and death, but between one form of 'abnormal' response to another, both imposed by a situation that was in no way of the victim's own choosing."[73] The Levite man is in a situation that forces him to send his concubine to the outside mob and to lose "his dignity and self-respect as a man" because of his inability to protect her.[74] In this sense, the Levite resembles Jewish men during the Nazi oppression who were forced to betray loved ones in order to survive. One of them is Holocaust survivor Calel Perechodnik, who acknowledged in his autobiography that, as a Jewish ghetto policeman in 1943, he was forced to load his wife and toddler daughter onto a train that was headed to the death camps. Von Kellenbach explains that "[l]ike the Levite," Perechodnik experiences "powerlessness and fear."[75] He was forced to secure his survival by abandoning his family members and choosing between his life and their lives; he became implicated in their torture and murder.

Von Kellenbach observes that this "choiceless choice" has "spiritually devastating effects."[76] Perechodnik admits that he did not see a future for himself anymore after the war. In his autobiography, he states: "After this that I have lived through, I cannot live a normal life. . . . I will never be a useful member of society."[77] He is overwhelmed by feelings of rage and revenge, and the Holocaust survivor experiences guilt and torment for the rest of his life. For von Kellenbach, the Levite faces a similar situation, which explains why he simply puts the half-dead or already dead woman on his donkey, takes her home, cuts her into twelve pieces, and demands justice from the other tribes. The Levite turns into an emotional zombie and "does not think about what might be best for his concubine."[78] The responses of Perechodnik and the Levite are thus bound up in the larger "structures of domination"[79] in which they are forced to operate.

Von Kellenbach also questions the extent to which the Levite and Perechodnik can be held accountable for their actions. Are they morally and legally guilty since "their involvement in the betrayal of the other is more complex" than the "clear-cut" guilt of "the Benjamite and Nazi perpetrators"?[80] Von Kellenbach wonders if the women of the Benjaminite tribe are implicated. Are they guilty because they stand in solidarity with their men, the gang-rapists of the Levite's concubine? Von Kellenbach asks: "Were the Benjamite women innocent victims of retributive bloodshed or were they rightly punished for their entanglement in the crime of their husbands?"[81] No easy answers present themselves, and there is no happy end because the biblical story line presents "a bewildering and contradictory path . . . between punishing the perpetrators (involving more violence) and accepting their reintegration and future (victimizing more women)."[82] What seems clear to von Kellenbach is that suffering is meaningless because God does not require it. The only constructive response for readers is to give witness to the suffering of "the other as our neighbor." She

observes: "As their neighbor, we are required to answer for their violation by testifying against the perpetrators and grieving the victims.
Their betrayal and senseless anguish compels us to engage in protest,
lamentation and mourning."[83]

Yet rape and murder of the unnamed woman do not end the story.
As Erik Eynikel observes perceptively: "[R]ape frames the whole story;
it starts with rape in Judges 19 and ends with rape in chapter 21."[84]
In summary, pervasive misogyny, grounded in a phallocentric order
that advances compulsory heterosexuality and combines with other
forms of discriminatory practices, leads to further sexual violence; this
time against women of other lands and customs. Inquiries in grammar, hermeneutical observations, and social location provide important
insights into the relationship of misogyny and rape in Judges 19 in times
of peace. The story continues with more rape, this time during war.

. . . In Times of War

When the other tribes realize what has happened in Gibeah, the Israelites gather in Mizpah and ask the Levite: "Tell us, how did this evilness
(hārā'â, הרעה) happen?" (Judg 20–21) Identified as "the man of the
woman," the Levite gives an answer that crucially modifies the events
that lead to the woman's murder. He does not mention that the male
Benjaminites first asked for him and that it was the Levite himself who
later pushed the woman to the outside. He explains:

> I came to Gibeah that belongs to Benjamin, I and my concubine,
> to spend the night. The lords of Gibeah rose up against me,
> and surrounded the house at night. They intended to kill me,
> and they raped ['innâ, ענה piel] my concubine until she died.
> Then I took my concubine and cut her into pieces, and sent her
> throughout the whole extent of Israel's territory; for they have
> committed a vile outrage [něbālâ, נבלה] in Israel. So now, you
> Israelites, all of you, give your advice and counsel here. (Judg
> 20:4b-7) [NRSV]

His summary omits the threat of rape toward him and his own par-
ticipation in the concubine's death because he grasped (ḥāzaq, חזק

hiphil) her and led (*yāṣā'*, יצא *hiphil*) her to the outside, where the mob gang-raped her the entire night (19:25). The Israelites listen to his report and then decide to request that the Benjaminites release the "wicked sons" of Gibeah. The Benjaminites refuse, fight against the Israelites, and kill twenty-two thousand Israelites. The defeated Israelites mourn their loss and pray to God, who tells them to fight again. The following day, they advance against the Benjaminites but again lose, and eighteen thousand Israelites are dead. After burnt offerings and other sacrifices, they receive divine encouragement to battle again. On the third day, they devise a military strategy and trick the Benjaminites into defeat. Initially, they kill 25,100 Benjaminites, and when they move into the city of Gibeah, they kill the entire city, all inhabitants and all animals. Yet six hundred Benjaminite warriors escape and flee into the wilderness.

After an unspecified time, the Israelites begin to weep because they realize that Israel lost one tribe. Then they remember that several male Benjaminites survived, and they vow not to marry any of their daughters to male Benjaminites. But they also wonder:

> What shall we do for them, for those who are left, [to get] wives, as we have sworn to Yahweh that we do not give them any of our daughters as wives? (21:7)

They come up with a solution. In Mizpah, they had also promised that "[w]hoever did not come up to Yahweh in Mizpah" (21:5) shall be killed. The men from Jabesh-gilead had not been in Mizpah (21:8-9), and so the Israelites send twenty thousand warriors to kill them, "every male and every woman who knows the bed of a male" (21:11). They also capture four hundred unmarried young women "who did not know a man [*'iš*, איש] at a bed of a male [*zākār*, זכר]" (21:12) and bring them back to the Israelite camp in Shiloh.[85] Then, the Israelites make peace with the remaining six hundred male Benjaminites and hand over the captured four hundred women. Since two hundred male Benjaminites still lack a woman, the Israelite elders devise yet another plan, which involves the abduction of two hundred "daughters of Shiloh." The Israelites tell the two hundred male Benjaminites: "Go and lie in wait in the vineyards, and watch; when the young women of Shiloh come out to dance in the dances, then come out of the vine-yards and each of you carry off a wife for himself from the young women of Shiloh, and go to the land of Benjamin" (21:20-21). The two hundred male Benjaminites follow the advice and abduct two hundred dancing women. Then they return with the women to their land, rebuild their towns and live in them (21:23).

The narrative does not report any resistance from the women of Jabesh-gilead or Shiloh, and they never speak.[86] Moreover, the fake excuse the Israelite elders invent for them is not needed:

> Then if their fathers or their brothers come to complain to us, we will say to them, "Be generous and allow us to have them; because we did not capture in battle a wife for each man. But neither did you incur guilt by giving your daughters to them." (21:22)

This narrative piles horror upon horror. Some interpreters explain that the story is a reminder of what happens when there is no king in Israel. It is a "pro-monarchic propaganda" that characterizes the book of Judges as a whole and also the end of chapter 21, which states: "In those days there was no king in Israel; a man [אִישׁ, אישׁ] did what was right in his eyes" (21:25).[87] Other interpreters suggest that is incumbent upon a reader to "inhabit the gap, the silence, and through the power of imagination break the silence of the women of Shiloh" because "[t]o leave them in silence is gynocide."[88] This is a "national rape of the daughters of Shiloh," which should be read not as part of "political exigencies" or a "holy war sanctioned by YHWH" but as "the perfect psychological backdrop" for men "to give vent to their contempt for women."[89]

Alas, the story's misogynistic perspective is often adopted by many interpreters when they explain that the search for women is a "political problem" that tries to resolve a tribe's survival. Interpreters neglect the sexual violence present in the story because they sympathize with the male characters' goal of progeny. This "familiar excuse"[90] appears in commentaries that have been widely read by clergy and scholars. For instance, Robert G. Boling explains Judges 19–21 in this way: "It is impossible to do justice to this story without looking ahead to the last two chapters of the book, for the finale (ch. 20–21) represents the confederacy as utterly leaderless. The Israelites will overreact to one case of injustice in such a way as to compound the tragedy a thousand times over, and permit the situation to develop into a full-scale civil war."[91] For Boling, these chapters are about "civil war and its sequel,"[92] and he does not mention that the civil war and its sequel include repeated gang rape on the individual and collective levels in both peacetime and wartime.

Other commentators hesitate to be explicit about the nature of the violence in Judges 19–21. J. Clinton McCann talks about the "victimized concubine" and characterizes the "civil war" as one that moves "from the victimization of one to the victimization of many."[93] With a reference to the "prevailing customs" of the time, McCann explains that the "rape" of the Levite would be "a greater breach" than the "rape of his own daughter and the Levite's concubine."[94] McCann also acknowledges that "the mistreatment of women may have been the lesser of the evils, according to prevailing customs," but still "an act of terror."[95] For McCann, all of these narratives "present the actions of the men of Gibeah as a worst-case scenario—that is, an example of how horrible things are when people act out of self-assertion rather than divine direction."[96] But is this the lesson of the story? Does it indeed suffice to define mass-rape as an "act of self-assertion" of people, of "human beings," when they lack "divine direction"?

The gender ambiguity in McCann's explanations is peculiar. After all, the women—daughters or concubine—do not commit any "horrible things" but are the victims of male sexual violence and aggression. Yet gender ambiguity permeates McCann's interpretation, which concludes with a generic reflection on "Chaos and Crisis, Then and Now," which does not explicitly mention the described chaos and crisis. In fact, McCann stresses that within the "larger canonical context" of these chapters the stories "portray a God who would not—indeed, could not stop loving a persistently idolatrous and frustratingly faithless people," and so he characterizes the book of Judges as "a call to covenant loyalty" that illustrates "God's incredible perseverance—an unfailing love that is inevitably manifest as grace."[97] While McCann probably does not mean to excuse the mass rapists and capturers of women, his interpretation misses a unique opportunity to address the problem of sexual violence in one of the most horrific biblical stories. As such, whatever its merit, this interpretation proves dangerous, for it omits and obfuscates rape in Judges 19–21, in a time and world in which rape prevails during peace and war.

Some commentaries, however, unequivocally address the concubine's gang-rape and the war rapes of the women of Jabesh-gilead and Shiloh. Susan Niditch names "the rape and murder of the Levite's concubine" and the "violent but socially sanctioned 'traffic in women'" as key elements in Judges 19–21.[98] She stresses that the narratives are "told from a male-dominated perspective, and little comfort is provided for feminist appropriation."[99] Tammi Schneider goes even further when she observes that "[m]ost commentaries place the rape [of the concubine] in the context of the military event that follows" and "do not refer to it as the abandonment and rape but the 'Outrage of the Gibeonites.'"[100] Schneider states that "[o]n a basic level the Israelites offered kidnap and rape as a viable method of obtaining a wife,"[101] and she equates the Benjaminite quest for wives with rape. The male Benjaminites rape six hundred women when they make them into "wives in a fashion that was condoned, in fact recommended, by Israel."[102] Hence, for Schneider, it is obvious that the actions of the male Benjaminites "led to death and rape/marriage for many others."[103]

Similarly clear is Carolyn Pressler. She acknowledges that in Judges 20–21 "mass slaughter and mass rape" shape the story[104] and "[e]ach effort entails further violence and violation."[105] Pressler writes: "A brutal act of gang rape/murder triggers intertribal war and more mass killings and rape. The account of Israel's escalating disobedience ends with violence and chaos."[106] It is apparent that "rape leads to additional rape,"[107] and so "the rape/murder of the Levite's wife and the kidnapping and rape of the daughters of Shiloh"[108] end the book of Judges. Although there is little hope and no mercy in these texts, Pressler seeks hermeneutical "redemption." She finds it in the canonical order of the books of Judges and Ruth. Following the horrific tales, the book of Ruth contrasts with Judges and models "covenant faithfulness and loyalty, illustrating how communal life is intended to be lived."[109] Pressler seeks a redemptive quality in the biblical canon and does not want to be left with the bleak brutality depicted in Judges 19–21. In her view, the story of Ruth and Naomi provides some justice for victims of sexual violence. She thus stresses the canonical order, in which the book of Ruth follows the horrific tales in the book of Judges.

"Take My Daughters . . .": Concluding Comments

The narratives in Judges 19–21 show that misogyny, rape, and war are interrelated structures of oppression and link to other social categories of domination. In such structures, women are viewed as goods, to be used and even abused, eventually murdered and cut into pieces. Sometimes they are there "for the taking" and to be married off. They are objects of the male actors whose needs they are fulfilling. In such an androcentric setting, the problem posed for readers is what to do with such stories. Shall we be complicit and accept assumptions of phallocentric superiority, or be aware of the links of misogyny, rape, and established hierarchies of sociopolitical and economic life? Unquestionably, the latter is required because it turns the meaning of Judges 19–21 into highly relevant literature that illustrates destructive societal forces. They create sociopolitical, economic, and religious hierarchies that place some people above others. In the narratives of Judges 19–21, all women become victims of a phallocentric order that benefits the male characters. This order begets violence, and so Judges 19–21 is brutal and bloody. It begins with one woman's gruesome fate, her gang-rape and subsequent murder, followed by wartime murder of a whole tribe and the gang-rape of many women. In the metaphoric language of biblical prose, Judges 19–21 illustrates the misogyny during so-called peacetime and the prevalence of rape during war. The ordeal is a reminder of the pervasive and persisting problem in androcentric societies: misogyny and rape are connected problems within a long tradition that stretches back to the stories in the book of Judges. They can help even contemporary readers to face the horrors of today's ongoing sexual violations of women, children, and some men during peacetime and war.

LOSING POWER

6

THE RAPE OF MEN
AS MALE FEAR AND REALITY

From the Top to the Bottom

Criminologists, psychologists, and social scientists have long called male rape a "hidden crime"—a taboo subject, according to Gillian C. Mezey and Michael B. King.[1] Susan Estrich, too, recognizes that "[t]he general invisibility of the problem of male rape, at least outside the prison context, may reflect the intensity of stigma attached to the crime."[2] A male rape survivor confirms this problem when he states: "I suspect juries have less sympathy for victims and less understanding of the concept of male rape."[3] Richie J. McMullen confirms that "ninety per cent of male rapes are not reported,"[4] and he lists five reasons why men are often reluctant to charge rape. Male survivors are in shock; they are embarrassed about the rape and afraid of losing loved ones if they found out. They fear stigmatization, and they blame themselves for failing to fend off the rapist.

This does not sound so different from women and girls who survive rape. Men and boys, too, are often ashamed to speak openly about a sexual violation, and they may face prejudices from the larger public. Such prejudices have decreased somewhat for women and girls after several decades of feminist struggle. Yet in the case of men, many people have never even heard of men becoming rape victim-survivors and do not understand why a man, strong as he supposedly is, would be unable to fend off an attacker. They assume that men are raped in prison when they are gay, if at all.

The hidden nature of male rape relates to enduring notions of masculinity that emphasize physical strength, size, and initiative, as well as male agency and aggression, as supreme male characteristics.

Rape survival, however, produces the opposite. One rape survivor explains:

> Society doesn't allow men to be victims of such a crime. They're expected to be strong . . . capable of protecting themselves. There's a lot of stigma that comes with being raped as a man. Loss of manhood is so destructive and adds to all the other traumas.[5]

When men are overpowered, threatened, and subjected to sexual violence, society views them as not male enough, as too much like women. Many heterosexual male rape survivors also worry about their sexual orientation when they are attacked by another man. Noreen Abdullah-Kahn quotes several male victim-survivors. One acknowledges that "[a]t one time I thought I might be bisexual because of the attack but I stopped about five minutes into it before it went any further. I'm glad I did it because I now know for sure, I like women." Another survivor, however, admits: "I feel confused. I think maybe I'm bisexual because I let it happen. I'm still very much attracted to women. I never had thought of men before. I definitely didn't want anything to happen." Yet another survivor explains: "[I]n society, people do link together that . . . you know, if you've been sexually assaulted and you're a man, then you're probably gay . . . or you probably did something to ask for it in some way." One man was told by the rapist, "I must be gay as well as I didn't stop him. He said he'd tell people I was gay. He said 'you obviously enjoy it'."[6]

Most male rapes happen between men, and the survivors often resist vehemently. One survivor remembers, "I screamed and screamed," whereas another admits, "I agreed to sex in the end but never to anal penetration." Other efforts at resistance include pleas to stop: "(I said) Please don't; I don't want this." One man explains that "I just froze, shocked." Another man describes his response to the attack: "I was really frightened and didn't know what to do, whether to shout or yell out loudly. I didn't say anything. I didn't struggle because I was afraid. I began crying and was very upset. I was worried about my safety and what might happen when it was over."[7] These few quotations illustrate that Mezey and King correctly assess male rape as "an aggressive attack on their [male] sexuality and a violation of their physical and psychological boundaries."[8] Male rape survivors need support and treatment programs that take this violation seriously and approach men with respect, care, and understanding.

An unknown number of men are attacked by women, as Wendy Stock indicates when she writes that "it is most probably that male sexual victimization by women is significantly underreported."[9] Peter B. Anderson attributes this lack of reporting to the lack of studies about women's sexual aggression.[10] Sometimes these cases make it into the newspapers as flashy pieces,[11] and movies treat the topic of "love" between an older woman and a male teenager, such as *The Graduate* (1967) or *Harold and Maude* (1971). Do these references to women's sexual aggression toward males serve as a "backlash against feminist activists working to end violence against women," as Charlene L. Muehlenhard fears?[12] The scant existing data suggest that women rely less on physical force than men to overwhelm a male victim-survivor and instead employ "sexual enticement," "altruism or a desire to help," and intoxication, as well as "social pressures related to male stereotypes, including the expectation that men should always want sex and always be ready to perform with an erection."[13] Cindy Struckman-Johnson and David Struckman-Johnson assert that "between the ages of 16 and 40 years, as few as 1% to as many as 50% of boys and men may experience sexually coercive contact with a woman" but that "most men were not very upset by the incident—only one-fifth reported strong negative reactions."[14]

Considering the rarity of male rape by men or women, it is perhaps surprising that several biblical narratives address the problem of male-on-male and female-on-male rape. Still, only a few references are identifiable, and for the most part in the history of interpretation, they have not been read this way. The story of Ehud (Judg 3) is a possible example of male-on-male rape. The stories of Ms. Potiphar and Joseph (Gen 39), Lot's daughters and their father (Gen 19:30-38), and Delilah and Samson (Judg 16) hint at female-on-male rape. The following section discusses these stories and their interpretations to indicate that male rape can be identified in biblical literature when the hermeneutical attention is focused on this silenced topic.

Ehud, a Judge, and His Left-Handed Murder

While the story of Ehud (Judg 3:12-30) is strange, it follows the classic pattern in the book of Judges. It begins with Israel doing "evil in the sight of Yahweh" (3:12); subsequently, King Eglon of Moab goes to war against the Israelites and defeats them "because they had done what was evil in the sight of Yahweh." Eventually the Israelites cry out to Yahweh (3:15), who raises up for them a savior (*môšîaʿ*, מושיע; v. 15)—in this case, Ehud "son of Gera, the Benjaminite, a left-handed man" (v. 15). The story then proceeds to describe Ehud's preparation for the eventual killing of the king and the liberation of the Israelites from Moabite oppression.[15] Ehud hides a sword under his clothing on the right side of his loins and brings gifts to the king. When Ehud tells the king, who is described as very fat, that he has a "secret thing" for him, Eglon sends away his court personnel and approaches Ehud. In the very moment when the king gets closer, Ehud pulls his sword with his left hand from his right thigh, and pushes it into the king's belly (*beṭen*, בטן; v. 21). The description presents in great detail how the sword disappears in the king's fatty flesh: "Then Ehud reached with the left hand, took the sword from his right thigh, and thrust it into Eglon's belly; the hilt also went in after the blade, and the fat closed over the blade, for he did not draw the sword out of his belly; and the dirt came out" (vv. 21-22). Ehud flees the scene after carefully locking the door. Meanwhile, the royal servants, coming back and waiting for the king to unlock the door, think: "He must be relieving himself in the cool chamber" (v. 24). They wait patiently but eventually open the door to find the king lying dead on the floor (v. 25). Ehud blows the trumpets, gathers the Israelites, and leads them into battle against the Moabites, whom they subdue. The story concludes: "And the land had rest eighty years" (v. 30).

An obvious question arises: Where is the male-on-male rape in this narrative? According to Deryn Guest, three elements turn the assassination of Eglon into a figurative male rape scene: the emphasis on Ehud's left-handedness, the repeated references to his "hand" as a euphemism for male genitals, and his Benjaminite affiliation.[16] Guest builds her argument on observations made by commentators such as Robert Alter, who observes:

> Ehud "comes to" the king, an idiom also used for sexual entry, and there is something hideously sexual about the description of the dagger-thrust. There may also be a deliberate sexual nuance in the "secret thing" that Ehud brings to Eglon, in the way the two are locked together alone in a chamber, and in the sudden opening of locked entries at the conclusion of the story.[17]

Guest also explains that the reference to the sword as being "a *gomed* in length contributes further to the sexual connotations of this narrative" because "*gomed* has an Arabic cognate meaning 'to be hard'."[18] Timothy R. Koch also ponders the size of the "sword": "A 'cubit' (roughly 19 ins.) would certainly be an impressive measurement for *anything* found snaking down (OK, OK, 'fastened' to) a young man's right thigh!"[19]

In addition, the characterization of Ehud as a Benjaminite "should be viewed in a negative or at least dubious light,"[20] possibly as a deliberate strategy to describe Ehud in conjunction with King Saul's problematic leadership. Perhaps the Ehud story foreshadows some of the problematic events during the rivalry of David and Saul, including the relationship of David to another Benjaminite man, Jonathan, with whom he has a homoerotic relationship. Thus, Guest wonders if the "author of Judges had this in mind and that in 20:16's reference to the Benjamites as a tribe of expert 'left-handers' we seem to have a satirical jibe at the Benjamites that gives double pleasure to the assumed Judean reader who can laugh not only at the Moabites but also at their tribal brothers who gave their loyalties to the wrong king and whose sexuality is questioned."[21]

Other textual ambiguities support this reading of Judg 3:12-30, and three are of particular significance. First, the emphasis on the Moabite king's body size stands out. In. v. 17, he is called "very fat" (*bārî'*, בריא), and in v. 22, the sword is mentioned as completely disappearing in the king's belly fat: "The hilt also went in after the blade, and the fat closed over the blade." Guest maintains that the mention of Eglon's body size indicates not only the king's gullibility, stupidity, greed, and opulence but also his feminized status in the narrative.[22] That he ends up dead and "with his pants down" (v. 25) is yet another "metaphor of feminization of the enemy."[23] The sexist attitude also includes "ethnic humour and scathing satire" about the Moabites, all of which contribute to the dehumanization of the "other" and to labeling them as "sexual deviants." The story legitimizes mockery and violence against the foreign nation, whose male leader is depicted in the position of a penetrated woman.[24]

Second, the king's fatness is not the only rhetorical strategy that hints at the male-on-male rape scenario in Judg 3:12-30. The detailed description of how the sword disappears in the fat belly of the king supports the idea that this narrative depicts male-on-male rape. Susan Niditch points to this idea, observing that the image "of the fat closing around the blade is strongly vaginal." For Niditch, the entire story plays between "eroticism and death," and the sword, "the short blade," is "a phallic symbol" dangling at the "male erogenous zone,"[25] that is, the thigh.[26] This phallic symbol is presented as penetrating the king's belly fat in a rape-like fashion. J. Clinton McCann adds to this perspective, noting that the sword "apparently pierces Eglon's bowels, so that 'the dirt' (v. 22) that is released is probably excrement."[27] For McCann, the narrative is "quite literally . . . bathroom humor," and this bathroom "comedy" depicts "figuratively and literally" how "Ehud beats the crap out of Eglon."[28] Moreover, the noun for the king's belly (*beṭen*, בטן) is ambiguous, signifying both the female womb and the abdomen in general. It is thus possible to view Ehud's sword as a phallic symbol that penetrates the king's "belly" or "womb." Read as a male rape, the scene refers implicitly to anal intercourse between Ehud and Eglon in which the king is the dominated one. The vague reference to the king releasing "something" (*paršĕdōn*, פרשדן, a *hapax legomenon*, perhaps from *pereš*, פרש, fecal matter)[29] could mean filth, dirt, or excrement, as various translations indeed specify.[30]

Third, the location of Ehud and Eglon's encounter indicates that something "unspeakable" may be going on between the two men.

After the only direct discourse between the two characters (v. 19), the king sends his attendants away (v. 19). In the next verse (v. 20), the location changes to a place about which commentators always speculate. Did the two men move up to a "cool roof chamber," an "upstairs room," or the "toilet room"?[31] Or does "the semantic range" of the noun (*mĕqērâ*, מקרה; root קרה) not hint at the possibility of a "seminal emission"?[32] If the latter, the depiction of Ehud as "coming upon" (*bô'*, בוא; v. 20) Eglon and that of the hilt as "coming" (*bô'*, בוא; v. 22) into the king's belly make it possible to read this text as a male-on-male rape story. That Eglon is later found dead after his servants believe that their king "covered his feet" (*raglāyw*, רגליו), a Hebrew euphemism for genitals, reinforces the idea that the king was involved in an activity involving the baring of his private parts. Niditch phrases it this way: "What Eglon's servants imagine him [Eglon] to be doing in his upper chamber is ambiguous. The colloquialism offered in the translation implies some sort of private bodily function."[33]

This clouded and amorphous depiction of the interaction between the Israelite judge and the Moabite king ends in murder, from which Ehud escapes successfully. It leads to Israelite liberation from Moabite oppression. Yet Ehud's success has not received unambiguous endorsement in the history of interpretation. According to Guest, "Ehud's exploits are described variously by commentators as peculiar, unnatural, devious, sinister—but perhaps the word they are all looking for is 'queer'."[34] Interpreters emphasize Ehud's masculinity, his "hardened professional warrior" qualities, his "daring" fighter status as one of the "most admirable of the judges."[35] In other words, this story does not diminish but rather enhances Ehud's masculinity. Yet at least for Guest, the characterization of Ehud is complex because Ehud's action is condemned in Leviticus and Deuteronomy in prohibitions of male-male sex.[36] Should Ehud be viewed similarly to other biblical characters, such as Ruth, Abraham, Jacob, and David, who emerge as heroic figures with obvious flaws? Guest upholds that Ehud should be classified as such an exonerated figure but also cautions that "such exoneration comes at a cost for contemporary readers who identify as gay men or as transgendered."[37] She explains that "[s]traight-identified readers who side with the Israelite 'hero' may be able to afford such luxuries [i.e. the comical assumptions about the Moabites' feminized and hence rape-able characteristics], but for the reader who has to read against their own interests, the text's rhetoric and assumptions are problematic and cannot be shared."[38]

Ms. Potiphar's Attempted Coercion

Another story that hints at the possibility of male rape, but this time with a woman as the attacker, is the narrative of Ms. Potiphar and Joseph in Genesis 39. This story, popular in Jewish, Christian, and Muslim traditions,[39] goes like this:

> Joseph, already exiled to Egypt due to the jealousy of his older half brothers, has been bought by Potiphar, an Egyptian official. In time, Potiphar gave Joseph full responsibility for running his household, in the exercise of which the Israelite had the full run of the house. Potiphar's wife thus had ample opportunity to see him and, finding him attractive, made multiple efforts to get him to sleep with her. Joseph repeatedly denied her, stating that to sleep with her would be wicked and a sin against God. One day, however during one of these attempts, she managed to grasp his garment, which he left behind in her hand as he fled. She then called the servants and claimed that he had attempted to seduce [sic] her. On hearing his wife's tale, Potiphar had Joseph arrested and thrown into prison, effectively removing him from his position of status.[40]

The motif of a presumably older woman pursuing a younger male who refuses her advances and whom she then accuses of rape to her husband has many parallels in ancient Near Eastern, Greek, rabbinic, Indian, Persian, and even German story worlds.[41] In all of these versions, the woman is the villain, and sometimes she is characterized as "the lusty wife"[42] or even "a filthy whore."[43] Yet in the version in Sura 12 of the Qur'an, the story has an interesting twist. There Ms. Potiphar's women neighbors gossip about her attraction to a slave; in turn, she invites them to her house so that they may see for themselves the attractiveness of "Yusuf." She gives them fruit knives when Joseph enters the room. Because the women cannot take their eyes off him, they end up cutting themselves into their fingers and exclaim: "Glory be to God, this is not a human being; this is an honorable angel" (Sura 12:31).[44] They agree that "the woman's love for him can and should be understood."[45] In the Sufi tradition, this story has even been elevated "to symbolize a love relationship between the human and the divine."[46]

The question is whether this narrative depicts an attempted rape story in which a younger male is indeed threatened with rape by a woman of higher status, or whether the androcentric bias in Genesis 39 presents a powerful woman "with suspicion, as unnatural and evil," "the female personification of anti-wisdom: disloyal to her husband, quick to seek satisfaction in forbidden places, strongly sexual, and duplicitous."[47] Many commentators combine both options, although they hesitate to characterize the story as a rape threat. They are ready to condemn Ms. Potiphar and to side with Joseph. Some interpreters compare Joseph's position with Hagar's, Bilhah's, and Zilpah's predicament.[48] For instance, Jon Pirson proposes that the word order in Ms. Potiphar's speech in v. 17 is ambiguous and may entail that Mr. Potiphar brought Joseph into the house to father a child with his wife. Thus, "this might support the idea that Joseph has a role comparable to Hagar, Bilhah and Zilpah."[49] Others find Ms. Potiphar's response similar to Amnon's mood change from "sexual desire" to hate.[50] They indicate that the narrative includes verbs that express the inherent violence in Ms. Potiphar's insistence to sleep with Joseph. For instance, Gordon J. Wenham explains that "[t]he verb תפש 'grab' implies violence (cf. Deut. 9:17; 22:28; 1 Kgs 11:30)" and that "'[t]o fool with us' is a nicely ambiguous phrase used of sexual intimacy in [Gen.] 26:8 and of insulting behavior in [Gen.] 21:9."[51] Other commentators are more cautious and speak of an "unwelcome embrace,"[52] "temptation,"[53] her (attempted) seduction[54] and "advances,"[55] or "the bluntness of the mistress's sexual proposition."[56] They do not define Ms. Potiphar's "proposition" as a rape threat to Joseph. Considering the ongoing difficulties of conceptualizing men as rape victims, particularly by women, the reluctance does not surprise. What is surprising is that, in contrast to most other rape stories, interpreters take Joseph's side unhesitatingly. They read *with* the androcentric narrative that "wages for Joseph's innocence" and "embraces the ideological structure which Joseph serves, namely, the male desire for an exclusive bond between men," in this case between Mr. Potiphar and Joseph, and—since this relationship does not work out—the bond is later established between Pharaoh and Joseph (Gen 41:44ff.).[57]

It is important to recognize the literary-rhetorical design of Gen 39:1-23, which is structured by the phrase "and it was" (*wayhî*, ויהי). This phrase occurs fifteen times in vv. 2, 5, 6, 7, 10, 11, 13, 15, 18, 19, 20, and 21. The central verse in this structure is v. 10 because there the phrase appears for the eighth time, the numerical midpoint of fifteen, stating:

> And-it-was
> > when-she-kept-speaking to-Joseph day-after day,
> and-not he-listened-to-her
> > to-sleep beside-her,
> > to-be with-her.[58]

The verse describes the psychological pressure that Ms. Potiphar puts on Joseph "day after day" while he refuses her offers again and again. In a subtle way, then, her repeated and relentless requests constitute the literary center of the story, as if to acknowledge that, indeed, some men experience women's aggressive pursuit. Yet the story also reassures the androcentric ego that at least this woman does not succeed. She fails to force Joseph to sleep with her because he manages to escape, and she is left with his clothes in her hands (v. 12). Nahum M. Sarna acknowledges her forcefulness: "Her verbal assaults having failed to achieve their end, she resorts in desperation and frustration to physical aggression."[59] The literary structure confirms that Ms. Potiphar is, indeed, a sexually aggressive woman who pursues this young man regardless of his response.

Yet it is important also to look closely at the androcentric portrayal of Ms. Potiphar, as feminist interpreters have sometimes chosen to do. For Esther Fuchs, for instance, the narrative condemns the female character because, according to the androcentric ideology of the narrative, a married woman "must not have sexual access to any man other than her husband."[60] Accordingly, androcentric ideology ensures that Joseph is able to escape from Ms. Potiphar. Fuchs observes that this bias in favor of the male character is one-sided, and female characters who find themselves in similar situations do not fare well. Instead, "female prospective rape victims" seem destined to be raped because they are not "capable of defending [themselves] or being helped by God."[61] A prospective male rape victim, however, benefits from divine care, as in the case of Joseph.

Another feminist interpreter, Alice Bach, challenges the androcentric ideology that she sees in the biblical narrative as working against Ms. Potiphar, whom Bach calls Mut-em-enet. Bach wants to recover, "recreate" the female character's story and tell "her version of what happened in bed with Joseph."[62] Arguing to produce a text that "gives speech to the silenced or suppressed female figure," Bach wants "to understand how social restrictions have shaped women's lives."[63] A comparison of Ms. Potiphar's depiction in postbiblical literature, such as the *Testament of Joseph*, is therefore central to Bach's analysis, because there Ms. Potiphar emerges as a woman who not only initiates the purchase of Joseph but also cares for him when he is in prison. In postbiblical retellings, Ms. Potiphar emerges as a sympathetic figure because her female neighbors agree that Joseph is irresistible. Accordingly, she is depicted as a character similar to other women falling in love with a man, such as Abigail, who falls in love with King David (1 Sam 25). Bach emphasizes that "Abigail shares with Mut-em-enet the impediment of a husband blocking the fulfillment of her desire for the beloved." But unlike Ms. Potiphar, "Abigail is lucky" because her husband dies, and so she "gets her man."[64] Thus, for Bach, the biblical story and its later retellings present Ms. Potiphar as a female character who reflects masculine identity, and so the stories suppress the woman's perspective and seduce readers into the ideology of the writers. Feminist deconstructions should, therefore, help readers to "resist the writer's view that Mut-em-enet behaves 'just like a woman'."[65] Yet even in a deconstructive retelling untainted by androcentric interests,

Ms. Potiphar's character does not fully emerge, because her portrayal as a "vengeful and conniving woman"[66] is pervasive even today. Ms. Potiphar ends up accusing a man of rape although readers know that she is the sexually aggressive partner. Bach concludes that this androcentric story does not lend itself easily to a sympathetic reading on Ms. Potiphar's behalf.

This is also the conviction of Laura Donaldson, who approaches Ms. Potiphar as a "cyborg" that "requires us to construct a radically different character."[67] Ms. Potiphar emerges "simultaneously [as] harassed and harasser, weak and strong, marginalized and centered, generated from within and produced from without: a 'condensed image of both imagination and material reality'."[68] Donaldson relies on James Kugel's summary of the Jewish tradition to press her point. The rabbinic Midrashim emphasize the phrase "after these things" in vv. 6b-7 as a crucial ambiguity in the narrative. Kugel explains:

> *Midrash Tanhuma* provides not one explanation, but two. The first takes the Hebrew words *debarim* in our biblical text not as "things" at all, but as "words" (an equally common meaning of the Hebrew term). What "words"? Why, words of Mrs. Potiphar—idle chatter, perhaps, or suggestive phrases, or little terms of endearment—anything to get him to desire her . . . the words themselves are not in the Bible, but their existence is hinted at in this phrase, and so, Tanhuma says, she "enticed him with words," and it was, therefore, "after these *words*" had been spoken that the rest of the story ensued. The other explanation put forward in Tanhuma is quite separate from this one and in fact incompatible with it, since it goes back to the other meaning of *debarim*, "things." What things? Things again unreported in the biblical text, but whose existence is being hinted at in the phrase "after these things," things designed to get Joseph to desire her. And so, in the absence of specifics in the Bible, our midrashist supplies them. Mrs. Potiphar kept changing her clothes, three times a day in fact, one spectacular dress after the next—"and to what purpose? Only that he desire her."[69]

In this sense, then, the literary nexus of Genesis 39, the description of the repetitive actions of Ms. Potiphar, present her as a sexual harasser that "masculinist ideologies"[70] want to curtail. Sometimes, Donaldson observes, even feminist interpreters fall prey to the binaries of the androcentric construction of the female character when they present Ms. Potiphar as an example of the Foreign Woman's negativity in biblical literature.[71] In contrast, Donaldson stresses that the female character resists male ideology, which favors male lineage, when she "uses her sexuality as a weapon to prevent the household's passing from man to man (from Potiphar to Joseph) rather than from man to woman (from Potiphar to Potiphar's wife)."[72] Donaldson explains:

> And it is precisely in terms of a negotiation for empowerment that we can understand the actions of Potiphar's wife toward Joseph. By asserting herself sexually, she can potentially gain some leverage with the man who has so abruptly invaded her daily world. When that strategy fails, Potiphar's wife hurriedly devises another ruse: a self-serving explanation of the incident that convinces her husband and effects the very removal of Joseph she so desperately desires.[73]

Although ultimately Ms. Potiphar does not succeed—eventually the Pharaoh places Joseph into his lineage—her action "dissolves into a much more contradictory and subversive socio-narrative structure."[74] This is an ambiguous story that does not present a clear-cut description of what is going on between Ms. Potiphar and Joseph. And this is perhaps advantageous for a hermeneutical process that looks for male rape in biblical literature.

Lot's Daughters and Their Father

The tale of Lot presents a scenario in which the male character is an unambiguous rape victim; Lot is depicted as the victim of daughter-forced incest. In Gen 19:30-38, Lot's two daughters believe that they are the last humans on earth, and so they decide to make their father drunk and have sex with him to secure progeny. Their plan works.

They become pregnant and give birth to two sons. The story explains that one of them is the ancestor of Moab and the other of Ammon.

Strangely, commentators do not always express horror about these events. For instance, Walter Brueggemann suggests that "no stigma is attached to the action of the mothers in the narrative" and that "Lot and his daughters are clearly treated as members of the family of promise."[75] Some speak in an admiring tone about the boldness and fertility of the daughters and approve of their resorting to "emergency incest,"[76] which secures their family's future. Others try to avoid any kind of ethical stance when they comment on this narrative and explain in a matter-of-fact tone that the daughters' "actions are motivated by a desire to preserve offspring . . . , not for their own sakes, but for their father's sake,"[77] and so "the daughters simply want to reproduce" and "eliminate the possibility of perpetual barrenness."[78] Others, however, note their alarm about this short but potent story. For instance, Carol Smith states that here "we have the closest approximation possible to a female's rape of a male"—the daughters make "their father a helpless sexual victim."[79] Yet all of these interpretations share a hermeneutical conviction that does not question the basic story line. They accept that the daughters are indeed the perpetrators of the sexual intercourse, sometimes suggesting that 19:30-38 is a countermove to the father's offer in Gen 19:8. There Lot offers his daughters as substitutes to the men of Sodom when they demand the male guests to be brought out to them (Gen 19:5).[80] Again, commentators read "with" the text, accept the daughters' sexual aggression as reasonably appropriate considering the situation in which they find themselves, and do not dwell on the narrative's questionable moral standard.

Yet several feminist readers are not satisfied with these options and propose alternative views of this biblical story. They take seriously that, according to research on incest, daughters do not initiate sexual contact with their fathers. Fathers do that. Accordingly, Elke Seifert stresses that fear and a deepening of hierarchical dynamics within the family are characteristics of father–daughter incest, and this characteristic appears also in Gen 19:30-38.[81] For instance, the fear that grips Lot and makes him leave the town of Zoar—the absence of the mother, and the sibling hierarchy between the older and the younger daughter—contribute to the rituals of power and submission that are typical of incest situations in which a father dominates his children. When the narrative presents the daughters as the agents of the incest violation, it creates an implicit contradiction. It "contradicts our knowledge and reality: The reality is that daughters do *not* want sexual contact with their fathers and that they are forced to such contacts and that fathers do indeed *know* what they are doing."[82] Consequently, Seifert suggests reconstructing Gen 19:30-38 as an incest story from the perspective of violated girls. Incest between fathers and daughters is "abuse of power by the fathers, . . . manipulation and exploitation of dependencies that create deep wounds within the victims."[83] Daughters, if allowed, tell a different story; this biblical tale is not theirs.[84] In Gen 19:30-38, the perspective of the daughters is reversed and the power dynamic between father and daughters is changed to protect the father. The narrative promotes the view of an incestuous father claiming that his daughters, not he, sought the sexual contact.

Seifert's hermeneutics of suspicion is also endorsed in J. Cheryl Exum's examination of the narrative. Exum focuses on "the cultural or collective unconscious,"[85] as it is expressed in Gen 19:30-38, because the story is "a literary production that allows the collective male narrative unconscious to engage in its forbidden fantasies." In this case, the forbidden fantasy centers on "the Father's wish (that is, the desire of the spokesperson for the collective cultural unconscious) to have sex with his daughters."[86] Accordingly, daughters emerge as characters that fit with this collective androcentric unconscious, and the narrative aims "to manage forbidden desires within an ordered discourse."[87] The fantasy is played out in the text; it is confessed, but its truth is modified, changed, and obfuscated. It requires that the daughters devise and execute strategies to have sex with the father. They are portrayed as "wanting it," not the father.

According to Exum, this unconscious desire of the collective "Father" is only part of an even deeper androcentric fantasy, which is played out in Gen 19:1-29. There the fantasy entertains "the wish for homosexual sex in a distorted form,"[88] Exum maintains, and it can be presented only in a distorted, evaded, and suppressed fashion within the narrative. The homoerotic desire is thus countered by Lot's offer of his daughters to the male Sodomites. Exum describes the dynamics between vv. 1-29 and vv. 30-38 in this way:

> In order to allow himself [the male collective unconscious] to entertain a fantasy of incest with his daughters, he imagines something even more abhorrent to him—homosexual sex. This, too, is a desire that he is unable to acknowledge, an unaccept-able wish that must be rejected, and it is thus dismissed in favor of another one—what for him is the lesser of the two evils, the wish for sex with his daughters. But he is unable to carry the incest fantasy through, presumably because his guilt is so great. The solution to his conflicting impulses is a temporary narrative resolution. He punishes himself with castration, which is sym-bolically represented in the text by blindness, so that he cannot act out his forbidden sexual fantasies in his narrative. Instead he gropes in vain for "the opening" (הפתח, v. 11), possibly, through the distortion of fantasy, an allusion to his frustrated desire for sexual intercourse with his daughters.[89]

In Exum's reading, Genesis 19 is a "symptom of collective guilt"[90] that the collective male unconscious has about its fantasy to have sex with daughters. It involves even deeper desired sexual scenarios so that the incestuous desire becomes tolerable in comparison to the alternative portrayed in the beginning of Genesis 19—homosexual rape.[91] Michael Carden sees in this reversal of power "a poetic justice perhaps."[92]

The repetitive literary structure of vv. 30-38 is another indication to Exum that the collective male unconscious seems to take pleasure "in imaging being the object of sexual abuse."[93] After setting the scene in v. 30, the repetitions are striking. In the first stanza (vv. 31-32), the older sister tells her younger sister in direct speech (vv. 31-32) what she then executes in narrated discourse (v. 32). In the second stanza (vv. 34-35), the older sister tells her younger sister in direct speech (v. 34) what she needs to do now, and the younger sister follows the instructions in narrated discourse (v. 35). A conclusion reports the birth of the two sons. The phrase "to lay him" is repeated five times, the phrase "to make him drink wine" four times, and the noun "night" three times. The direct speech of the older daughter is always repeated in the narrated discourse, so as to give the collective male unconscious ongoing opportunity to take delight in the repetitively described situations of incest. For Exum, "the narrator obviously enjoys replaying the scene in his mind, for it is hardly necessary for him to repeat, almost verbatim and in detail, both the proposal and the act in such detail."[94] This narrative does not present an undistorted depiction of father–daughter incest, but one that aims to absolve the father from any responsibility or accountability for the incestuous desires. Hidden underneath may, in fact, lie another even more forbidden desire: homosexual rape. If so, this narrative too might be categorized as a male-on-male rape story.

The Charms of Delilah

The story of Delilah and Samson (Judg 16:4-22) is widely known through film, opera, the visual arts, and children's Bibles, but Delilah's charms are rarely appreciated. Perhaps Mieke Bal said it best: "In our culture, the story of Samson and Delilah is the paradigmatic case of women's wickedness."[95] Delilah seduces and betrays Samson, and as a result he must die. This couple's relationship serves as a warning to every man not to trust any woman because he might find himself in Samson's unlucky position. In popular culture, Delilah is the paradigmatic *femme fatale*, a woman who tempts, seduces, and ultimately destroys any man in her path.[96] Cultural appropriations tackle whether Delilah loves Samson, why she betrays him for money, or whether she is a prostitute who in the end feels no guilt about his fate.[97]

This final section of the Samson cycle tells of Samson falling in love with "a woman in the valley of Sorek, whose name was Delilah" (Judg 16:4). Philistine men approach her and offer her money to find out the source of Samson's strength. The narrative describes in a stylistically repetitive manner how Delilah asks Samson three times "how he could be bound" (vv. 6, 10, 13), how three times the Philistines try to overwhelm him (vv. 9, 12, 14), and how each time Samson defeats them (vv. 9, 12, 14). The fourth time Delilah uses a different strategy and says: "How can you say, 'I love you,' when your heart is not with me? You have mocked me three times now and have not told me what makes your strength so great" (v. 15). She then reportedly nags and pesters him day after day until he "was tired to death" (v. 16). Eventually, he tells her his whole secret" (v. 17; literally, "his whole heart"): "A razor has never come upon my head; for I have been a nazirite to God from my mother's womb. If my head were shaved, then my strength would leave me; I would become weak, and be like anyone else" (v. 17). Delilah informs the Philistines that this time Samson told her the truth. When he falls asleep "between" her "knees" (v. 19),[98] Delilah initiates the shaving of his hair. Then the Philistines come and attack him. As usual, Delilah shouts: "The Philistines are upon you, Samson!" (vv. 9, 12, 14, 20), but this time he does not succeed because "he did not know that Yahweh had left him" (v. 20). The Philistines blind, shackle, and put Samson into prison, but his hair begins to grow back—a hint at what is to come in the second part of the narrative (vv. 23-31).

So where is the male rape? The ambiguity of the text plays a crucial role for arguing that the Philistines and Delilah attempted to "rape" Samson. The infinitive of *'innâ* (עָנָה *piel*) in vv. 5, 6, and 19 is key, although most interpreters do not comment on the verb and simply present a translation that varies from "afflict," to "weaken," "make helpless," "humble," or "subdue."[99] The one term that commentators do not use is "rape," perhaps because they believe it is impossible for a woman to rape a man or because they assert that this verb does not always signify rape.[100] Yet the interpretative possibility exists. It is a "rhetorical game" in which the text plays on the verb's ambiguous meaning ranging from "humiliate" to "force/use sexually."[101] The connotations of rape appear in vv. 5, 6, and 19, and the possibility of indirect sexual references can be discerned in vv. 25 and 27 when Samson is forced to "play" or "perform" for the Philistines.[102]

The linguistic ambiguities are creatively exploited in Lori Rowlett's reading, which defines "the pattern of domination" in Judg 16:4-31 as "a tale of bondage and degradation" and a S/M role-play scenario.[103] Rowlett grounds her characterization of the relationship between Delilah and Samson in artistic adaptations of the biblical story in which, as she observes, the gender characterizations were less static than in the biblical account. In early musical versions, men played the female roles, but even when these roles are played by women, they are enacted with great drama and exaggeration. In literary creations, Delilah also turns into "another example of 'gender performance'" in which she impersonates "a hyperfeminine ideal" that emphasizes her desire for love only.[104] In these artistic renderings Delilah appears "with a butch bottom and a dominatrix femme or either indeterminate gender or gender so overdetermined as to verge on the camp sensibility of gender impersonation."[105]

When this pattern is applied to the interpretation of the biblical narrative, Rowlett argues, Samson desires Delilah as "dominatrix," and he is willing to submit to "sexual games of dominance and submission."[106] Accordingly, he allows Delilah repeatedly to bind him with various ropes and materials, always successfully terminating the game when he is almost "overwhelmed" by the methods of domination. Yet he tires after winning three times and "delves into an act of deeper submission"[107] that plays at the edge of life-threatening danger. Samson loses in this final game when Delilah leaves the game instead of keeping him at the edge of this dangerous "sex play," and consequently she disappears from the story (19:20ff.).[108] At this point Yahweh steps into the "cat-and-mouse game."[109] Initially, God abandons Samson and puts him into the violent hands of the Philistines (v. 20f.), but later God reappears (v. 28) and enables Samson to kill the Philistines in the temple and himself. Rowlett wonders if God, or at least the author of this character, the Deuteronomistic historian, derives "sadistic pleasure"[110] from this cycle of violence. When the story is read within such a hermeneutical context, however, it is clear that Samson deliberately participates in such violence. Therefore, Rowlett rejects the notion that it was his "absolutely incredible stupidity" leading to his eventual demise in Judges 16. Instead, his "fascination with the forbidden, the lure of 'the other,' his compulsion to mix sex with danger"[111] bring him down. Samson is not "a fool for love"[112] but rather is into "classic bondage games."[113] Yet perhaps the story is also a subtle recognition of the possibility that men may be raped by other men, and even by women, in the game for power and control.

The Subjugation of Men

The discussion of this chapter demonstrates that the Hebrew Bible does not contain explicit male-on-male or female-on-male rape stories. Certainly this literary situation does not surprise, because this hidden crime challenges androcentric views on masculinity, heterosexist notions of sexual violence, and a one-sided conceptualization of women as rape victim-survivors. There is only one biblical narrative that depicts explicit female-on-male rape, a story in which a male is overpowered by two women: the story of Lot and his two daughters. Since this narrative is so disturbing, commentators often hesitate to mention it. When they do, they usually avoid any terminological references to rape. So far, only feminist interpreters have chosen a different hermeneutical strategy. For them, the narrative presents an androcentric fantasy that obfuscates actual father–daughter incest dynamics, and so feminists do not consider Gen 19:30-38 to be a realistic depiction of a female-on-male rape scenario.

The tales about Ehud, Ms. Potiphar, and Delilah and Samson are even further removed from realistic male-on-male or female-on-male rape depictions. Only vague, ambiguous, and veiled allusions allow for the possibility of viewing these stories as male rape texts. The interpretations are by no means obvious and require an ardent search for hermeneutical possibilities that read the texts as incidences of rape. Several strategies can be called upon to identify the possibilities of male rape in biblical literature. Sometimes textual ambiguity provides hints, as in the case of Judg 3:12-30. There, the location of the sword on Ehud's hips, the king's physical size, and the penetration of the sword into the king's belly allow for manifold hermeneutical possibilities. At other times, such as in the story of Delilah and Samson, neglected verbal clues help to suggest that rape rhetoric *may* be part of the dynamics, even if only implied and not directly specified. Still another strategy seeking to identify male rape texts relies on observations from within the history of interpretation itself. The story of Ms. Potiphar provides ample opportunity to explore this history, because commentators have often emphasized the role of this woman as the sexual aggressor and Joseph as the persecuted male. Joseph then emerges as a victim of sexual harassment and even as a survivor of attempted rape.

Yet none of these narratives offers a clearly defined tale about male rape. They contain clues, traces, and hints for interpreters looking to identify male rape in the Hebrew Bible—though too often the idea is mired in silence. This topic is too deeply buried in the sociocultural and religious imagination of the literature to provide uncensored, truthful discourse. Yet it is remarkable that clues, traces, and hints appear when readers look for them. They prove again the maxim that sacred literature is inherently ambiguous, flexible and elastic and that readers create meaning(s). When the topic is male rape, the Hebrew Bible is not altogether silent, but gives witness to this hidden crime in ambiguous stories about murder, female desire, incest, and betrayal.

7

RESISTING the THEOLOGY OF A RAPIST
AGAINST the POETICS OF RAPE IN PROPHETIC LITERATURE

Rape Metaphors in Contemporary Language

Contemporary language is rife with metaphors about rape, although such vocabulary often goes unnoticed. It is commonly understood that the "rape of nature" refers to the industrial exploitation of the earth's resources or that the "rape of Nanjing" describes the massacre by Japanese troops of the Chinese city of Nanjing between December 1937 and March 1938. Similarly, when a white male professor claimed to have "felt like a rape victim,"[1] he was using metaphoric speech to describe a conflict he had with students. The expression does not literally refer to rape; it is a figure of speech that compares two unlike entities and aims to connect emotionally with the audience, often to move them to political action.

According to the analysis of linguist George Lakoff and his collaborator, Tim Rohrer, such a metaphoric call for action occurred in 1991 when U.S. president George Bush tried to convince the American public of the need for going to war against Iraq. Many of the metaphors portrayed the nation of Kuwait as raped by the military invasion of Iraq and its then-president, Saddam Hussein, and called for American intervention to help the "victim." Quoted in Rohrer's analysis, Bush stated:

> But I simply say the "rape" and the systematic dismantling of Kuwait defies description. . . . Saddam Hussein's unprovoked "invasion"—his ruthless, systematic "rape" of a peaceful neighbor—"violated" everything the community of nations holds dear. . . . Kuwait was the "victim," Iraq the aggressor.[2]

This kind of metaphoric language, which according to Rohrer is characteristic of U.S. foreign policy rhetoric, assumes that nations are persons, that a ruler stands for the nation, and that if one nation bullies its neighbor leading to "crimes," America has the "moral" obligation to help the violated state.[3] In this particular case, Kuwait turns into a nation-person and is cast rhetorically as raped by the bully, Saddam Hussein, from whom the U.S. military is compelled to defend the victim, to do what is morally right.

According to Rohrer and Lakoff, Bush's rape metaphors obfuscated the prevailing sociopolitical and economic dynamics between Kuwait and Iraq. For instance, Lakoff suggests that Kuwait was not innocent like a classic rape victim "but an innocent ingénue."[4] Previously, the government of Kuwait had been allied with Iraq and had assisted Iraq in financing its war against Iran. Yet, after the war, Kuwait claimed to have given loans and demanded repayment from Iraq. Kuwait had also used its oil production to keep oil prices down to the disadvantage of Iraq, and it did not want to provide resources for rebuilding postwar Iraq, although the Kuwaiti government was investing in Europe, America, and Japan at the time and had the resources. In addition, most foreign workers and many Kuwaiti citizens experienced severe discriminatory practices in Kuwait, and wealthy Kuwaiti men indulged themselves with cheap Iraqi goods and sexual services from Iraqi widows and orphans. In "real" life, Kuwait was powerful, and according to Lakoff, it was "badly miscast as a purely innocent victim."[5] When Bush used the rape metaphor, his vocabulary hid the strength of the Kuwaiti monarchy.

Not only did the rape metaphor misrepresent the actual power dynamics between Kuwait and Iraq, Rohrer and Lakoff argue, but it also added insult to Arab androcentric sensibilities. The metaphor correlates "weakness" with femininity, which even an Iraqi proverb finds unacceptable, saying: "It is better to be cock for a day than a chicken for a year."[6] In short, the metaphor describes the socioeconomic and political interests of the involved countries, particularly the United States, in a woefully inadequate fashion. Instead of rational discourse and explanation grounded in an understanding of society, politics, economics, religion, and history, the metaphor functions as propaganda that rallies people's deep-seated fears and irrationalities. In Lakoff's view, "it hides the main ideas that drive Middle Eastern politics."[7]

Rohrer notes that it is difficult to develop metaphoric speech, and he therefore suggests that we "refine the one we have." His suggestion makes sense, especially in light of the long tradition of viewing nations as women (raped or not). Yet refining existing metaphors is not easily accomplished, especially when we look at the prophetic literature in the Hebrew Bible. This poetry contains the so-called marriage metaphor, which describes powerful cities in the ancient Near East: Jerusalem, Babylon, Nineveh, Sidon, and Edom. Prophetic poems describe these cities as raped women, violated by military powers and even by God. In the latter case, the prophetic metaphor presents God as the husband of his wife, Jerusalem; God is enraged by his wife's infidelities and prescribes and executes the rape of his wife. A more disturbing and destructive metaphor can hardly be envisioned, and even contemporary politicians do not go that far. It is to these prophetic poems we turn next.

Divinely Authorized Rape Rhetoric in Prophetic Speech

Throughout the androcentric history of interpretation, biblical poems that depict God as the angry punisher of the idolatrous actions of the biblical and ancient Near Eastern cities of Jerusalem, Babylon, Nineveh, Sidon, or Edom have been largely ignored. Yet, since the emergence of feminist interpretation, these poems have gained recognition, and the theologically problematic implications of the metaphors have been brought to light, exposing the prophetic poetics of rape as violent and pornographic. The poems contain rape metaphors that justify sexual violence as divinely mandated punishment. Many of these poems were written during the time of the Babylonian exile in the sixth century B.C.E.[8] and depict major cities as personified women. The poems present God as decreeing sexual violence upon the women-cities, who are punished for their misbehaviors. Crude, brutal, and violent vocabulary prevails. In the case of Jerusalem, the charge is that she prostituted herself to other male nation-persons and disobeyed her husband/

God; the charge in the case of the other ancient Near Eastern cities is that they destroyed Israel. The metaphors are prophetic speech gone awry; the images have to be resisted by rereading them against the misogynist ideology of text and interpreters.[9]

"Lifting Up Her Skirt":
The Besieged City of Jerusalem as a Raped Woman

Several prophetic poems imagine female figures—women of Jerusalem and also the city of Jerusalem itself personified as a woman—as punished by God through acts of sexual violence. As Rachel Magdalene explains, "Metaphorically, then, God is seemingly quite willing to perpetrate repeated sexual assaults and abuse on women. Such texts are the ultimate in biblical texts of terror."[10] Four texts are discussed here: Isa 3:16-17; Jer 13:22, 26; Ezekiel 16; and Ezekiel 23.

In the first poem, Isa 3:16-17, God prescribes sexual attacks and rape of Jerusalem's female population. The poem characterizes the daughters of Zion as "haughty" and "walk[ing] with outstretched necks, glancing wantonly with their eyes, mincing along as they go, tinkling with their feet" (v. 16).[11] Fashion-conscious in look and posture, women of Jerusalem are the recipients of androcentric mockery. They are viewed as "serious infractions of the social order,"[12] and their exaggerated obedience to androcentric standards of femininity makes them fair game for sexual attacks, at least according to the prophetic imagination. Once the poem of Isaiah 3 establishes the women's arrogance and pride, God appears as the authorizer and executer of pornographic attacks. Verse 17 describes God's action against the women:

> The Lord will afflict with scabs the heads of the daughters of Zion,
> and the Lord [Yahweh] will lay bare their secret parts [*pōt*, פֹת].
> [NRSV]

The sexual candor of this poem makes many translators nervous, and so they read the second line as a reference to the head rather than the genital area, "and Yahweh will lay bare their forehead."[13] Translators substitute for sexual violence a description that presents captive women as being humiliated when their hair is shorn off because grammatical ambiguity allows for a changed meaning from the genitals to the head. In question is the Hebrew noun *pōt* (פת), which appears only one other time in the Hebrew Bible—in 1 Kgs 7:50 it refers to a "door socket." Some scholars recognize that the text offers "coarse language" and refers to female genitals in a vulgar and colloquial expression.[14] Accordingly, J. Cheryl Exum translates Isa 3:17 thus: "The Lord will make bald the heads of the daughters of Zion, and the Lord will bare their cunts."[15] Biblical literature is often flexible and elastic, and this is a theologically problematic setting, in which God is portrayed as the violator of Jerusalem's women. Why be plain when an image of a door socket in which a door swings will do?

The rhetoric of this poem leads Johnny Miles to declare the poem "an act of violence" that "screams 'abuse of power'—poetically, metaphorically, and ideologically."[16] He explains:

> The undercurrents of misogynist biases within this poem actuate its rape story despite attempts to deflect our attention. The "daughters of Zion" become unwitting victims in a poetic abuse of power as they are raped by the pen. . . . In an act of poetic collusion, (male) poet and God mock . . . and degrade the "daughters of Zion," the effects of which relegate Woman to the point of erasure as "other."[17]

What is needed in reading such rape rhetoric is "a voice of advocacy" that names the violence, holds the perpetrators accountable, and questions the divinely sanctioned abuse of power. Such an interpretation also emphasizes that "this misogynist text really says nothing about YHWH" because in this poem androcentric culture and history have "culturally inscribed" God in the poetics of rape.[18]

Jeremiah 13:22, 26 contains similarly troubling metaphoric speech. God announces the rape of Jerusalem—here the city itself is personified as a woman. In v. 22, the verb is in the passive voice, which avoids mentioning the identity of the rapist. But in v. 26, the verb is active and God the subject. God is the sexual violator.[19] The following translation is close to the syntax of the Hebrew text:

(22) On account of the greatness of your iniquity
exposed/uncovered are your skirts,
violated are your heels/genitals. . . .
(26) and also I myself I shall strip your skirts over your face,
so that is seen your shame.[20]

The passage is part of a larger poem in Jer 13:20-27. The personal pronouns in vv. 22 and 26 are in the second person feminine singular ("you"). God addresses the feminine city and decrees sexual punishment for her transgressions. In v. 22, the two verbs, "to uncover" and "to violate," are in the passive voice and the focus is on the woman's situation. In v. 22, the perpetrator remains unnamed, although the scene is "clearly"[21] one of rape. Robert P. Carroll suggests that Jeremiah uses euphemisms in vv. 22 and 26, perhaps to "conceal an obscene practice of exposing women by drawing their legs over their heads in order to uncover their vulvas completely"[22]—in itself an astonishing act of conjecture by the commentator.

Interpreters usually assume that in v. 24 the rapists are the victorious Babylonian soldiers, because Jeremiah's predictions often warn about the Babylonian siege and ultimate victory. Trying to ignore the "raw sexuality and violence" of this rape poem, commentators offer little or "no resistance to the powerful, ideological effects of this misogynist text upon a rape culture"[23] and omit that in v. 26 God is the rapist. They perpetuate the poetics of rape in Jer 13:20-27, in which the female is the victim and the male dominates, even violates, her. The poem proclaims that the woman brought this fate upon herself and she is to be blamed for it, while the prophet sides with the sexually violent perpetrators, viewing the attack as deserved and God as justifying it. Rape poetics endorses "masculine authoritarianism" and the "dehumanization of women," perhaps especially when the subject is God.[24] As Miles observes correctly, "violence unnamed is tacitly violence condoned."[25] Interestingly, commentators acknowledge freely that the passage is loaded with sexual metaphors. The nouns "skirt" and "shame" carry several sexual connotations, and two verbs (gālâ, גלה, "to uncover"; rā'â, ראה, "to see") appear also in other contexts of sexual violence, such as Isa 47:3; Ezek 16:36, 37; 23:29; and Nah 3:5.[26]

The prophetic poem in Jeremiah 13, then, envisions God as relishing the rape of woman Jerusalem, a rape that is presumably perpetrated by the Babylonian army and supported by the male God. It represents a climax of androcentric fury, and as such it constitutes a major theological problem. God turns out to be a rapist.[27]

Commentators are uncomfortable with this passage, define it as "a difficult section,"[28] and sometimes classify it as a rape scene. Carroll states: "Jerusalem has become a violated woman, a typical victim of invading warriors"; this is an oracle of "outrage and violence of rape."[29] He points to the suffering of the women who are brutally raped by the invading army and finds it difficult to excuse the metaphor in which the rapist is God. He states further: "[M]etaphors and reality combine to portray a sickening picture of battered sexuality and torn flesh, an image of a culture invaded, raped and devastated."[30] Yet he does not reject the prophetic sense of justice in which God turns into a sexual predator. He reads with the metaphor even while wondering, "Why are these outrages Yahweh's portion for the city?"[31]

This lack of what might be termed "readerly resistance" is not unusual. Other readers tolerate God punishing Jerusalem with sexual violence, and they read the poem from the prophet's perspective. For instance, R. E. Clements muses:

> [T]he people were eagerly placing the blame for their tragic misfortunes upon God and regarding themselves self-pityingly as the unfortunate victims of a fate that they had not deserved. It was the concern of the prophet, as well as of his editors and followers, to show that the people could not evade the acceptance of responsibility for what they had suffered.[32]

Like other interpreters, Clements does not reject androcentric extremism that characterizes God as a perpetrator of rape. Instead, he approves of the prophetic criticism that scorns the contemporaries of the prophet for their mistaken political allegiance. The prophet tells his listeners that they are not victims, as they believe, but brought their fate upon themselves because they did not follow God. Their own actions led to war, national annihilation, and exile because they abandoned God. Hence, they themselves are responsible for the national disaster in the form of foreign occupation. For Jeremiah, the Israelites are like a raped woman who is told to blame herself for the sexual violence. Many interpreters are caught in this prophetic perspective and endorse the prophetic position, which promotes a "theology of the rapist." The question is why interpreters find it so easy to accept this prophetic argument. Do they find it too difficult to go against prophetic authority, which takes for granted androcentric assumptions that portray God as "Father, Lord, Master, King, or Judge?"[33]

There are those, however, who question the depiction of God as a sexually violent retaliator. One of the first feminist commentators to struggle with this passage in Jeremiah was Gracia Fay Ellwood.[34] She identifies God as a rapist and also discusses the poem's implications. She worries what the image of God as a rapist might mean for the prevalence of violence against women and cautions that perhaps God speaks through these texts "in a different sense than we had thought." Ellwood insists that the prophetic metaphor cannot mean what it seems to imply. It cannot be that God commands the rape of women. In her opinion, there has to be another meaning, but she does not offer an alternative.

Other feminist interpreters pick up on her question and continue wrestling with it. Gerlinde Baumann, after an extensive linguistic and grammatical discussion, states: "Here we definitely have a rape scene" and "if the verse [v. 22] is read together with v. 26 . . . YHWH would be represented as a perpetrator of sexual violence."[35] She emphasizes that "[i]n v. 26 YHWH appears explicitly as a perpetrator of sexual violence"[36] who punishes woman Jerusalem for breaking the covenant with her husband, God. Baumann also observes that woman Jerusalem does not have an opportunity to repent; her punishment is rape prescribed and executed by God. Like Ellwood, Baumann worries that rapists might use this and similar texts to justify their behavior because even God "lives within damaged relationships" and punishes his wife.[37]

This concern resonates in feminist readings. Exum observes that "God not only endorses it [that is, rape], he participates in the attack."[38] The problem is that most readers read "with" God and privilege the prophetic perspective to justify rape as the proper form of punishment for idolatry and adultery. The metaphor, read accordingly, can be used to excuse men who use sexual violence against women. Thus, the rape metaphor has real-life consequences and "reinscribes patriarchal hierarchy" in the lives of women and men.[39] As Pamela Gordon and Harold C. Washington put it, "[T]he city as an object of violence is always a feminine Other, reinforcing the status of the feminine as secondary, and facilitating a pornographic objectification of women by setting the female as the model victim."[40]

The problem of a pornographic objectification of Jerusalem as the wife of her husband, Yahweh, is most dramatically depicted in two additional poems in Ezekiel 16 and 23. They are among the most extreme representations of God as the advocate and executor of rape. The city-wife is the target of verbal rape threats that in length and detail go far beyond the poems in Isaiah and Jeremiah. The prophet Ezekiel portrays the following words as those of God:

> The adulterous wife,
>   though subordinate to her husband,
> takes foreign men
>   who give payment to all prostitutes.
> . . . .
> Thus, prostitute, hear the word of YHWH:
> Thus says the Lord YHWH:
> Because your cunt was exposed
> and uncovered were your genitals in your prostitution with your
>   lovers
>   and with all your abominable idols . . .
> and for the blood-guilt of your children
>   that you gave them;
> therefore, I will gather all your lovers
>   with whom you had pleasure,
> and all whom you loved
> and all whom you hated;
> I will gather them against you from everywhere.

I will uncover your genitals to them
and they shall see all of your genitals.
I will give you into their hands.

. . . .

They shall strip you of your clothes
and they shall take away all of your fine jewels
and they shall leave you naked and uncovered.
They shall bring up a mob against you,
and they shall stone you
and they shall cut you into pieces with their swords.

. . . .

I will satisfy my fury on you
and my jealousy will turn away from you.
I will be calm
and I will not be angry anymore. (Ezek 16:32, 35-37, 39, 40)[41]

These violent words obscure the perspective of the woman, and the accusations are presented solely through the eyes of the accuser, Yahweh.[42] God speaks, accuses his wife of adultery, and prescribes the punishment in the form of public stripping, violation, and killing. In the prophetic imagination, the woman is not given an opportunity to reply. She is the exclusive recipient of divine wrath, and her point of view is absent. The woman's body is the focus of the attention, as is the treatment with which Yahweh curses her, and repetitive terminology hammers it home. She is to be stripped naked. Stoned and cut into pieces, the woman is ordered to be killed, and God expresses satisfaction about the prospect of her being thus punished. Carroll characterizes "the texture and intensity of the violent images" as "shocking," stating, "The YHWH of these narratives is a tyrant and a bully—an abusive husband of a kind utterly unacceptable to modern readers" and "a monster, guilty of bouts of pornographic violence."[43]

The emphasis on the woman's nakedness stimulates androcentric pornographic fantasy. The objectified and naked woman is the forbidden sight of the perverse desire for more. Ezekiel 23 satisfies that desire. Two women feature prominently in it: Oholah as Samaria and Oholibah as Jerusalem, both portrayed as wives of the divine husband.

Oholah prostituted herself,
    though (she was) subordinate to me,
and she yearned for her lovers,
    the Assyrians who approached her.
They were dressed in blue,
governors and commanders,
young and handsome all of them,
mounted horsemen . . .
Therefore I gave her into the hands of her lovers,
    into the hands of the Assyrians
        for whom she had yearned. (Ezek 23:5-6, 9)[44]

In accordance with pornographic fantasy, the text depicts Oholah's transgression as sex with uniformed men whose status signifies power and hierarchy. The extensive description of the wife's sexual partners follows the punishment by the divine husband. The pronouncement suggests that Samaria (Ohola) brought the destruction by the Assyrian empire upon herself.[45] The prophet portrays the military defeat of the nation of Samaria, by the other nation, Assyria, as a sexual violation:

They uncovered her genitals,
her sons and her daughters they took.
They killed her with the sword.
And so she became a warning sign for women
and they applied the laws on her. (Ezek 23:10)

The poem depicts Oholah being publicly stripped and killed, as God commanded. Mercy is not an option because, according to the prophet, this is God's way of punishing the wife for her infidelities.

The fate of the sister, Oholibah (Jerusalem), is similarly violent, and the divine rage prescribes torture for the woman:

Therefore, Oholibah, thus says the Lord YHWH:
I will rouse against you your lovers
    from whom you turned in disgust,
and I will bring them against you from every side.
. . . .

I will direct my indignation against you,
in order that they may deal with you in fury.
They shall cut off your nose and your ears,
and your survivors shall fall by the sword.
They shall seize your sons and your daughters,
and your survivors shall be devoured by fire.
They shall also strip you of your clothes
and take away your fine jewels.
So I will put an end to your lewdness and your whoring
       brought from the land of Egypt;
you shall not long for them,
or remember Egypt any more.
For thus says the Lord YHWH:
I will deliver you into the hands of those
       whom you hate,
              into the hands of those
       from whom you turned in disgust;
and they shall deal with you in hatred,
and take away all the fruit of your labor,
and leave you naked and bare,
and the nakedness of your whoring shall be exposed.
Your lewdness and your whorings have brought this upon you,
because you played the whore with the nations,
and polluted yourself with their idols.
You have gone the way of your sister;
       therefore I will give her cup into your hand. (Ezek 23:22, 25-31)

As Mary E. Shields points out, "the language in these verses is clearly rape language."[46] The women are stripped in public, mutilated, raped, and murdered, all of which is initiated and commanded by God, the husband. The other nations—Babylon, Assyria, and Egypt—follow God's order and sexually violate and murder the women with whom they had sex before (see also Mic 4:11). Most important, in the classic fashion of absolving the abusers, God's speech blames the women for the sexual violence they experience; the women brought it upon themselves by not listening to their divine husband and by following, even inviting, other men (that is, nations) to sexual play (that is, idolatry). The prophet portrays God as justified for punishing his wives with rape and murder.

The poem also stresses that women should remember Oholah's and Oholibah's fate as a warning to adhere to their husbands. Already Ezek 23:10 includes such a warning ("And so she became a warning sign for women"), but a later verse is even more direct:

> Thus will I put an end to lewdness in the land,
> so that all women may take warning
> and not commit lewdness as you have done. (Ezek 23:48)

The prophetic rape metaphor turns the tortured, raped, and murdered wives into a warning sign for all women. It teaches that women better obey their husbands, stay in their houses, and forgo any signs of sexual independence. This "masculine fantasy of punishment and violence"[47] threatens women in particular because it cements male domination, hierarchy, and supremacy with God's authority. This prophetic fantasy constructs women as objects, never as subjects, and it reduces women to sexualized objects who bring God's punishment upon themselves and fully deserve it. Male control in the form of the divine husband and military men/nations defines women's sexuality—metaphoric men force metaphoric women into a submissive role.

Some commentators also reflect on the consequences of the prophetic rape metaphor that portrays God as a sexually violent punisher. Shields observes that interpreters often empathize with the deity, downplay divine rage and jealousy, and consider God's rage as a sign of love for his wife.[48] Yet, from a postmodern perspective, the raped and murdered women/cities simultaneously threaten the power and identity—the subject role—of God. Accordingly, "YHWH is actually the antireflection of the sisters" and the subject position attributed to male characters is "harmful to men as well."[49] Shields's analysis tries to deconstruct the binary gender perspective of the rape metaphor and to return some power to the female characters and perhaps to women in general. Yet the argument underestimates the historical pervasiveness of rape metaphors. Even if one recognizes that violators, torturers, and rapists are also victims of their own weakness, which makes them employ violence, and if one even sympathizes with the psychological weakness of oppressors, they have hurt untold numbers of people in theory and practice throughout the ages. Their dysfunctional notions about love and relationships have brought death to women, children, and even some men. Commenting on this problem, Shields contends: "it is dangerous . . . to let the male figure off the hook here, even if that figure is God," and she encourages readers to look closely and to endure being "repelled by what we see" and "to call into question this text's validity as 'the word of God'."[50] Ultimately, Shields wants to move beyond "a divine figure who is identified in such violent, horrific ways."[51] Unlike Renita Weems, who identifies with the abused and battered woman Jerusalem, Shields maintains that the image of a raping God does not leave any room for grace.[52] Thus, she wonders how we will be reconciled with a prophet who presents God as a raping murderer of women.

Shields suggests deconstructing this image of God so that it cannot any longer be read as a justification of sexual violence.[53] While she herself does not offer such a deconstructed reading, she locates the metaphor firmly within the male prophetic psyche and insists that androcentric imagination links God with misogyny and sexual violence. The prophet who justifies male violence pictures God as a sexually violent punisher of women. In Shields's opinion, readers have to remember at all times that Ezekiel 16 and 23 are words of the prophet. It is he who speaks his androcentric truth, and this truth comes in words that are not the words of God.

Daniel L. Smith-Christopher goes even further, proposing that the portrayal of "a sadistic God," as described in Ezekiel 16 and 23, might actually be an empowering ideology for the victims of imperial oppression. Perhaps sixth-century Israelites, after being defeated by the Babylonians and displaced in exile, used "self-blaming ideologies to take away the ultimate victory of the conqueror by attributing defeat to one's own failures or sins."[54] The self-blaming ideology includes the notion that the "male and military images of violence" describe the exilic conditions of lost power and control. As customary in ancient Near Eastern war (and mentioned also in Isa 19:16;

Jer 50:37; and Jer 51:30), the images present the unsuccessful army as metaphoric "women"—weak, stripped naked, and lacking control. Hence, Smith-Christopher proposes that perhaps "the image of stripped and humiliated Jerusalem may not have 'titillated' the male hearer at all, but rather shocked them precisely because it reminded them of their own treatment at the hands of the Babylonian conquerors! Accordingly, they would have identified with the female Jerusalem, rather than the 'male God'."[55] Thus, for Smith-Christopher, Ezekiel's rape metaphors give evidence not only of gendered hierarchies but of "degrading imperial hierarchies"[56] that oppress people—women and men—who are forced to endure life under military occupation and imperial power.

Yet another very powerful analysis comes from Linda Day. She observes that "the profile of YHWH in Ezek. 16 matches that of real-life batterers in significant ways."[57] Day agrees with the notion, as outlined by Smith-Christopher, that "woman abuse" originates "in a patriarchal system of society at large" and depends on "a hierarchical stratification of power."[58] Hence, she focuses on the battering relationship between God and his wife, as depicted in Ezekiel 16, and identifies a three-stage cycle in the poem that is typical of battering relationships. The first phase, illustrated in vv. 1-26, consists of "tension building," during which the male batterer increases the violence and the battered woman tries to avoid the escalation by overlooking the verbal tirades and psychological pressures. The second phase, described in vv. 27-41, begins with "an acute violent incident," during which the batterer cannot control himself anymore; he attacks the woman. She is no longer able to manipulate his anger and rage; she is powerless. The ensuing violence inflicts physical injuries, and her only safeguard is to escape until the batterer decides to stop the violence. The third phase, as presented in vv. 42-63, is characterized by the batterer's return to kindness, regret, and the plea to the battered woman to come back.[59]

According to Day, the problem is that the mostly male commentators have bought into the perspective of the battering husband, God. They consider "the man YHWH . . . to be perfectly justified, even obligated, to react to the woman as he does, and the punishment is appropriate."[60] These male commentators accept that God is justified in being angry about his wife's infidelities and strongly believe in God's love and grace as God's main character trait. They view divine rage as "romantic passion"[61] and emphasize God's love and benevolence in taking Jerusalem back, even suggesting that human husbands emulate God's attitude. Like battered women, commentators find little fault with the abusive divinity and express gratitude for God's willingness to forgive them like Jerusalem.

This attitude toward divine rage and love demonstrates, according to Day, that commentators themselves often behave like battered women. Day explains:

> A battered woman tends to see only the positive side of her abuser. She chooses to believe that the loving, caring behavior before and after a physically abusive incident shows the man's true character. Abused women will state that they love their men and that they believe that their men, deep down, really do love them. Idealizing the relationship, they hope that phases one and two will not happen again. Time and time again the woman chooses to return to the man, believing again in her original dream of how wonderful love is.[62]

Commentators, too, want to believe in divine goodness and generosity. They see only the "beauty and grace of divine love," all of which proves them to be completely dependent on their God. Yet for Day, this exclusive belief in God's goodness reflects a battered woman's consciousness.

It can be deduced from Day's explanations that a post-battered faith in God would not limit God to goodness alone. Rather, such a faith is based on a theology that challenges hierarchies and rejects power differentials. It also requires an unambiguous acknowledgment of prophetic rape metaphors as violent, harmful, and ultimately unacceptable. Katheryn Pfisterer Darr pursues such a theological path. Responding to Ezekiel's insistence that suffering and exile are appropriate divine punishment, she exclaims: "No, in this, I cannot follow you."[63] Only a rejection of the binary characterization of the divinity avoids the prophetic projection of God as a rapist. A post-battered faith requires a critical engagement of these rape metaphors, so that readers can develop post-hierarchical ways of thought and ways of life. Katheryn Pfisterer Darr expresses this insight best when she states:

> Yet even if they [students] decide to say "no" to him [Ezekiel], that does not mean that the text in question is ill-suited to the canon and should be discarded, or relegated beyond the borders of their "canon within the canon." Sometimes, we continue to embrace hurtful texts not because we affirm their answers, but rather because they force us to confront the important questions.[64]

"Uncovering Their Nakedness": The Besieged Cities of Babylon, Nineveh, Sidon, and Edom as Raped Women

Prophetic androcentrism does not rest with the depiction of Jerusalem as a woman cursed by God and punished with rape, abuse, and murder. The cities of Babylon, Nineveh, Sidon, and Edom receive similar metaphoric treatment. Several divine oracles address Babylon, and in Isa 13:16 the women of Babylon are threatened with rape. The NRSV offers this English translation of verse 16:

> Their infants will be dashed to pieces before their eyes;
> their houses will be plundered,
> and their wives ravished.

The oracle presents a violent and graphic depiction of the violence perpetrated on the Babylonian inhabitants, especially children and women, but the important text is the last line of v. 16. The verb connoting sexual violation is *šāgal* (שׁגל), which appears also in Deut 28:30 and Zech 14:2.[65] The NRSV translates it as "ravished." Interestingly, Hans Wildberger notes that already the Masoretes recognized the verb *šāgal* as a "gutter term." They wanted to soften the "offensive" meaning and often substituted another verb, "to sleep with" (*šākab*, שׁכב),

because, in their view, "[p]assages written with unclean expressions are changed to more seemly readings."[66]

Many translators and commentators follow this convention and avoid terminology that specifies what was actually done to women in Isa 13:16—although some express revulsion at the extent of the violence. Others admit that such violence is common in today's world as well, but they still do not describe what exactly happens to the women in Isa 13:16. For instance, Joseph Blenkinsopp makes a connection to contemporary sensibilities and realities: "By closing with the scene, not unfamiliar in our day, of refugees trying to escape a victorious army bent on murder and mayhem, the stanza provides an appropriate transition to the capture and sack of the city of Babylon."[67] Yet, despite an explicit, if welcome, comparison to "our day," Blenkinsopp does not address the women's fate.

Even when commentators mention the gross violations prescribed in the Isaian poem and point to its androcentric bias, they still refrain from clearly defining the women's fate. For instance, Gene M. Tucker writes:

Among the most horrible of lines in Scripture are those in v. 16 promising that "their infants will be dashed to pieces . . . and their wives ravished." As if those violent acts were not sufficient, one must notice that the perspective is not that of the children and women, but of the men. The picture stresses their pain at seeing such horrors. The loss of the children is a punishment for their fathers.[68]

Tucker recognizes the destructive violence pictured in the poem, but he does not specifically deal with the verb *šāgal*. Similar to the NRSV and other translations, he uses the archaic term "to ravish" for a commentary published in 2001. He also seems unaware of the androcentric bias. He silently accepts the omission of rape when he speculates what the murder of the children might mean for the fathers, ignoring what the women's rapes might mean to spouses, children, and the women themselves. These details remain unspoken and are left to a reader's imagination.

The tendency to ignore the women's plight is apparent also in the Isaiah commentary by Otto Kaiser, who describes v. 16 thus: "In a few bold strokes the poet draws a picture of total defeat and complete abandonment to the conqueror, describing the conquest of the city only indirectly, as it is reflected in what happens to its defenders and its inhabitants."[69] This kind of fatalistic acceptance of the prescribed punishment of the civilian population makes Kaiser and other commentators compliant with the poem's envisioned "total defeat." To them, the fate of the women in v. 16 remains an unspoken horror, a silenced fact of war that is not openly characterized as unacceptable. Whether it is fatalism or the reliance on antiquated and indirect terminology in v. 16, the androcentric perspective—consciously or unconsciously—eliminates rape discourse from the biblical text and interpretation.

Only a few interpretations provide a translation that lifts the rape out of the poetic shadows. For instance, Brevard S. Childs translates Isa 13:16c as "and their wives (will be) raped," although he, too, reverts to the old-fashioned "ravish" in the exposition of his commentary: "The final description (vv. 14-16) leaves the arena of the heavenly judgment and returns to the description—all too well known in the ancient Near East—of the cruel massacre of a helpless people by an invading army: infants dashed on the rocks, wives ravished, and houses looted."[70]

The fate of the Babylonian women, as depicted in this prophetic oracle, is a horrible one, as is the fate of the infants (see also Ps 137:9). The problem is not that the oppressed nation fantasizes about revenge, but that the revenge relies on such androcentric images in the first place. Nor does the latter part of the poem propose to take on the men (except for the "boys" [*nĕ'ārîm*, נערים] in v. 18), but it presents "wombs" (*beṭen*, בטן), children (*bānîm*, בנים), and animals as the victims of the destructive fantasy. Isaiah 13:18 states:

Their bows will slaughter the young men;
they will have no mercy on the fruit of the womb;
their eyes will not pity children.

In other prophetic poems, the androcentric fantasy of revenge goes even further in oracles about the city of Babylon. In Isa 47:2-3, the prophet envisions God as cursing the city of Babylon personified as a young woman.

> Take the millstones
> and grind meal,
> take off [gālâ, גלה] your veil,
> strip off your robe,
> uncover [gālâ, גלה] your thigh,
> pass through the rivers.
> Your genitals ['erwâ, ערוה] shall be uncovered [gālâ, גלה]
> and your vagina [ḥerpâ, חרפה] shall be seen.
> I will take vengeance,
> and I will spare no human. (Isa 47:2-3)[71]

This poem contains the same features that prophetic speech uses to refer to Israelite cities,[72] as Blenkinsopp explains: "[T]his type of saying can very easily also be 'recycled' in accordance with the changing international scene. . . . Feminine personification was traditional for cities (Babylon, Jerusalem, Nineveh, Sidon in Isa. 23:12) and peoples."[73] Here the "ritualized verbal humiliation" is addressed to Babylon, "the dishonored queen" who is "the mirror image" of "the female *persona* of Jerusalem-Zion."[74] In Isaiah 47, Babylon is a woman whom God threatens to strip, to lead around naked, and to expose her genitals, whereas elsewhere in Deutero-Isaiah Jerusalem is a woman for whom God cares (for example, 52:1-2; 54:1-4). Blenkinsopp recognizes that in chapter 47 the oracle contains violent, "at times pornographic imagery" that clearly "involves rape," similar to other prophetic sayings on Jerusalem as a woman (for example, Jer 13:22, 26).[75] Blenkinsopp notes that the notion of Babylon "grinding" grain in v. 2 has "a dreadful double entendre"; it is "a euphemism for coercive sexual activity."[76] Already in 1968, commentator John L. McKenzie acknowledged the passage's reference to rape:

> Babylon is addressed in terms similar to those prophets and poets used in addressing Jerusalem when it was threatened; they

personify her as a young woman, the most helpless of the cap-
tives of ancient warfare. She is enslaved, put to hard labor, or
forced to submit to sexual abuse.[77]

Others point also to the "sexual connotation" of the phrase in v. 2,
although they do not use plain and direct vocabulary. For instance, Klaus
Baltzer translates the verse as: "Your nakedness will be exposed . . .
your shame will become visible," and remarks: "But this is not actually
shown. Drastic though Deutero-Isaiah can be, here—especially since
this is divine speech—the utmost limit has been reached."[78] Brevard S.
Childs identifies the action as "sexual humiliation."[79] What is missing
in these comments is a simple and declarative statement that recognizes
rape in this poem.

The reticence disappears when the metaphor applies to
Nineveh, another ancient Near Eastern city. In Nah 3:5-7, this
Assyrian city appears as a woman whom God threatens with sexual
violence:

I am against you, says Yahweh of hosts.
I will take off [gālâ, גלה] your skirts over your face;[80]
I will let nations look at your genitals [ma'ar, מער]
and kingdoms at your disgrace [qālôn, קלון].
I will throw filth at you,
I will sexually violate you [nibbēl, נבל piel],[81]
I will make you a gazing stock.
Then all who see you will shrink from you
and they will say:
"Wasted is Nineveh;
who will bemoan her?"
Where shall I seek comforters for you?[82]

Familiar imagery dominates the poem, "typical of the *Prophecy of
Punishment against Foreign Nation*" genre.[83] God is said to act as a
sexually violent force. The terms "skirts," "nakedness," and "shame"
are references to female genitals.[84] Marvin A. Sweeney explains: "At
this point, verse 5 turns to the treatment of women by a conqueror by
metaphorically portraying Nineveh as a woman who is exposed before

her captors, presumably to be raped."[85] The sentence "I will sexually violate you" uses the Hebrew verb *nābal* (נבל) in the *piel,* which appears also in rape narratives such as Gen 34:7, Judges 19-21, and 2 Sam 13:12.[86] In the entire poem of Nah 3:1-19, Nineveh is depicted as succumbing to the military attack. The enemy's horses overrun the city. Citizens die by the sword, fire destroys the houses in the town, and no one is there to assist the victims. As in other prophetic poems, sexual violence intermingles with sexual harassment and murder. Rape is a predictable ingredient of complete destruction; it is the climax of this gruesome prophetic poem.[87] To some commentators, the woman's punishment is justified because she is characterized as a prostitute[88] who is "made the object of scorn and an example to all who see her."[89] To others, Nahum's abusive words are questionable not because they try to provide justice in words, but because they engender "verbal and physical abuse of women" in the name of God.[90]

The question, though, is why God is upset about Nineveh's sexual promiscuities, since Nineveh does not have a relationship with God. Gerlinde Baumann proposes that the allusions of sexual promiscuity have broader meaning. They describe pejoratively how a feminized nation makes political deals with the other national powers of its day. The poem characterizes "Ms. Nineveh" ironically as a "prostitute" who receives due punishment for her unacceptable behavior.[91] In the prophetic imagination, God takes revenge on this previous oppressor of Israel and hands her over to the next powerful empire for systematic annihilation. The prophet sees no greater penalty, no superior depiction of total destruction than rape. Thus, in this poem God acts again as a rapist; this time against a hated oppressor of Israel. Does it make the rape metaphor less abhorrent? Francisco O. García-Treto takes exception to this portrayal of woman Nineveh, contending:

> [T]oday's reader must question Nahum's choice of poetic expression for God's activity. . . . The image of God's humiliation of the prostitute is particularly abhorrent to modern readers. Nahum clearly speaks as a male representative of a patriarchal culture. . . . Add to this the harm that an image of God abusing

and humiliating a woman can do, and it is clear that these verses in the book of Nahum must be treated as dangerous territory.[92]

Nahum stands in a considerable tradition of prophetic poetry that applies the rape metaphor to nations and cities, foreign or Israelite. All of them are "dangerous territory," and all of them demonstrate the dangerous power of androcentric hierarchical thought. A brief passage in Isa 23:12 cites another Mediterranean town, Sidon, as "destroyed" or "crushed" by God. Baumann contends that here, too, God threatens a non-Israelite city with rape. The line "O virgin daughter Sidon who was treated violently" contains the verb 'āšaq (עשׁק) in the *pual*. Elsewhere, the verb describes the oppression of widows, orphans, foreigners, or poor people and connotes an unjust condition of exploitation that should be opposed.[93] Only in Isa 23:12 does the verb refer to violence that is directed against a woman. It is thus possible to conjecture, Baumann argues, that the "exploitation" endured by virgin Sidon is indeed rape.[94]

Finally, a one-line reference to Edom, a neighboring country south of Judah, appears in Lam 4:21, and this foreign nation, too, is personified as a woman. The short address begins with a sarcastic appeal to "daughter Edom," asking her to "rejoice and be glad." A brief description of her "ugly and hurtful . . . violation"[95] follows. She is to be punished, probably for being a vassal of Babylonia under Nebuchadnezzar after 605 B.C.E. She is made drunk and ordered to strip herself, similar to an earlier divine speech on daughter Jerusalem, who in Lam 1:8-10 is imagined as naked and violated.[96] In other words, prophetic poetry personifies foreign and Israelite cities as women who, according to the prophetic imagination, are publicly abused and raped. Divine authority, "Thus says YHWH," sanctions the sexual violence as legitimate punishment for these women's disobedience to God and sexual independence. Often the imagined abusers and rapists are military men from Israel or from other nations. In the case of Ezekiel 16 and 23, the divinity—projected as a husband—orders the rape and murder of his wives, Jerusalem and Samaria. Yet elsewhere in biblical prophecy, God rapes even the prophet himself. The next section discusses briefly two such scenarios.

"You Overpowered Me and Prevailed": Prophetic Responses to the Experience of Divine Rape

In two poems, God appears to rape the male prophet. The poems are ambiguous and leave room for interpretation, but when the hermeneutical interest focuses on rape it is difficult to exclude these texts. The image of God as a violator is indeed a most disturbing theological possibility, and perhaps for that very reason the poems are of elastic meaning and, at least in one case, grammatically unclear.

In the first case, Jer 20:7, the prophet's reference to the experience of divine rape is part of a longer lament about his unfortunate fate of being deceived and despairing (20:7-18).

> You seduced [*pātâ*, פתה, *piel*] me, YHWH, and I was seduced.
> You overpowered/raped [*ḥāzaq*, חזק] me, and you prevailed.
> I have become a laughingstock all day long,
> everyone mocks me.[97]

Already Abraham Joshua Heschel saw the connotation of rape in the combined verbs of "persuade" (פתה) and "overpower" (חזק).[98] William L. Holladay also finds it "clear that in the present passage Jeremiah is engaged in a bitter complaint to Yahweh, that Yahweh led him into the situation of misery and danger." For Holladay, "[i]t is possible that the image of seduction is carried forward in the verb חזק 'overcome' in the second colon."[99] He thus suggests that the verse stands in a "semantic field of sexual violence" that is not only "deeply rebellious" but even "blasphemous" because it presents God as "brute force, as deceptive, beyond any conventional norm."[100] Angela Bauer agrees with this interpretation because, in her view, the verbs "seduce" and "overpower" "embody a forceful accusation" in which "[J]eremiah identifying as female accuses YHWH of seduction and rape."[101]

This is a challenging image of God, and so, perhaps predictably, several commentators reject a reading of Jer 20:7 that emphasizes rape. Robert P. Carroll cautions that such a "literalist" reading would "put v. 7 into the mouth of Jeremiah" and create "the bizarre image of the *celibate* prophet . . . accusing the deity of *rape*."[102] For Carroll, the notion of "a disgruntled prophet complaining about divine rape in a life devoted to ranting about his neighbour's sexual excesses . . . is an image too grotesque and modern to be the likeliest reading of the text." He claims that this meaning *"can* be derived from v. 7" but he finds other possibilities more convincing,[103] especially when they do not correlate with the prophet's life.

Other interpreters, among them Patrick D. Miller, point to Jer 20:11 to hint at the theological complexities in the prophetic God-talk: "But YHWH is with me like a dread warrior; therefore my persecutors will stumble, and they will not prevail. They will be greatly shamed, for they will not succeed." To Miller, the poem praises God as a mighty warrior who makes Jeremiah's persecutors stumble and fail. The verse stands in sharp contrast to v. 7, in which the prophet portrays God as his prosecutor, perhaps even rapist. Miller tries to resolve the contradiction:

> That jarring juxtaposition, however, is significant for the character and context of prayer. It reflects a fundamental tension that may run against our tendency to seek logical connections but is a part of the dialogue of faith that prayer becomes. It is the one who trusts in God who complains to God. The complaints and accusations, no matter how extreme, arise out of a fundamental relationship that is asserted as the grounds for the petition and thus a part of the urging of God that goes on in prayer. It is only the person who truly believes that God can and will help who dares to challenge the Lord so forthrightly.[104]

For these interpreters, the prophet's closeness to God enables both rape and faith, lament and prayer, because without a believer's relationship with the divinity neither complaint nor faith is possible. Miller asserts that the prophetic poem in Jeremiah 20 provides evidence for this theological dynamic

Another hermeneutical solution to Jer 20:7 comes from Ken Stone, who questions whether the verse describes the rape of the prophet.[105] In his view, a connection between power and sex does not find expression only in sexual violence, and so he suggests an alternative. He observes, like Miller, that the literary context of v. 7 does not indicate the prophet's distrust of God but just the opposite. Jeremiah praises God and rejoices in the power of the divinity. In addition, commentators previously observed that the prophet is both attracted to and coerced by God. Hence, Stone finds in Jer 20:7-13 a power dynamic that entails both "attraction and coercion. Appeal and pressure. Charm and stress. Overwhelming and irresistible. Power and trust."[106] This description sexualizes a religious experience, and there is no indication that the prophet did not consent. Stone emphasizes that the prophet enjoys the experience, although he also complains "about the *social* disapproval that accompanies his status as Yahweh's partner." Stone maintains, "[T]he text can therefore be construed, I think, as replicating dynamics at least associated with an S/M [Sadomasochism] scene."[107] Read accordingly, the poem depicts a male homoerotic experience of sadomasochism between the prophet and God that needs to be evaluated differently from "the now common hermeneutics of rape."[108] For Stone, the text requires a "distinct" ethical critique that relates to male homoerotic sadomasochism and engages parallels between "the dynamics of S/M and the dynamics of prayer," as articulated in ethical discussions on the use of sadomasochism in religion.[109]

Shall Stone's call for a "hermeneutics of sadomasochism" be applied to another poem, one that describes the sexual violation of the main character in the book of Job, or is a "hermeneutics of rape" more appropriate? The highly ambiguous verse Job 30:11, which depicts Job's struggle with divine forces, allows for the possibility that Job's encounter with the divinity is a violation. Job exclaims in v. 11: "Because God has loosed my bowstring and humbled ['*innâ*, ענה *piel*] me, they have cast off restraint in my presence." The verse is part of a longer poem in chapter 30 that depicts "the misery of his [Job's] present condition"[110] and Job's treatment by God and his enemies in vv. 11-15.[111] In the early twentieth century, Samuel Rolles Driver and George Buchanan Gray submitted that "the text . . . is so uncertain or ambiguous that it is impossible to determine with confidence whether these vv. refer" to God, the men in the rest of the chapter, or partially to God and partially to the men.[112] Hence, Driver and Gray ask if it can really be that "God has weakened me and tormented me" or is it rather that "God loosened his cord and tormented me so that they have cast off restraint in my presence"?[113] In Job 30:21, God is Job's tormenter for sure, and Job exclaims that God is "assaulting me with your heavy hand."[114] In v. 11, the verb *'innâ* (עִנָּה) further connotes oppressive violence and, in fact, rape. Perhaps the text is ambiguous and corrupted because it contains such a radical notion of God; God is the rapist of Job, opens his pants ("loosening his rope"[115]), and rapes Job—truly a metaphor that seems blasphemous. E. Dhorme's translation of Job 30:11 demonstrates the problem: "As soon as he [God] has untied his rope, he handles me [Job] roughly."[116] Is it possible that "rope" is a euphemism for the male genital? The Hebrew text is ambiguous and the possible meaning is not only irritatingly andromorphous but also theologically disconcerting. Its content is so thoroughly indefensible, it "could scarcely be."[117]

The Difficulties with the Prophetic Poetics of Rape: Concluding Comments

So what shall we do with these poems that promote a theology of the rapist? They are likely to be shocking to anybody who was not aware of these metaphors before reading this chapter, but they also contain the power to disturb those who knew of them before. Who included these texts in the Sacred Scriptures of Christianity and Judaism, and why were they not omitted? They have been part of the canon for so long; why were they not more vigorously discussed, deconstructed, or even rejected? It is upsetting to realize that androcentric bias has hindered, prevented, and obstructed intellectually and theologically honest debates on the theology of rape in biblical literature. Only when feminist scholars began studying the Hebrew Bible did they uncover these prophetic metaphors, make them central to feminist interpretations, and expose androcentric bias. In short, the theological problem of rape has become unavoidable, and the prophetic poetics of rape cannot stay hidden any longer.

During Talmudic times, the rabbis understood the grave theological challenges of these passages and prohibited the liturgical reading of a text such as Ezekiel 16. They explained: "R. Eliezer says: We do not read the chapter, 'Cause Jerusalem to know' as the concluding recitation following a Torah reading" (*m. Meg.* 4.10).[118] They ordered the biblical poetics of rape to remain unread in public settings. Yet, despite the various efforts to keep these texts out of sight from "ordinary readers," they have always been part of the biblical canon. The question is how we should engage them now that we know they exist.

Over the past few years, different hermeneutical strategies have been proposed to help readers cope. In fact, four strategies have proven effective in the hermeneutical process of wrestling with these highly problematic passages. One strategy teaches readers to renounce metaphors that depict women as the victim-survivors of rape and murder. Pamela Gordon and Harold C. Washington promote this strategy: "So we suggest in conclusion that it is necessary for us to renounce, for a moment, the use of the raped woman as a metaphorical figure of something else—a feminine city assaulted by an army of men."[119] Gordon and Washington give permission to reject the rape metaphors as inadequate, unacceptable, and hateful language about raped women.[120] No longer are readers required to side with the prophet and the image of God, but they are advised openly to reject the poetics of rape. We may say no to the poetics of rape and define these passages as "beyond salvation not only for feminists but also for any objector to violence."[121] This is probably the most "spontaneous" reading strategy when one encounters the prophetic texts for the first time.

Another closely related reading strategy locates the metaphors in the historical context from which they emerged. Johnny Miles reminds us of this approach when he writes that the prophetic texts do not "really" tell us what Yahweh says or does. Rather, the texts inform us about "the perspectives of an ancient culture on men, women, and, yes, God."[122] Perhaps it makes sense to justify the poetics of rape when we recognize that, historically, "Nineveh . . . certainly deserved to be humiliated," and the announcements of punishment stand in line with ancient Near Eastern understanding of justice.[123] Christl M. Maier holds a similar position, advising on how best to deal with prophetic metaphors: "Readings that merely name texts like Jer 13:20-27, Ezekiel 16 and 23 'prophetic pornography' without any discussion of the historical background take the sexual imagery literally and do not provide an appropriate interpretation of the metaphors," although she also suggests that "feminist scholars should focus on explaining the implications of these metaphors for readers then and now." The historical description, Maier argues, would disclose gender bias and androcentric rhetoric in the biblical texts and allow contemporary readers "to distance ourselves from their implicit message and their image of the violent deity."[124] Yet Athalya Brenner, along with some other feminist readers, questions this line of argument, stating: "Ultimately, no reconsideration of 'original circumstances,' whether grounded in reconstructed history or anthropology or religious studies or psychology or developmental theory or positivism, can change that [that is, that depictions of God in the Hebrew Bible are also violent] or serve as an excuse of 'understanding'."[125]

Yet another strategy correlates the prophetic metaphors with other biblical books and seeks to counteract the rhetorical violence against women in Isaiah, Jeremiah, and Ezekiel. Carleen Mandolfo follows this approach when she recovers Zion's voice in the book of Lamentations and defines it as a challenge to "God's abusing voice."[126] Daughter Zion talks back to God and refuses to submit to the prophetic charges of her guilt and punishment in the form of rape, abuse, and murder. In Lamentations, says Mandolfo, Zion disputes the validity of these charges and questions "the hegemony" of God's authority over her. Only when readers recover the different voices from the biblical text will they take on their "responsibility to protect victims of abuse."[127]

Finally, some commentators encourage wrestling with the difficult texts and trying to take them back. Julia M. O'Brien acknowledges that "I find myself less willing than in the past to write off texts that offend me. . . . I tend to wrestle with them instead,"[128] because in this way androcentrism does not have the last word. As Miles puts it:

"Taking back the text" becomes a means of liberation; it marks an act of inhabiting the gap and breaking the silence through the power of imagination. . . . It does not leave, in this case, the "daughters of Zion" as silent and as victim, an act of gynocide. Instead, it offers them a voice of advocacy by naming the violence committed against them and holding their perpetrator(s) accountable. Confronting the androcentric perspectives (en)gendering the divinely sanctioned abuse of power perpetrated against Woman within this rape text is crucial to breaking the cycle of a patriarchal ethos of violence perpetuated by its uncritical readers. Only by critically engaging in a resistant reading can we re-inscribe valuation for devaluation and reverse the (circum)(in)scribed fate of the "daughters of Zion" from victimization, from textual marginalization, from "other." Only by re-reading can we begin to envision a society that fosters values of sharing, warmth, and equality among gender relations.[129]

Reading the text and rereading the readings of the text help one to come to grips not only with metaphoric rape in the text but also with rape in the world. The goal of this strategy is that readers learn to connect texts, interpretations, and the world and to interpret toward justice, peace, and the integrity of creation, including animals and nature. As a *via negativa*, rape metaphors provide direction and purpose in the negative, guiding toward the healing of the world, what the Jewish mystics called *tikkun olam*. Perhaps readers of the prophetic poetics of rape will come to understand that a "raping God" does not exist. Such a god is an invention of biblical prophecy. Majella Franzmann said it well: "The metaphor is a scandal—a scandal for the human persons who thought it worthwhile to express some aspect of God in this way, rather than a scandal about this God."[130] As problematic image, then, the biblical rape metaphor should not be classified as a "sacred" witness.

CONCLUSION
THE BLESSING OF A SACRED WITNESS

"In naming it [sexual violence], we reclaim the truth which we know, that the way things are is not the way they have to be," writes feminist ethicist Marie M. Fortune.[1] This study has accomplished just that: it has named the manifold versions of rape, as understood from feminist perspectives, and located these versions in biblical texts of prose and poetry. We visited acquaintance rape in the stories of Dinah, Tamar, Abishag the Shunammite, and Susanna. We encountered the rape of enslaved women in the narratives of Hagar, Bilhah and Zilpah, and the royal concubines to understand how rape links both to gender and class. We examined marital rape fantasies about Sarah, Rebekah, Ms. Gomer, and Bathsheba. We evaluated biblical and ancient Near Eastern rape laws and also noted the connection of rape to legislation on incest and bestiality. The link between misogyny and rape in times of peace and war occupied us in the stories about the unnamed concubine and the women of Jabesh-gilead and Shiloh. That the recognition of male rape is a possibility became clear in the narratives about Ms. Potiphar, Delilah, and Lot's daughters. These stories indicated also that androcentric interests might have had a say in disguising Joseph's and Samson's accountability for sexual violence and, in Lot's case, incest. Finally, our investigation considered the prophetic "theology of a rapist," which depicts even God as an endorser and perpetrator of sexual violence, probably the theologically most disturbing chapter of this book.

All of these investigations were necessary to assert "that the way things are is not the way they have to be." Biblical texts do *not* prescribe rape as an unavoidable fact in life. Instead, they are a "sacred witness" to the ongoing pervasiveness, existence, and harm of rape in the world then and now. This is the theo-ethical conviction from which biblical rape literature is read in this book. It assumes that readers create biblical meanings. Yet this hermeneutical principle is also cause for much theo-epistemological sorrow, because the history of interpretation is so exhaustively filled with missed recognition of rape in the Hebrew Bible and, worse, misclassification of rape as seduction, marriage, or even love. The disconnection between the biblical literature and the history of interpretation could not be more drastic. It has also led to the absence of biblical rape texts from religious teaching, preaching, and learning. As a result, naming rape in biblical literature, as feminist interpreters have done since the 1970s, continues to be a subversive, power-destabilizing, liberative, and deconstructive undertaking in both religious and secular settings.

The hope of this study, then, is that the naming of biblical rape texts and the expression of discontent with the violent status quo—both grounded in a feminist hermeneutics—will eventually make it less likely that readers, religious or secular, will remain *silent* about the "unmentionable sin."[2] The ongoing pervasiveness of rape makes such silence dangerous and complicit, because silence keeps the violent status quo alive and enables it. Considering the daily rapes of women, girls, boys, men, old, young, married, single, in peacetime and in war, silence adds to resignation and acquiescence. Fortunately, such silence is broken here and there, mainly at the fringes, but often rape is still not yet viewed as the responsibility of the rapist and of the society that tolerates it. Victim-survivors are still blamed and they still blame themselves. Otherwise, how can it be explained that so few people have protested the terrible violence suffered by women and girls in Congo—violence in which female bodies are mutilated by soldiers to such an extent that it can only be explained as "women hatred"?[3] Otherwise, Western societies would no longer tolerate or indirectly promote the trafficking of women and girls of impoverished countries into brothels for male "pleasure." Otherwise, human rights organizations such as Amnesty International would not be among the most active opponents of rape and sexual violence, especially in contrast to Christian and Jewish organizations.

Perhaps it should also be emphasized that the existence of so many rape texts in the Hebrew Bible establishes this literature's inherent "morality." It does not endorse violence and bloodthirstiness—in sharp contrast to the manifold anti–Old Testament attitudes of the Christian tradition. At least since Marcion in the second century C.E., Christian followers have often, even today, disqualified the Hebrew Bible as the "book of the Jews" because they view it as superseded by New Testament statements of love, grace, and peace. Christians still articulate this classic anti-Jewish position whenever they explain why, to them, the Hebrew Bible is less important than the New Testament.[4] Yet biblical rape texts signify the Hebrew Bible's ongoing theo-ethical relevance, sociopolitical meaningfulness, and cultural-religious significance in our contemporary rape culture. When Christians and Jews affirm the Hebrew Bible as a sacred witness to rape, they are ready to confront a major injustice in today's world. Then they are ready to resist, dismantle, and oppose rape-prone assumptions, conventions, and conduct on individual and collective levels.

The recognition that the Hebrew Bible is a sacred witness to rape does not require a lighthearted theo-ethical attitude. As the previous chapters have shown, there are some horrifying passages on rape in biblical literature that cannot be excused, mollified, or easily reconciled. They demand an "ongoing wrestling match," as Julia M. O'Brien argues,[5] and we have to be deliberate in "taking back the text," as Johnny Miles declares.[6] Katheryn Pfisterer Darr is correct when she explains that "[s]ometimes, we continue to embrace hurtful texts not because we affirm their answers, but rather because they force us to confront the important questions."[7]

When we follow these strategies, the Jewish and Christian Scriptures turn into a treasure trove, as they have often been throughout the ages. Only this time, we are the readers, and in our time the Hebrew Bible becomes a sacred witness to the prevalence of rape in past and present lived experiences of women, children, and men. This is how biblical literature contributes to an understanding of the various settings in which we live. That is the promise of this body of literature for this time, for this generation. It will change again, but in the meantime the Hebrew Bible, as read *today*, is our sacred witness in a world still torn apart, as it was in the time of Dinah and Tamar, Susanna, Hagar, and Bilhah, by the terrors of rape.

NOTES

Acknowledgments

1. For data, see, for example, these Web sites: http://www.rainn.org/ statistics; http://www.ovw.usdoj.gov/; http://www.amnestyusa.org/women/ rapeinwartime.html (accessed April 7, 2009).

2. Jeffrey Gettleman, "Rape Victims' Words Help Jolt Congo into Change," *New York Times*, October 17, 2008: http://www.nytimes .com/2008/10/18/world/africa/18congo.html (accessed March 18, 2009).

3. Jeffrey Gettleman, "Rape Epidemic Raises Trauma of Congo War," *New York Times*, October 7, 2007: http://www.nytimes.com/2007/10/07/ world/africa/07congo.html (accessed April 7, 2009).

4. "Rape Victim Stoned to Death in Somalia Was 13, U.N. Says," *New York Times*, November 5, 2008: http://www.nytimes.com/2008/11/05/ world/africa/05somalia.html?pagewanted=print (accessed April 7, 2009).

5. Ibid.

6. See also the film by Helke Sanders *BeFreier und Befreite*, which created a storm of controversy when it came out in Germany in 1992. The film is based on interviews of German women raped by soldiers of the invading Russian army in Berlin in 1945. Most recently, the film *Anonyma—Eine Frau in Berlin* (2008) directed by Max Färberböck again engages the topic of the rape in Berlin in 1945, although many, if not most, of the victim-survivors have passed away by now.

7. The article is accessible at http://www.lectio.unibe.ch/04_1/Scholz .Enslaved.pdf.

8. The article is accessible at http://publications.epress.monash.edu/ toc/bc/1/4.

Introduction

1. Herbert Kupferberg, "Song of Samson," *Metropolitan Opera Stagebill* (February 1998), 16.

2. Anita Diamant, *The Red Tent* (New York: Picador, 1997); see also Ita Sheres, *Dinah's Rebellion: A Biblical Parable for Our Time* (New York: Crossroad, 1990).

3. For an overview of this development, see, for example, Philip R. Davies, *In Search of "Ancient Israel,"* Journal for the Study of the Old Testament Supplement Series 148 (Sheffield: Sheffield Academic Press, 1992); Lester L. Grabbe, ed., *Can a "History of Israel" Be Written?* Journal for the Study of the Old Testament Supplement Series 245 (Sheffield: Sheffield Academic Press, 1997); Keith W. Whitelam, *The Invention of Ancient Israel: The Silencing of Palestinian History* (London: Routledge, 1996); Thomas L. Thompson, "Text, Context and Referent in Israelite Historiography," in *The Fabric of History: Text, Artifact and Israel's Past*, ed. Diana Vikander Edelman, Journal for the Study of the Old Testament Supplement Series 127 (Sheffield: Sheffield Academic Press, 1991), 65–92; John Van Seters, *In Search of History: Historiography in the Ancient World* (New Haven/ London: Yale University Press, 1983). For linguistic arguments, see, for example, Avi Hurvitz, "The Relevance of Biblical Hebrew Linguistics for the Historical Study of Ancient Israel," in *Proceedings of the Twelfth World Congress of Jewish Studies, Jerusalem, July 29–August 5, 1997, Division A*, ed. Ron Margolin (Jerusalem: World Union of Jewish Studies, 1999), 21–33. For a discussion about archaeological dating, see, for example, William G. Dever, "Histories and Nonhistories of Ancient Israel," *American Schools of Oriental Research Bulletin* no. 315 (November 1999): 89–105; Israel Finkelstein, "The Rise of Early Israel: Archaeology and Long-Term History," in *The Origin of Early Israel—The Current Debate: Biblical, Historiographical and Archaeological Perspectives*, ed. Shmuel Ahituv and Eliezer D. Oren (Beer-Sheba: Ben-Gurion University of the Negev Press, 1998), 7–39. For other arguments supporting earlier dates for the Hebrew Bible, see, for example, Baruch Halpern, "Erasing History: The Minimalist Assault on Ancient Israel," in *Israel's Past in Present Research: Essays on Ancient Israelite Historiography*, ed. Philips V. Long (Winona Lake, Ind.: Eisenbrauns, 1999), 415–26; H. G. M. Williamson, "The Origins of Israel: Can We Safely Ignore the Bible?" in Ahituv and Oren, *Origin of Early Israel*, 141–51.

4. Johannes Pedersen, *Israel: Its Life and Culture*, 2 vols. (London: Oxford University Press, 1926, 1940; repr., 1959).

5. Ibid., 1:67, 69–70, 73.

6. Ibid., 1:71.

7. Ibid., 2:1–32.

8. Carol L. Meyers, *Discovering Eve: Ancient Israelite Women in Context* (New York: Oxford University Press, 1988).

9. See, for example, Lester L. Grabbe, ed., *Did Moses Speak Attic? Jewish Historiography and Scripture in the Hellenistic Period*, Journal for the Study of the Old Testament Supplement Series 317 (Sheffield: Sheffield Academic Press, 2001); Philip R. Davies, *The Origins of Biblical Israel* (New York/London: T&T Clark, 2007).

10. See, for example, Susanne Scholz, "Religion," in *Encyclopedia of Rape*, ed. Merril D. Smith (Westport, Conn.: Greenwood, 2004), 206–9.

11. Ibid.

12. See the descriptions in Sally J. Sutherland, "Sītā and Draupadī: Aggressive Behavior and Female Role-Models in the Sanskrit Epics," *Journal of the American Oriental Society* 109, no. 1 (1989): 63–79.

13. Scholz, "Religion," 208. Other stories exist, at least in the oral tradition, as a comment by Rita M. Gross illustrates in "Is the Goddess a Feminist?," in *Is the Goddess a Feminist? The Politics of South Asian Goddesses*, ed. Alf Hiltebeitel and Kathleen M. Erndl (New York: New York University Press, 2000), 104–12, here 108: "I was once quite struck by a male guide telling, with great enthusiasm, the story of a virgin goddess of South India who had killed her would-be rapist."

14. Mary Pellauer, "Augustine on Rape: One Chapter in the Theological Tradition," in *Violence against Women and Children: A Christian Theological Sourcebook*, ed. Carol J. Adams and Marie M. Fortune (New York: Continuum, 1998), 207–41, here 207.

15. Ibid., 225.

16. Susan Brownmiller, *Against Our Will: Men, Women and Rape* (New York: Bantam, 1975).

17. Catharine A. MacKinnon, *Toward a Feminist Theory of the State* (Cambridge, Mass.: Harvard University Press, 1989).

18. Jacquelyn Dowd Hall, "'The Mind That Burns in Each Body': Women, Rape and Racial Violence," in *Powers of Desire: The Politics of Sexuality*, ed. Ann Snitow, Christine Stansell, and Sharon Thompson, New Feminist Library (New York: Monthly Review Press, 1983), 328–49; Bettina Aptheker, *Woman's Legacy: Essays on Race, Sex, and Class in American History* (Amherst: University of Massachusetts Press, 1982).

19. Susan Griffin, "Rape: The All-American Crime," *Ramparts* 10 (1971): 26–35, here 35.

20. Angela Y. Davis, *Women, Race & Class* (New York: Random House, 1981), 201.

21. For a history of the creation of rape crisis centers, see, for example, Diane Kravetz, *Tales from the Trenches: Politics and Practice in Feminist Service Organizations* (Lanham, Md.: University Press of America, 2004). For rape statistics in the United States, see National Victim Center and Crime Victims Research and Treatment Center, *Rape in America: A Report to the Nation*, April 23, 1992. See, for example, Diana E. H. Russell, *The Politics of Rape: The Victim's Perspective* (New York: Stein & Day, 1984); Joyce E. Williams and Karen A. Holmes, *The Second Assault: Rape and Public Attitudes* (Westport, Conn.: Greenwood, 1981); Nancy Gager and Cathleen Schurr, *Sexual Assault: Confronting Rape in America* (New York: Grosset & Dunlap, 1976). For a historical-cultural account, see Sylvana Tomaselli and Roy Porter, eds., *Rape* (New York: Basil Blackwell, 1986). For international studies see, for example, Patricia d. Rozee, "Forbidden or Forgiven? Rape in Cross-Cultural Perspective," *Psychology of Women Quarterly* 17 (1993): 499–514; Alice Armstrong, *Women and Rape in Zimbabwe*, ISAS Human & People's Rights Project 10 (Lesotho: Institute of Southern African Studies, 1990); Jane Held, "The British Peace Movement: A Critical Examination of Attitudes to Male Violence within the British Peace Movement, as Expressed with Regard to the 'Molesworth Rapes'," *Women's Studies International Forum* 11, no. 3 (1988): 211–21; *Rape in Malaysia: The Victims and the Rapists, The Myths and the Realities. What Can Be Done* (Penang, Malaysia: Consumers' Association of Penang, 1988); K. P. Krishna, "Rape and Its Victims in India," *Journal of Social and Economic Studies* 10 (1982): 89–100.

22. Judith Butler, *Gender Trouble: Feminism and the Subversion of Identity* (New York: Routledge, 1990), 33.

23. Sharon Marcus, "Fighting Bodies, Fighting Words: A Theory and Politics of Rape Prevention," in *Feminists Theorize the Political*, ed. Judith Butler and Joan W. Scott (New York: Routledge, 1992), 385–403, esp. 393, 387.

24. Brownmiller, *Against Our Will*, 4.

25. O. Oyewumi, *The Invention of Women: Making an African Sense of Western Gender Discourses* (Minneapolis: University of Minnesota Press, 1997), 11.

26. Christine Helliwell, "It's Only a Penis: Rape, Feminism, and Difference," *Signs* 25, no. 3 (Spring 2000): 789–816, here 798.

27. Ibid., 808. For a recent article on the psychological and legal difficulties of defining oneself as a raped woman, see Laura Hengehold, "Remapping the Event: Institutional Discourses and the Trauma of Rape," *Signs* 26, no. 1 (Autumn 2000): 189–214.

28. Helliwell, "It's Only a Penis," 812.

29. Ibid., 799.

30. Ibid., 807.

31. Ibid., 812.

32. Paula Gunn Allen, *Off the Reservation: Reflections on Boundary-Busting, Border-Crossing, Loose Canons* (Boston: Beacon, 1998), 76, 78.

33. Ibid., 82.

34. Linda Nicholson, "Interpreting Gender," *Signs* 20 (Autumn 1994): 79–105, here 103.

35. Winifred Woodhull, "Sexuality, Power, and the Question of Rape," in *Feminism and Foucault: Reflections on Resistance*, ed. Irene Diamond and Lee Quinby (Boston: Northeastern University Press, 1988), 167–76, here 174.

36. Julie Peters and Andrea Wolper, eds., "Introduction," in *Women's Rights/Human Rights: International Feminist Perspectives*, ed. Julie Peters and Andrea Wolper (New York: Routledge, 1995), 5. For further information on the movement, "Women's rights as human rights," see http://www.unhchr.ch/html/menu2/womenpub2000.htm (accessed March 18, 2009).

37. Ibid., 5.

38. Rhonda Copelon, "Gendered War Crimes: Reconceptualizing Rape in Time of War," in Peters and Wolper, *Women's Rights/Human Rights*, 197–214. For some statistics on the international prevalence of rape, see also, in the same volume, the article of Lori L. Heise, "Freedom Close to Home: The Impact of Violence against Women on Reproductive Rights," 238–55. See also the UN Resolution 1820 (2008), which "[n]otes that rape and other forms of sexual violence can constitute a war crime, a crime against humanity, or a constitutive act with respect to genocide, *stresses the need for* the exclusion of sexual violence crimes from amnesty provisions in the context of conflict resolution processes, and *calls upon* Member States to comply with their obligations for prosecuting persons responsible for such acts, to ensure that all victims of sexual violence, particularly women and girls, have equal protection under the law and equal access to justice, and *stresses* the importance of ending impunity for such acts as part of a comprehensive approach to seeking sustainable peace, justice, truth, and national reconciliation." See http://www.un.org/Docs/sc/unsc_resolutions08.htm (accessed March 18, 2009).

39. Phyllis Trible, *Texts of Terror: Literary-Feminist Readings of Biblical Narratives* (Philadelphia: Fortress, 1984).

40. Jon D. Levenson, review of *Texts of Terror* by Phyllis Trible, *Journal of Religion* 65, no. 3 (July 1985): 448.

41. Trible, *Texts of Terror*, 28–29, 36, 65, 87.

42. Renita J. Weems, *Battered Love: Marriage, Sex, and Violence in the Hebrew Prophets* (Minneapolis: Fortress Press, 1995).

43. Ibid., 105.

44. J. Cheryl Exum, *Fragmented Women: Feminist (Sub)versions of Biblical Narratives*, Journal for the Study of the Old Testament Supplement Series 163 (Valley Forge, Pa.: Trinity Press International, 1993).

45. J. Cheryl Exum, "Raped by the Pen," in eadem, *Fragmented Women*, 170, 200, 201.

46. Jonathan Kirsch, *The Harlot by the Side of the Road: Forbidden Tales of the Bible* (New York: Ballantine Books, 1997).

47. Ibid., 2.

48. Ibid., 6.

49. Ibid., 11.

50. Ibid., 12.

51. Ibid.

52. See, e.g., Ellen J. van Wolde, "Does *'innâ* denote rape? A Semantic Analysis of a Controversial Word," *Vetus Testamentum* 52, no. 4 (2002): 528–44.

53. Stanley E. Fish, *Is There a Text in This Class? The Authority of Interpretive Communities* (Cambridge, Mass.: Harvard University Press, 1980).

54. Dorothee Soelle, *The Silent Cry: Mysticism and Resistance* (Minneapolis: Fortress Press, 2001).

55. Mohandas K. Gandhi, "Appendix: The Message of the Gita," in Stephen Mitchell, *Bhagavad Gita: A New Translation* (New York: Harmony Books, 2000), 211.

56. Bernard Williams, ed., *Theaetetus/Plato*, trans. M. J. Levett, rev. Myles Burnyeat (Indianapolis: Hackett, 1992).

57. Todd Penner and Lilian Cates, "Textually Violating Dinah: Literary Readings, Colonizing Interpretations, and the Pleasure of the Text," *Bible and Critical Theory* 3, no. 3 (2007): 37.12. Available at http://publications.epress.monash.edu/toc/bc/3/3.

58. Ibid.

59. Ibid., 37.14.

60. All Bible verses here and elsewhere in the book are taken from the New Revised Standard Version, except when noted otherwise.

61. Erhard S. Gerstenberger, "ענה, *'ānāh*," in *Theologisches Wörterbuch zum Alten Testament*, ed. Heinz-Joseph Fabry and Helmer Ringgren (Stuttgart: Kohlhammer, 1989), 6:252–53.

62. See, for example, Yael Shemesh, "Rape Is Rape Is Rape: The Story of Dinah and Shechem (Genesis 34)," *Zeitschrift für die alttestamentliche Wissenschaft* 119 (2007): 2–21; Hilary Lipka, *Sexual Transgression in the Hebrew Bible*, Hebrew Bible Monographs 7 (Sheffield: Sheffield Phoenix, 2006); Sandie Gravett, "Reading 'Rape' in the Hebrew Bible: A Consideration of Language," *Journal for the Study of the Old Testament* 28, no. 3 (March 2004): 279–99.

1. Breaking the Silence

1. Susan Estrich, *Real Rape* (Cambridge, Mass.: Harvard University Press, 1987).

2. Ibid., 4.

3. Robin Warshaw, *I Never Called It Rape: The Ms. Report on Recognizing, Fighting, and Surviving Date and Acquaintance Rape* (New York: Harper & Row, 1988).

4. Ibid., 32.

5. Christine Kim, "True Love," in *The Other Side of Silence: Women Tell about Their Experiences with Date Rape*, ed. Christine Carter (Gilsum, N.H.: Avocus, 1995), 117–26, esp. 123.

6. James D. Brewer, *The Danger from Strangers: Confronting the Threat of Assault* (New York: Plenum, 1994), 146.

7. For an analysis of the history of interpretation of Genesis 34, see, for example, Susanne Scholz, *Rape Plots: A Feminist Cultural Study of Genesis 34*, Studies in Biblical Literature 13 (New York: Peter Lang, 2000); Mary Anna Bader, *Tracing the Evidence: Dinah in Post-Hebrew Bible Literature*, Studies in Biblical Literature 102 (New York: Peter Lang, 2008).

8. See, for example, Mayer I. Gruber, "A Re-examination of the Charges against Shechem son of Hamor" (in Hebrew), *Beit Mikra* 157 (1999): 119–27.

9. Tikva Frymer-Kensky, "Virginity in the Bible," in *Gender and Law in the Hebrew Bible and the Ancient Near East*, ed. Victor H. Matthews, Bernard M. Levinson, and Tikva Frymer-Kensky, Journal for the Study of the Old Testament Supplement Series 262 (Sheffield: Sheffield Academic Press, 1998), 79–96, here 89.

10. Ibid., 91.

11. Lyn M. Bechtel, "What if Dinah is Not Raped? (Genesis 34)," *Journal for the Study of the Old Testament* 62 (1994): 19–36.

12. Ibid., 27. For a full discussion of this and other interpretations on Genesis 34, see Scholz, *Rape Plots*, 91–127.

13. Ibid., 31.

14. See, for example, Joan E. Cook, "Rape and Its Aftermath in Genesis 34," *Bible Today* 44 (2006): 209–14; Gershon Hepner, "The Seduction of Dinah and Jacob's Anguish Reflect Violations of the Contiguous Law of the Covenant Code," *Estudios bíblicos* 62 (2004): 111–35; Parry Robin Allinson, *Old Testament Story and Christian Ethics: The Rape of Dinah as a Test Case* (Bletchley, Milton Keynes, U.K./Waynesboro, Ga.: Paternoster, 2004); Joseph Vlcek Kozar, "When 'Circumfession' Is Not Enough: Understanding the Murder of the Newly Circumcised Shechemites Subsequent to Shechem's Rape of Dinah," *Eastern Great Lakes and Midwest Biblical Society Proceedings* 23 (2003): 55–64; Ellen van Wolde, "The Dinah Story: Rape or Worse?" *Old Testament Essays* 15 (2002): 225–39. The title of another article is misleading and does not refer to date or acquaintance rape: Michael M. Homan, "Date Rape: The Agricultural and Astronomical Background of the Sumerian Sacred Marriage and Genesis 38," *Scandinavian Journal of the Old Testament* 16, no. 2 (2002): 283–302.

15. See, for example, van Wolde, "Dinah Story," 225–39. For a discussion of the problem, see Susanne Scholz, "Was It Really Rape in Genesis 34? Biblical Scholarship as a Reflection of Cultural Assumptions," in *Escaping Eden: New Feminist Perspectives on the Bible*, ed. Harold C. Washington, Susan Lochrie Graham, and Pamela Thimmes (New York: New York University Press, 1998), 182–98; Caroline Blyth, "Terrible Silence, Eternal Silence: A Consideration of Dinah's Voicelessness in the Text and Interpretive Traditions of Genesis 34" (Ph.D. thesis, University of Edinburgh, 2008). See also n. 62 in chapter 1 above.

16. See, for example, Solomon Mandelkern, *Veteris Testamenti Concordantiae Hebraicae atque Chaldaicae* (Tel Aviv: Schocken, 1967), 902; Francis Brown, S. R. Driver, and Charles A. Briggs, eds., *Hebrew and English Lexicon of the Old Testament, based on the Lexicon of William Gesenius* (1906; Oxford: Oxford University Press, 1951), 776; Wilhelm Gesenius, *Hebräisches und Aramäisches Handwörterbuch über das Alte Testament* (1915; Berlin: Springer, 1962), 604.

17. A. A. Anderson, *The Book of Psalms*, 2 vols., New Century Bible (London: Marshall, Morgan & Scott, 1972), 2:458.

18. Ibid., 1:702.

19. Gesenius, *Hebräisches und Aramäisches Handwörterbuch*, 152: "an einem Besitz festhalten."

20. G. Wallis, "אהב, *'āhāb*," in *Theologisches Wörterbuch zum Alten Testament*, ed. Heinz-Josef Fabry and Helmer Ringgren (Stuttgart: Kohlhammer, 1973), 1:111, 115.

21. Phyllis Trible, "Tamar: The Royal Rape of Wisdom," in eadem, *Texts of Terror: Literary-Feminist Readings of Biblical Narratives* (Philadelphia: Fortress Press, 1984), 58 n. 6.

22. The phrase appears ten times: Gen 34:3; 50:21; Judg 19:3; 1 Sam 1:13; 2 Sam 19:8; Isa 40:2; Hos 2:16; Ruth 2:13; 2 Chr 30:22; 32:6.

23. Georg Fischer, "Die Redewendung דבר על לב im AT—Ein Beitrag zum Verständnis von Jes 40,2," *Biblica* 65 (1984): 244–50, here 249.

24. Ibid., 244–50.

25. For an early feminist description of this phenomenon, see Andra Medea and Kathleen Thompson, *Against Rape* (New York: Farrar, Straus & Giroux, 1974), 21.

26. See, for example, William H. Propp, "Kinship in 2 Samuel 13," *Catholic Biblical Quarterly* 55 (1993): 39–53, here 39; A. A. Anderson, *2 Samuel*, Word Biblical Commentary 11 (Dallas: Word Books, 1989), 177. See also Frank M. Yamada, *Configurations of Rape in the Hebrew Bible: A Literary Analysis of Three Rape Narratives*, Studies in Biblical Literature 109 (New York: Peter Lang, 2008).

27. Bruce B. Birch, "The First and Second Books of Samuel: Introduction, Commentary, and Reflections," in *The New Interpreter's Bible* (Nashville: Abingdon, 1998), 2:947–1383, here 1302.

28. See, for instance, Anderson, *2 Samuel*, 175.

29. Fokkelien van Dijk-Hemmes, "Tamar and the Limits of Patriarchy: Between Rape and Seduction (2 Samuel 13 and Genesis 38)," in *Anti-Covenant: Counter-Reading Women's Lives in the Hebrew Bible*, ed. Mieke Bal, Journal for the Study of the Old Testament Supplement Series 81 (Sheffield: Almond Press, 1989), 135–56, here 145.

30. Pamela Tamarkin Reis, "Cupidity and Stupidity: Women's Agency and The 'Rape' of Tamar," *Journal of the Ancient Near Eastern Society* 25 (1998): 43–60, here 43. The following quotations are from various pages in this article.

31. Walter Brueggemann, *First and Second Samuel*, Interpretation: A Bible Commentary for Teaching and Preaching (Louisville: John Knox, 1990), 288.

32 Birch, "First and Second Books of Samuel," 1305.

33. This is the position of van Dijk-Hemmes, "Tamar and the Limits of Patriarchy, 135–56.

34. Carl Friedrich Keil, *The Books of the Kings*, trans. James Martin (German original 1876; Grand Rapids: Eerdmans, [1950]), 16.

35. Adele Berlin, "Characterization in Biblical Narrative: David's Wives," *Journal for the Study of the Old Testament* 23 (1982): 69–85, here 74.

36. Thus argues Martin Jan Mulder, "Versuch zur Deutung von *Sokènèt* in 1. Kön. I:2, 4," *Vetus Testamentum* 22 (1972): 43–54.

37. Mordechai Cogan, *1 Kings: A New Translation with Introduction and Commentary*, Anchor Bible 10 (New York: Doubleday, 2002), 156.

38. Two manuscripts add the phrase "and be his bedfellow" to v. 2, probably in an attempt to solve the ambiguity; see Simon J. De Vries, *1 Kings*, Word Biblical Commentary 12 (Waco, Tex.: Word Books, 1985), 4.

39. Cogan, *1 Kings*, 156.

40. For a translation of the "Old Greek" manuscript text that is not based on Theodotion, see John J. Collins, *Daniel: A Commentary on the Book of Daniel*, Hermeneia (Minneapolis: Fortress Press, 1993), 420–24.

41. For a translation of the Arabic Samaritan manuscript, see Moses Gaster, *Studies and Texts in Folklore, Magic, Mediaeval Romance, Hebrew Apocrypha and Samaritan Archaeology*, 3 vols. (London: Maggs Bros, 1925–28), 201–6.

42. For references to the sources of these versions and a brief discussion, see Max Wurmbrand, "A Falasha Variant of the Story of Susanna," *Biblica* 44, no. 1 (1963): 29–45.

43. For the Syriac translation, see the discussion in Leona G. Running, "The Problem of the Mixed Syriac Mss of Susanna in the Seventeenth Century," *Vetus Testamentum* 19 (1969): 377–83. For Origin's letter, see N. R. M. De Lange, "The Letter to Africanus: Origen's Recantation," in *Papers Presented to the Seventh International Conference on Patristic Studies Held in Oxford, 1975*, ed. E. A. Livingstone, Studia Patristica 16, Pt. 2; Texte und Untersuchungen 129 (Berlin: Akademie-Verlag, 1985), 242–47.

44. All quotations are from Gaster's translation in *Studies and Texts* (see n. 41 above).

45. The verbal threat of rape does not appear in the Jewish versions, where the elders are reduced to asking the woman to marry one of them; the reason for the woman's rejection remains unspoken; see Wurmbrand, "Falasha Variant."

46. For analytical discussions, see, for example, Babette Bohn, "Rape and the Gendered Gaze: *Susanna and the Elders* in Early Modern Bologna," *Biblical Interpretation* 9, no. 3 (2001): 259–86. See also Mary D. Garrard, "Artemesia and Susanna," in *Feminism and Art History: Questioning the Litany*, ed. Norma Broude and Mary D. Garrard (New York: Harper & Row, 1982), 147–71.

47. For a wide selection of reprinted paintings, see Joe H. Kirchberger and Dorothee Soelle, eds., *Grosse Frauen der Bibel in Bild und Text*—English

edition (Minneapolis: Fortress Press, 2006). For an analysis of Rembrandt's paintings on Susanna, see Mieke Bal, "The Elders and Susanna," *Biblical Interpretation* 1, no. 1 (1993): 1–19.

48. For a general description of the story in art, see Carey A. Moore, "A Case of Sexual Harassment in Ancient Babylon: Susanna," *Bible Review* 8 (1992): 20–29, 52. For a synopsis of Floyd's opera's story line, see Louise T. Guinther, "April 3, 1999: Susannah," *Opera News* 63, issue 10 (April 1999): 60–63. For a critical discussion, see Barrymore L. Scherer, "Southern Revival," *Opera News* 63, issue 10 (April 1999): 16–21. For a scholarly analysis, see Lisa S. Ramer, "A Critical Analysis of Carlisle Floyd's Opera, Susannah" (M.A. in Music thesis, University of Washington, 1993). See also Lauren F. Winner, "Whoa, Susannah: It's great music, but its portrayal of Christian hypocrisy will make you wince," *Christianity Today* 43, no. 11 (October 4, 1999): 86.

49. Quoted in Jennifer A. Glancy, "The Accused: Susanna and Her Readers," *Journal for the Study of the Old Testament* 58 (1993): 103–16, here 111. The quotations are from R. Dunn ("Discriminations in the Comic Spirit in the Story of Susanna," *Christianity and Literature* 31 [1980–81]: 31) and Carey A. Moore (*Daniel, Esther, and Jeremiah: The Additions. A New Translation with Introduction and Commentary*, Anchor Bible 44 [Garden City, N.Y.: Doubleday, 1977], 97).

50. See the detailed discussion of this verb in Sarah J. K. Pearce, "Echoes of Eden in the Old Greek of Susanna," *Feminist Theology* 11 (1996): 10–31, here 14 n. 13.

51. Collins, *Daniel*, 431.

52. For a discussion on the historical dating of the Old Greek version compared to Theodotion's version, see, for example, Klaus Koenen, "Von der todesmutigen Susanna zum begabten Daniel: Zur Überlieferungsgeschichte der Susanna-Erzählung," *Theologische Zeitschrift* 54, no. 1 (1998): 1–13.

53. For this expression, see Bal, "Elders and Susanna," 5.

54. See, for instance, Wurmbrand's brief discussion of the various versions, which focuses almost entirely on the question of how many witnesses were considered necessary in Jewish antiquity, two or three ("Falasha Variant").

2. Subjugated by Gender and Class

1. Harriet A. Jacobs, *Incidents in the Life of a Slave Girl* (Cambridge, Mass.: Harvard University Press, 1987), 27.

2. Ibid., 53.

3. Ibid., 57.

4. Quoted in Kelly Brown Douglas, *Sexuality and the Black Church: A Womanist Perspective* (Maryknoll, N.Y.: Orbis, 1999), 40.

5. Mentioned in Deborah Gray White, *Ar'n't I a Woman: Female Slaves in the Plantation South* (New York: W. W. Norton, 1985), 78ff.

6. Phyllis Trible, "Hagar: The Desolation of Rejection," in eadem, *Texts of Terror: Literary-Feminist Readings of Biblical Narratives* (Philadelphia: Fortress Press, 1984), 9–35; Elsa Tamez, "The Woman Who Complicated the History of Salvation," in *New Eyes for Reading: Biblical and Theological Reflections by Women of the Third World*, ed. John S. Pobee and Bärbel von Wartenberg-Potter (Geneva: World Council of Churches, 1986), 5–17; Delores S. Williams, *Sisters in the Wilderness: The Challenge of Womanist God-Talk* (Maryknoll, N.Y.: Orbis, 1993); Renita J. Weems, "A Mistress, a Maid, and No Mercy (Hagar and Sarah)," in eadem, *Just a Sister Away: A Womanist Vision of Women's Relationships in the Bible* (San Diego, Calif.: LuraMedia, 1988), 1–21.

7. Gerhard von Rad, *Genesis: A Commentary*, trans. John H. Marks, 3rd rev. ed., Old Testament Library (Philadelphia: Westminster, 1972), 335. For a different view, see Mar Jacob, Bishop of Serugh, "A Homily on Our Lord and Jacob, on the Church and Rachel, and on Leah and the Synagogue," *The True Vine* 4, no. 4 (1993): 50–64. This Christian interpretation offers an allegorical anti-Jewish perspective on Genesis 29–30: Leah stands for the synagogue, Rachel for the church, and Jacob for God. This perspective is illustrated by the following quotations (pp. 53, 60, 63): "How glorious is her sister Rachel in the readings! The beauty of the Church was hid in her, wherefore great is her glory;" "Jacob portrayed the entire path of the Son of God;" "The Synagogue and Leah could not enter without a veil, for they had no beauty for which to be loved. Devices, deceits, and cunning did they employ with God, as also with Jacob, who bore His likeness. But since artifice cannot stand before the truth, the Cross and the dawn exposed what had been done with guile. At daybreak Jacob saw Leah, that she was unsightly, and the dawning of the Son revealed the Synagogue, that she was double-minded. The Church's face was revealed and she stood before the truth. . . . She was depicted in Rachel, who was beautiful of appearance and fair of face."

8. Claus Westermann, *Genesis 12–36: A Commentary*, trans. John J. Scullion (Minneapolis: Augsburg, 1985), 469; Nahum M. Sarna, *Genesis* [= *Be-reshit*]: *The Traditional Hebrew Text with the New JPS Translation*, JPS Torah Commentary (Philadelphia: Jewish Publication Society, 1989), 206.

9. Victor P. Hamilton, *The Book of Genesis: Chapters 18–50*, New International Commentary on the Old Testament (Grand Rapids: Eerdmans, 1995), 265, 269.

10. See, for example, Ilana Pardes, "Rachel's Dream: The Female Subplot," in eadem, *Countertraditions in the Bible: A Feminist Approach* (Cambridge, Mass.: Harvard University Press, 1992).

11. Williams, *Sisters in the Wilderness*, 33.

12. Ibid., 198.

13. E. A. Speiser, *Genesis: Introduction, Translation, and Notes*, Anchor Bible 1 (Garden City, N.Y.: Doubleday, 1964), 119–21; John Van Seters, "Jacob's Marriages and Ancient Near East Customs," *Harvard Theological Review* 62 (1969): 377–95.

14. See, for example, Renita J. Weems, "Do You See What I See? Diversity in Interpretation," *Church & Society* 82 (September–October, 1991): 28–43, here 35.

15. Trible, "Hagar: The Desolation of Rejection," 13.

16. See, for example, Williams, *Sisters in the Wilderness*, 17.

17. Trible, "Hagar: The Desolation of Rejection," 16.

18. Katheryn Pfisterer Darr, *Far More Precious Than Jewels: Perspectives on Biblical Women*, Gender and the Biblical Tradition (Louisville: Westminster John Knox, 1991), 39–140.

19. Weems, *Just a Sister Away*, 3.

20. Williams, *Sisters in the Wilderness*, 21.

21. Trible, "Hagar: The Desolation of Rejection," 18; Sarna, *Genesis*, 121; von Rad, *Genesis*, 190.

22. Trible states that "patriarchy is well in control" in Gen. 16:15-16; see Trible ("Hagar: The Desolation of Rejection," 19).

23. As in interpretations of Genesis 16, scholars suggest that this practice was common in the Ancient Near East, and so they "normalize" the practice; see, for example, Raymond Westbrook, "The Female Slave," in *Gender and Law in the Hebrew Bible and the Ancient Near East*, ed. Victor H. Matthews, Bernard M. Levinson, and Tikva Frymer-Kensky, Journal for the Study of the Old Testament Supplement Series 262 (Sheffield: Sheffield Academic Press, 1998), 214–38, esp. 224–29.

24. Williams, *Sisters in the Wilderness*, 199.

25. Esther Fuchs, *Sexual Politics in the Biblical Narrative: Reading the Hebrew Bible as a Woman*, Journal for the Study of the Old Testament Supplement Series 310 (Sheffield: Sheffield Academic Press, 2000). For other feminist interpretations, see, e.g., Irmtraud Fischer, "Genesis 12–50: Die

Ursprungsgeschichte Israels als Frauengeschichte," in *Kompendium Feministische Bibelauslegung*, ed. Luise Schottroff und Marie-Theres Wacker, 2nd ed. (Gütersloh: Gütersloher Verlagshaus, 1998), 12–25, here 19.

26. Fuchs, *Sexual Politics*, 63.

27. Ibid., 63, 154–55, 158. For a parallelism between Hagar and the two enslaved women, see, for example, Cynthia Gordon, "Hagar: A Throw-Away Character among the Matriarchs?" in *Society of Biblical Literature 1985 Seminar Papers*, ed. Kent H. Richards (Cambridge, Mass.: Society of Biblical Literature, 1985), 271–77, here 273; Weems, "Do You See What I See?" 35; Ina J. Petermann, "'Schick die Fremde in die Wüste!' Oder: Sind die Sara-Hagar-Erzählungen aus Genesis 16 und 21 ein Beispiel (anti)rassistischer Irritation aus dem Alten Israel?" in *(Anti-)Rassistische Irritationen: Biblische Texte und interkulturelle Zusammenarbeit*, ed. Silvia Wagner, Gerdi Nützel, and Martin Kick (Berlin: Alektor Verlag, 1994), 137–50, here 140.

28. Hermann Gunkel, *Genesis*, trans. Mark E. Biddle, Mercer Library of Biblical Studies (German original 1910; Macon, Ga.: Mercer University Press, 1997), 324.

29. Von Rad, *Genesis*, 294.

30. Elyse Goldstein, *ReVisions: Seeing Torah through a Feminist Lens* (Woodstock, Vt.: Jewish Lights Publishing, 1998), 65. For the idea of God as the equalizer between the women, see also John Calvin, *Genesis*, trans. John King (Carlisle, Pa.: Banner of Truth Trust, 1992), 140.

31. Athalya Brenner demonstrated that Genesis 29–30 follows the "birth-of-the-hero" paradigm, which pursues androcentric interests; see her article "Female Social Behaviour: Two Descriptive Patterns within the 'Birth of the Hero' Paradigm," *Vetus Testamentum* 36, no. 3 (1986): 273.

32. Sharon Pace Jeansonne, *The Women of Genesis: From Sarah to Potiphar's Wife* (Minneapolis: Fortress Press, 1990), 79.

33. Peter Pitzele, "The Myth of the Wrestler," in *Our Fathers' Wells: A Personal Encounter with the Myths of Genesis* (San Francisco: HarperSanFrancisco, 1995), 181.

34. Francine Klagsbrun, "Ruth and Naomi, Rachel and Leah," in *Reading Ruth: Contemporary Women Reclaim a Sacred Story*, ed. Judith A. Kates and Gail Twersky Reimer (New York: Ballantine Books, 1994), 261–72, here 271.

35. Ibid.

36. For a discussion about the etymologies of the names, see, for example, Speiser, *Genesis*, 231–33; Westermann, *Genesis 12–36*, 473–77.

37. Isaac Unterman, *The Five Books of Moses. The Book of Genesis: Profoundly Inspiring Commentaries and Interpretations Selected from the Talmudic-Rabbinic Literature* (New York: Bloch, 1973), 250.

38. Sarna, *Genesis*, 208.

39. See also Hamilton, *Book of Genesis*, 271–72.

40. Terence E. Fretheim, "The Book of Genesis: Introduction, Commentary, and Reflections," in *The New Interpreter's Bible: A Commentary in Twelve Volumes*, ed. Leander E. Keck et al. (Nashville: Abingdon, 1994), 1:319–674, here 546.

41. Hamilton, *Book of Genesis*, 271–72.

42. Everett Fox, *The Five Books of Moses: Genesis, Exodus, Leviticus, Numbers, Deuteronomy. A New Translation with Introductions, Commentary, and Notes*, Schocken Bible 1 (New York: Schocken Books, 1995), 139. Francis I. Andersen also argues that the noun "God" should remain in Gen 30:8; see his brief comment, "Note on Genesis 30:8," *Journal of Biblical Literature* 88 (1969): 200.

43. Ramban (Nachmanides [Rabbi Moshe ben Nahman]), *Commentary on the Torah: Genesis*, translated and annotated with index by Charles B. Chavel (New York: Shilo, 1971), 368.

44. For the principles of translating the Hebrew text in this format, see Phyllis Trible, *Rhetorical Criticism: Context, Method, and the Book of Jonah* (Minneapolis: Fortress Press, 1994), esp. 101–6.

45. This is also the reading of Weston W. Fields, *Sodom and Gomorrah: History and Motif in Biblical Narrative*, Journal for the Study of the Old Testament Supplement Series, 231 (Sheffield: Sheffield Academic Press, 1997), 130–31.

46. Speiser, *Genesis*, 274.

47. George G. Nicol, "Genesis xxix. 32 and xxxv. 22a: Reuben's Reversal," *Journal of Theological Studies* 31 (1980): 536–39.

48. Mordechai Rotenberg, "The 'Midrash' and Biographic Rehabilitation," *Journal for the Scientific Study of Religion* 25, no. 1 (1986): 41–55.

49. Quoted in Rotenberg, "Midrash," 46. The quotation is from the Babylonian Talmud, tractate *Shabbat* 55b.

50. Michael L. Klein, "Not to Be Translated in Public," *Journal of Jewish Studies* 39, no. 1 (Spring 1988): 80–91.

51. Von Rad, *Genesis*, 341.

52. Richard J. Clifford and Roland E. Murphy, "Genesis," in *The New Jerome Biblical Commentary*, ed. Raymond E. Brown, Joseph A. Fitzmyer, and Roland E. Murphy (Englewood Cliffs, N.J.: Prentice Hall, 1990), 8–43, here 36.

53. See, for example, James E. Miller, "Sexual Offenses in Genesis," *Journal for the Study of the Old Testament* 90 (2000): 41–53, where Miller debates whether Bilhah's status as a concubine makes the interaction between Reuben and Bilhah "adultery" or "incest" (p. 49).

54. For a brief discussion of "slave concubines," see Westbrook, "Female Slave," 215–20.

55. For further explanations, see Karen Engelken, "*pilægæs*," in *Theologisches Wörterbuch zum Alten Testament*, ed. G. Johannes Botterweck, Helmer Ringgren, et al. (Stuttgart: Kohlhammer, 1987), 6:586–90. See also Engelken, *Frauen im Alten Israel: Eine begriffsgeschichtliche und sozialrechtliche Studie zur Stellung der Frau im Alten Testament*, Beiträge zur Wissenschaft vom Alten und Neuen Testament 130 (Stuttgart: Kohlhammer, 1990), 101, 124 . Engelken argues for a sharp distinction between the position of a concubine and a slave. For the opposite view, see Westbrook, "Female Slave," 233, who finds the term *pilegeš* (פילגש) "totally inappropriate" and considers it the author's effort "to spare Reuben, whose crime in sleeping with Bilhah would have been far more heinous if she were Jacob's wife."

56. A. A. Anderson, *2 Samuel*, Word Biblical Commentary 11 (Dallas: Word Books, 1989), 56.

57. See, for example, P. Kyle McCarter, *II Samuel: A New Translation with Introduction, Notes and Commentary*, Anchor Bible 9 (Garden City, N.Y.: Doubleday, 1984), 384–85; Fritz Stolz, *Das erste und zweite Buch Samuel*, Zürcher Bibelkommentare (Zürich: Theologischer Verlag, 1981), 199.

58. See, for example, Anderson, *2 Samuel*, 214.

59. John Rook, "Making Widows: The Patriarchal Guardian at Work," *Biblical Theology Bulletin* 27 (1997): 10–15, here 14.

60. Hans Wilhelm Hertzberg, *I & II Samuel: A Commentary*, trans. John Bowden, Old Testament Library (Philadelphia: Westminster, 1964), 371.

61. McCarter, *II Samuel*, 423; Anderson, *2 Samuel*, 214.

62. Ken Stone, "Sexual Power and Political Prestige," *Bible Review* (August 1994): 28–31, 52–53, here 53. See also Ken Stone, "1 and 2 Samuel," in *The Queer Bible Commentary*, ed. Deryn Guest, Robert E. Goss, Mona West, and Thomas Bohache (London: SCM, 2006), 195–221, here 219: "One can quite plausibly conclude that what we have in 2 Samuel 16 is a representation of rape, which is understood within the logic of the narrative of 2 Samuel as having been initiated by God. When considered from that point of view, the story in 2 Samuel 16 is arguably one of the most

disturbing texts in the Bible and needs to be evaluated critically on the basis of the fact that it incorporates (as does much of 1 and 2 Samuel) obviously patriarchal notions about the sexual use of women. In this instance, moreover, such views are not simply presupposed by the narrator or held by male human characters, but are projected onto the male divine character, Yhwh. Inasmuch as Yhwh uses the rape of ten women to humiliate, and thereby punish, David, Yhwh seems no more concerned about the actual fate of those women than are Absalom, Ahithophel or for that matter David."

63. Rook, "Making Widows," 13.

64. See also Jessica Grimes, "Reinterpreting Hagar's Story," *lectio difficilior: European Electronic Journal for Feminist Exegesis* 1 (2004), http://www.lectio.unibe.ch/04_1/Grimes.Hagar.htm (accessed November 11, 2008).

3. Controlling Wives

1. Diana E. H. Russell, *Rape in Marriage* (1982), expanded and rev. ed., with a new introduction (Bloomington: Indiana University Press, 1990).

2. Ibid., 123.

3. Ibid., 44.

4. Raquel Kennedy Bergen, *Wife Rape: Understanding the Response of Survivors and Service Providers*, Sage Series on Violence against Women, 2 (Thousand Oaks, Calif.: Sage, 1996), 19–24.

5. Ibid., 22.

6. David Finkelhor and Kersti Yllo, *License to Rape: Sexual Abuse of Wives* (New York: Holt, Rinehart & Winston, 1985), 64, 74.

7. Russell, *Rape in Marriage*, 44.

8. One of the most direct statements about marital rape is found in Gen 31:50. There Laban, the father-in-law of Jacob, warns his son-in law: "If you ill-treat my daughters . . . remember that God is witness between you and me." This NRSV translation of the verb *'innâ* (עִנָּה, *piel*) is obfuscating. The verse should be translated: "If you rape my daughters . . . ."

9. For a brief but informative comparison of the three stories, see Hermann Gunkel, *Genesis*, trans. Mark E. Biddle, Mercer Library of Biblical Studies (German original 1910; Macon, Ga.: Mercer University Press, 1997) 223–25.

10. See, for example, Gerhard von Rad, *Genesis: A Commentary*, trans. John H. Marks, 3rd rev. ed., Old Testament Library (Philadelphia: Westminster, 1972), 167. Von Rad uses the German noun *Gefährdung*, which is translated in the English as "jeopardizing." The translation of the German noun

as an adjective, "endangered," is, however, better because the noun "danger" has gained dominance in other commentaries translated from German to English. See, for example, the classic commentary by Claus Westermann, *Genesis 12–36: A Commentary*, trans. John J. Scullion, S.J. (Minneapolis: Augsburg, 1981). The title of Gen 12:10-20 in this originally German commentary is "The Ancestral Mother in Danger [*Gefahr*]." See also Robert Polzin, "The Ancestress of Israel in Danger' in Danger," *Semeia* 3 (1975): 81–98. For the use of the adjective "endangered," see Mark E. Biddle, "The 'Endangered Ancestress' and Blessing for the Nations," *Journal of Biblical Literature* 109 (1990): 599–611.

11. For the idea of "sister-wife," see the classic argument by E. A. Speiser, "The Wife-Sister Motif in the Patriarchal Narratives," in *Biblical and Other Studies*, ed. Alexander Altmann (Cambridge, Mass.: Harvard University Press, 1963), 15–28.

12. Gunkel, *Genesis*, 173, 223.

13. Scholars debate whether the wife or the husband was in danger. For the view that it was the wife, see, for example, Victor P. Hamilton, *The Book of Genesis: Chapters 18–50*, New International Commentary on the Old Testament (Grand Rapids: Eerdmans, 1995), 61. For the view that it was the husband, see, for example, David J. A. Clines, "The Ancestor in Danger: But Not the Same Danger," in idem, *What Does Eve Do to Help? And Other Readerly Questions to the Old Testament*, Journal for the Study of the Old Testament Supplement Series 94 (Sheffield: JSOT Press, 1990), 67–84.

14. Examples abound. For a recent and widely disseminated commentary, see Terence E. Fretheim, "The Book of Genesis: Introduction, Commentary, and Reflections," in *The New Interpreter's Bible: A Commentary in Twelve Volumes*, ed. Leander E. Keck et al. (Nashville: Abingdon, 1994), 1:319–674, here 427–28.

15. Ibid., 428, 430.

16. Ilona N. Rashkow, "Intertextuality and Transference: A Reader in/of Genesis 12:10-20 and 20:1-18," in eadem, *The Phallacy of Genesis: A Feminist-Psychoanalytic Approach*, Literary Currents in Biblical Interpretation (Louisville: Westminster John Knox, 1993), 48.

17. Matthias Augustin, "Die Inbesitznahme der schönen Frau aus der unterschiedlichen Sicht der Schwachen und der Mächtigen: Ein kritischer Vergleich von Gen 12,10-20 und 2 Sam 11, 2-27a," *Biblische Zeitschrift* 2 (1983): 145–54. The German word *Inbesitznahme* connotes ownership and possession of goods. To Pharaoh, Sarah is an object to be owned and possessed like a house or a piece of furniture.

18. J. Cheryl Exum, "Who's Afraid of 'The Endangered Ancestress'?" in *The New Literary Criticism and the Hebrew Bible*, ed. J. Cheryl Exum and David J. A. Clines (Valley Forge, Pa.: Trinity Press International, 1993), 91–113, here 110.

19. Hamilton, *Book of Genesis*, 61.

20. M. Delcor, "נגע *ngʿ* to touch," in *Theological Lexicon of the Old Testament*, ed. Ernst Jenni and Claus Westermann, trans. Mark E. Biddle (Peabody, Mass.: Hendrickson, 1997), 2:718–19.

21. So also, for example, Westermann, *Genesis 12–36*, 421.

22. The Rabbinical Assembly and the United Synagogue of Conservative Judaism, *Etz Hayim: Torah and Commentary* (New York: Jewish Publication Society, 1999), 150.

23. Hamilton, *Book of Genesis*, 63.

24. This, at least, is the meaning of the German expression *Mutwillen treiben*, which the translators used for Plaut's English "to dally with"; see W. Gunther Plaut, *Die Tora in jüdischer Auslegung* (Gütersloh: Kaiser, 1999), 336; for the English original, see Plaut, *The Torah: A Modern Commentary* (New York: Union of American Hebrew Congregations, 1981), 258.

25. See, for example, C. F. Burney, *The Book of Judges with Introduction and Notes* (London: Rivingtons, 1920), 387–88.

26. See, for example, Holman Christian Standard Bible (2003) or the New American Standard Bible (1977). The King James Version offers this translation: "and behold, Isaac was sporting with Rebekah his wife." See also C. F. Keil and F. Delitzsch, *Biblical Commentary on the Old Testament*, trans. James Martin (Grand Rapids: Eerdmans, 1949), 1:270: "sporting with Rebekah."

27. See, for example, the King James Version: "And he made them sport"; the NRSV: "And he performed for them"; the New Jerusalem Bible: "And he performed feats in front of them." For other biblical verses in which this verb occurs, see Gen 19:14; 21:9; Exod 32:6; Judg 16:25.

28. For a sampling of positions, see Howard Wallace, "On Account of Sarai: Gen 12:10—13:1," *Australian Biblical Review* 44 (1996): 32–41.

29. Fokkelien van Dijk-Hemmes, "Sarai's Exile: A Gender-Motivated Reading of Genesis 12:10—13:2," in *A Feminist Companion to Genesis*, ed. Athalya Brenner (Sheffield: Sheffield Academic Press, 1993), 222–34, here 231.

30. See, for example, Hans Walter Wolff, *Hosea: A Commentary on the Book of the Prophet Hosea*, Hermeneia (Philadelphia: Fortress Press, 1974), 44.

31. Ibid.

32. For a classic expression of this view, see Gerhard von Rad, *Old Testament Theology*, trans. D. M. G. Stalker, 2 vols., Old Testament Library (Louisville: Westminster, 2001), 138–46. For a feminist approach, see Gale A. Yee, "'She Is Not My Wife and I Am Not Her Husband': A Materialist Analysis of Hosea 1–2," *Biblical Interpretation* 9, no. 4 (2001): 345–83.

33. Dianne Bergant, C.S.A. "Restoration as Re-creation in Hosea 2," in *The Ecological Challenge: Ethical, Liturgical, and Spiritual Responses*, ed. Richard N. Fragomeni and John T. Pawlikowski (Collegeville, Minn.: Liturgical Press, 1994), 3–15, esp. 8; R. Abma, *Bonds of Love: Methodic Studies of Prophetic Texts with Marriage Imagery*, Studia Semitica Neerlandica 40 (Assen: Van Gorcum, 1999), esp. 153; Marie-Theres Wacker, *Figurationen des Weiblichen im Hosea-Buch*, Herders Biblische Studien 8 (Freiburg: Herder, 1996), esp. 58–88. For a thorough description of feminist interpretations of Hosea 1–3, see Yvonne Sherwood, *The Prostitute and the Prophet: Hosea's Marriage in Literary-Theoretical Perspective*, Journal for the Study of the Old Testament Supplement Series 212 (Sheffield: Sheffield Academic Press, 1996).

34. David J. A. Clines and David M. Gunn, "'You Tried to Persuade Me' and 'Violence! Outrage!' in Jeremiah xx 7-8," *Vetus Testamentum* 28 (1978): 20–27.

35. Fokkelien van Dijk-Hemmes, "The Imagination of Power and the Power of Imagination: An Intertextual Analysis of Two Biblical Love Songs: The Song of Songs and Hosea 2," *Journal for the Study of the Old Testament* 44 (1989): 75–88, esp. 84.

36. For a discussion of this phrase, see Susanne Scholz, *Rape Plots: A Feminist Cultural Study of Genesis 34*, Studies in Biblical Literature 13 (New York: Peter Lang, 2000), 141–42.

37. Naomi Graetz, "God Is to Israel as Husband Is to Wife: The Metaphoric Battering of Hosea's Wife," in *A Feminist Companion to the Latter Prophets*, ed. Athalya Brenner (Sheffield: Sheffield Academic Press, 1995), 126–45, esp. 142. For other feminist interpretations that focus on Hosea 2 in the context of sexual violence and pornography, see T. Drorah Setel, "Prophets and Pornography: Female Sexual Imagery in Hosea," in *Feminist Interpretations of the Bible*, ed. Letty Russell (Philadelphia, Pa.: Westminster, 1985), 86–95; Renita J. Weems, "Gomer: Victim of Violence or Victim of Metaphor?" *Semeia* 47 (1989): 87–104.

38. Renita J. Weems, *Battered Love: Marriage, Sex, and Violence in the Hebrew Prophets* (Minneapolis: Fortress Press, 1995), 49.

39. Ibid., 49.

40. Ibid.

41. Ibid., 50.

42. Ibid., 51, 52.

43. Ibid., 116.

44. Gale A. Yee, *Poor Banished Children of Eve: Woman as Evil in the Hebrew Bible* (Minneapolis: Fortress Press, 2003), 98.

45. Ibid.

46. Ibid., 99.

47. For a detailed discussion of these and other cultural artifacts in 2 Samuel 11, see J. Cheryl Exum, *Plotted, Shot, and Painted: Cultural Representations of Biblical Women*, Journal for the Study of the Old Testament Supplement Series 215 (Sheffield: Sheffield Academic Press, 1996), 19–53.

48. George G. Nicol, "Bathsheba, a Clever Woman?" *Expository Times* 99 (1988): 360–63, here 360. See also idem, "The Alleged Rape of Bathsheba: Some Observations on Ambiguity in Biblical Narrative," *Journal for the Study of the Old Testament* 73 (1997): 43–54; he argues against Exum's interpretation that both the biblical narrator and ensuing interpreters "symbolically" rape Bathsheba when they ignore her perspective. For the full argument of Exum, see her "Raped by the Pen," in eadem, *Fragmented Women: Feminist (Sub)versions of Biblical Narratives*, Journal for the Study of the Old Testament Supplement Series 163 (Valley Forge, Pa.: Trinity Press International, 1993), 170–201.

49. Lillian R. Klein, "Bathsheba Revealed," in *Samuel and Kings: A Feminist Companion to the Bible* (Second Series), ed. Athalya Brenner (Sheffield: Sheffield Academic Press, 2000), 47–64, here 53.

50. So, for instance, Exum, "Plotted," 22–23.

51. Ibid., 22.

52. Deryn Guest describes yet another reading strategy that disrupts the androcentric perspective in 2 Samuel 11. She suggests that lesbian readers "play butch to Bathsheba's femme." Guest explains that she reads the story from a lesbian butch position in which she does "not stand *as* David, but alongside David, vying for Bathsheba's attention, challenging his values, his performance of masculinity, offering Bathsheba a different option, and representing the presence of male homoeroticism in a scene otherwise far too overloaded with testosterone." Guest asserts that such a reading position "produces a criticism of the performance of masculinity that David embodies"; see Deryn Guest, "Looking Lesbian at the Bathing Bathsheba," *Biblical*

Interpretation 16 (2008): 227–62, here 249, 250. This is a highly intriguing suggestion, but is it one that will successfully prevent the powerful man, the king, from getting what he wants? After all, as Guest acknowledges in her discussion, often butches suffer from male violence and femmes are usually invisible in androcentric culture. Both face considerable difficulties in asserting their power and in gaining acceptance for it (ibid., 243–44).

4. Regulating Rape

1. For a comprehensive description of the state laws on rape in the United States, see Richard A. Posner and Katharine B. Silbaugh, *A Guide to America's Sex Laws* (Chicago/London: University of Chicago Press, 1996).

2. This New York State law is available online at http://public.leginfo .state.ny.us/frmload.cgi?MENU-46609910, where other laws can also be found (accessed November 24, 2009).

3. For informative and evaluative comments on the U.S. rape reform movement of the 1970s, see Vivian Berger, "Rape Law Reform at the Millennium: Remarks on Professor Bryden's Non-Millennial Approach," *Buffalo Criminal Law Review* 3 (2000): 513–25; Cassia C. Spohn, "The Rape Reform Movement: The Traditional Common Law and Rape Law Reforms," *Jurimetrics* 39 (1999): 119–30; Ronet Bachman and Raymond Paternoster, "A Contemporary Look at the Effects of Rape Law Reform: How Far Have We Really Come?" *Journal of Criminal Law & Criminology* 84, no. 3 (1993): 554–74; Carole Goldberg-Ambrose, "Unfinished Business in Rape Law Reform," *Journal of Social Issues* 48, no. 1 (1992): 173–85.

4. For a valuable explanation of New York State rape law, see http:// www.nycagainstrape.org/survivors_legal.html (accessed November 24, 2009).

5. See online at http://codes.ohio.gov/orc/2907.02 (accessed November 24, 2009).

6. For a listing of U.S. state laws, see http://www.law.cornell.edu/topics/ state_statutes2.html (accessed November 24, 2009).

7. See, for example, the German Strafgesetzbuch §177 (http://www .interpol.int/Public/Children/SexualAbuse/NationalLaws/csaGermany.asp) or the Philippine Laws Republic Act No. 8353 (http://www.chanrobles.com/ republicactno8353.htm) (accessed November 24, 2009).

8. See, for instance, the rape laws in many Latin American countries: http://www.ishr.org/sections-groups/germany/latinamericanwomen.htm (accessed November 24, 2009).

9. Berger, "Rape Law Reform at the Millennium," 524.

10. One of the oldest collections is the Laws of Eshnunna, which emerged from the ancient city of Eshnunna in Mesopotamia and probably preceded the Code of Hammurabi by two hundred years, or, as other commentators suggest, was its "near contemporary." The most renowned and comprehensive law collection of the ancient Near East is the Code of Hammurabi, named after the famous ruler of ancient Babylon. It is usually dated to the reign of Hammurabi from 1728 to 1686 B.C.E. Another ancient and incompletely recovered collection is the Codex of Ur-Nammu from Sippar which dates to around 2100 B.C.E. (see S. N. Kramer and J. J. Finkelstein, "Ur-Nammu Law Code," *Orientalia* 23 [1954] 40–51). A younger collection is the Middle Assyrian Laws, which developed between 1450 and 1250 B.C.E. For a discussion, see G. R. Driver and John C. Miles, *The Assyrian Laws*, Ancient Codes and Laws of the Near East (Oxford: Clarendon, 1935).

Finally, there are the Hittite Laws, which emerged in the middle of the second millennium. They are difficult to date, but tentatively suggested dates range from 1500 B.C.E. to the thirteenth century B.C.E. For a description of the various proposals, see E. Neufeld, *The Hittite Laws* (London: Luzac, 1951), 110–13. For an overview of the various law codes and their dates, see also Raymond Westbrook, "The Character of Ancient Near Eastern Law," in *A History of Ancient Near Eastern Law*, ed. Raymond Westbrook, Handbuch der Orientalistik, Nahe und der Mittlere Osten 72 (Leiden/Boston: Brill, 2003), 8–9. Importantly, all of these law codes precede the biblical laws by several centuries. The ancient Near Eastern laws were discovered in the early decades of the twentieth century C.E., when archaeological excavations in the Middle East were fashionable and excited the wider Western public. The discoveries led to abundant research and publications. The Code of Hammurabi was recovered in 1901–1902, and the Middle Assyrian Laws were found from 1903 to 1914. The Hittite laws were found in archaeological digs of 1906–1907 and 1911–1912. The Laws of Eshnunna were found only in 1945 and 1947. The Sumerian Codex of Ur-Nammu was originally discovered in 1952 but the passages relevant to our discussion were identified only in 1979; see Fatma Yildiz, "A Tablet of Codex Ur-Nammu from Sippar," *Orientalia* 50 (1981): 87–97, esp. 87. Other ancient Near Eastern law codes exist, but they do not contain references to rape, perhaps owing to their fragmentary survival. Examples of other ancient Near Eastern law codes are the Sumerian Laws, the Lipit-Ishtar Code, the Edict of Ammisaduqa, and the Nuzi laws and customs. Ancient Egyptian legal texts do not refer to rape, but some nonlegal texts do, such as the story of Enlil and Ninlil; see H. Behrens, *Enlil und Ninlil: Ein sumerischer Mythos aus Nippur*, Studia Pohl (Rome: Biblical Institute Press, 1978), 22.

11. Duane L. Christensen, *Deuteronomy 21:10—34:12*, Word Biblical Commentary 6B (Nashville: Thomas Nelson, 2002), 471; Jeffrey H. Tigay, *Deuteronomy [= Devarim]: The Traditional Hebrew Text with the New JPS Translation*, JPS Torah Commentary (Philadelphia: Jewish Publication Society, 1996), 194.

12. Ronald E. Clements, "The Book of Deuteronomy: Introduction, Commentary, and Reflections," in *The New Interpreter's Bible: A Commentary in Twelve Volumes*, ed. Leander E. Keck et al. (Nashville: Abingdon, 1994), 2:269-538, here 443.

13. Ibid., 445. This law was probably never observed. For instance, Harold C. Washington acknowledges that "there is reason to doubt that this law was extensively applied;" see his "'Lest He Die in the Battle and Another Man Take Her': Violence and the Construction of Gender in the Laws of Deuteronomy 20-22," in *Gender and Law in the Hebrew Bible and the Ancient Near East*, ed. Victor H. Matthews, Bernard M. Levinson, and Tikva Frymer-Kensky, Journal for the Study of the Old Testament Supplement Series 262 (Sheffield: Sheffield Academic Press, 1998), 185-213, here 202.

14. Christensen, *Deuteronomy*, 475.

15. Clements, "Book of Deuteronomy," 448.

16. Carolyn Pressler, *The View of Women Found in the Deuteronomic Family Laws*, Beihefte zur Zeitschrift für die alttestamentliche Wissenschaft 216 (Berlin/New York: de Gruyter, 1993), 10-15.

17. Ibid., 11.

18. Ibid. See also Cheryl B. Anderson, *Women, Ideology, and Violence: Critical Theory and the Construction of Gender in the Book of the Covenant and the Deuteronomic Law* (London: T&T Clark, 2004), 47.

19. Pressler, *View of Women*, 12.

20. Ibid., 43.

21. Elisabeth Schüssler Fiorenza, *Rhetoric and Ethic: The Politics of Biblical Studies* (Minneapolis: Fortress Press, 1999), 43.

22. Pressler, *View of Women*, 22.

23. Washington, "'Lest He Die in the Battle'," 186.

24. Ibid., 192.

25. Ibid., 187.

26. Ibid., 186.

27. Ibid., 205.

28. Alexander Rofé, "Family and Sex Laws in Deuteronomy and the Book of Covenant," *Henoch* 9 (1987): 131–59.

29. Tigay, *Deuteronomy*, 204; Christensen, *Deuteronomy*, 510.

30. S. R. Driver, *A Critical and Exegetical Commentary on Deuteronomy*, International Critical Commentary (Edinburgh: T&T Clark, 1895; latest impression 1965), 244.

31. Washington, "'Lest He Die in the Battle'," 208.

32. Tigay, *Deuteronomy*, 206.

33. Tikva Frymer-Kensky, "Deuteronomy," in *The Women's Bible Commentary with Apocrypha*, ed. Carol A. Newsom and Sharon H. Ringe (Louisville: Westminster John Knox, 1998), 63; Angelika Engelmann, "Deuteronomium: Recht und Gerechtigkeit für Frauen im Gesetz," in *Kompendium Feministische Bibelauslegung*, ed. Luise Schottroff and Marie-Theres Wacker, 2nd ed. (Gütersloh: Gütersloher Verlagshaus, 1999), 73; Anderson, *Women, Ideology, and Violence*, 43–44.

34. James B. Pritchard, ed., *Ancient Near Eastern Texts Relating to the Old Testament* (Princeton, N.J.: Princeton University Press, 1969), 181. For a more recent translation, see Martha T. Roth, ed., *Law Collections from Mesopotamia and Asia Minor*, Writings from the Ancient World 6 (Atlanta: Scholars Press, 1995).

35. Pritchard, *Ancient Near Eastern Texts*, 171.

36. According to some scholars, the harsh punishment is due to the fact that, different from ancient Near Eastern law, biblical law considers all crimes as transgressions against God, the lawgiver; see, for example, Moshe Greenberg, "Some Postulates of Biblical Criminal Law," in *A Song of Power and the Power of Song*, ed. D. Christensen (Winona Lake, Ind.: Eisenbrauns, 1993), 283–300, esp. 288–89.

37. All forms of punishment mentioned in these laws are at best unreasonable from a contemporary Western perspective on rape. First, only the rapist and not the victim-survivor should receive a penalty. Second, the Universal Declaration of Human Rights gives everyone the right to life in its Article 3, which, for instance, the organization Amnesty International interprets as a rejection of the death penalty. The Charter of Fundamental Rights of the European Union explicitly rejects the death penalty in its Article 2. It is highly unlikely, however, that any of the biblical or ancient Near Eastern penalties were ever carried out (since their status as practiced law is questionable).

38. See also Middle Assyrian Law 55 and §197 of the Hittite Laws, and the discussion of these laws below.

39. Tigay, *Deuteronomy*, 207.

40. Rofé, "Family and Sex Laws," 147.

41. Christensen, *Deuteronomy*, 51.

42. Engelmann, "Deuteronomium," 74.

43. Against the view of Tikvah Frymer-Kensky ("Deuteronomy," 93), who maintains that in this context the verb means "illicit sex," that is, sex with someone with whom one has no right to have sex. Frymer-Kensky's position is also supported by Mayer I. Gruber, "A Re-examination of the Charges against Shechem son of Hamor" (in Hebrew), *Beit Mikra* 157 (1999): 119–27; and Washington, "'Lest He Die in the Battle'," 208–12. For a recent study of these and related verbs, see Sandie Gravett, "Reading 'Rape' in the Hebrew Bible: A Consideration of Language," *Journal for the Study of the Old Testament* 28, no. 3 (March 2004): 279–99.

44. Sophie Lafont, *Femmes, droit et justice dans l'antiquité orientale: Contribution à l'étude du droit pénal au Proche-Orient ancien*, Orbis Biblicus et Orientalis 165 (Göttingen: Vandenhoeck & Ruprecht, 1999), 138. For an opposing view, see Anthony Phillips, "Another Look at Adultery," *Journal for the Study of the Old Testament* 20 (1981): 3–25, here 13.

45. Against Frymer-Kensky, who considers Exod 22:16 to be a "comparable law" to Deut 22:28-29; see Tikvah Frymer-Kensky, "Law and Philosophy: The Case of Sex in the Bible," *Semeia* 45 (1989): 93–94. Her arguments stand in a long tradition of premishnaic readers; see Robert J. V. Hiebert, "Deuteronomy 22:28–29 and Its Premishnaic Interpretations," *Catholic Biblical Quarterly* 56 (1994): 203–20. Anderson also considers the act in Exod 22:16 to be consensual when she uses the term "seduction" (*Women, Ideology, and Violence*, 40).

46. Washington, "'Lest He Die in the Battle'," 211.

47. See Henry McKeating, "Sanctions against Adultery in Ancient Israelite Society, with Some Reflections on Methodology in the Study of Old Testament Ethics," *Journal for the Study of the Old Testament* 11 (1979): 57–72, here 70: "What I am suggesting, to put it in another way, is that the ethics of the Old Testament and the ethics of ancient Israelite society do not necessarily coincide, and the latter may not be represented altogether accurately by the former. Old Testament ethics is a theological construction, a set of rules, ideals and principles theologically motivated throughout and in large part religiously sanctioned. Were the principles by which real Israelites actually lived quite so closely determined by religious faith? It may be that they were, but we cannot without further ado assume so."

48. Neufeld, *Hittite Laws*, 194.

49. J. J. Finkelstein, "Sex Offenses in Sumerian laws," *Journal of the American Oriental Society* 86 (1966): 355–72.

50. Ibid., 359. The choice of translating the Sumerian verb into English as "to deflower" reflects an inherently androcentric perspective.

51. Ibid., 360.

52. Raymond Westbrook, "Adultery in Ancient Law," *Revue biblique* 97 (October 1990): 542–80, here 562.

53. In this very context, Westbrook ("Adultery," 548 n. 26) refers to Finkelstein's study.

54. The 1995 translation of ancient Near Eastern rape laws, edited by Martha Roth, exhibits a similar reliance on Finkelstein's work. The index of "Selected Legal Topics and Key Words" lists the category "sexual offenses," under which the following terms appear: "adultery and fornication, consent, defloration, flirtatious behavior, incest, procuring, promiscuity, rape and sexual assault, seduction, sodomy." Why these terms are part of the category of "sexual offenses" is clear only when one studies the history of scholarship. Still, it is hard to believe that adultery, consent, and flirtatious behavior appear as "sexual offenses" in the index of a 1995 publication. See Roth, *Law Collections*, 282.

55. Lafont, *Femmes, droit et justice*, 133.

56. Erich Ebeling and Bruno Meissner, eds., *Reallexikon der Assyriologie und Vorderasiatischen Archäologie* (Berlin/New York: de Gruyter, 1928–). Even the new edition, currently in preparation, has not yet published a volume with an article on "*Vergewaltigung*"; see also n. 68 below.

57. Yildiz, "A Tablet of Codex Ur-Nammu," 96.

58. Lafont, *Femmes, droit et justice*, 467. In the original French: "Si un homme a fait violence à l'éspouse d'un jeune homme, qui n'était pas déflorée, et l'a déflorée, cet homme sera tué." The English is my translation from the French.

59. Yildiz, "A Tablet of Codex Ur-Nammu," 96–97.

60. For a discussion of the rape of enslaved women, see Lafont, *Femmes, droit et justice*, 144–45.

61. For an extensive discussion of classism in combination with androcentric co-optation of women in the Hebrew Bible, see Susanne Scholz, "Gender, class, and androcentric compliance in the rapes of enslaved women," *lectio difficilior: European Electronic Journal for Feminist Exegesis* 1 (2004): available at http://www.lectio.unibe.ch/04_1/Scholz .Enslaved.pdf.

62. Pritchard, *Ancient Near Eastern Texts*, 162.

63. Ibid., 171.

64. Finkelstein, "Sex Offenses in Sumerian Laws," 356.

65. Raymond Westbrook, *Old Babylonian Marriage Law* (Horn, Austria: F. Berger; 1988), 30. The terminology of "inchoate marriage" appeared initially in the early decades of the twentieth century; see Benno Landsberger, "Jungfräulichkeit: Ein Beitrag zum Thema 'Beilager und Eheschliessung'," in *Symbolae Iuridicae et Historicae: Martiono David Dedicatae*, ed. J. A. Ankum, R. Feenstra, W. F. Leemans (Leiden: E. J. Brill, 1968), 2:40–103, here 40–41.

66. Westbrook, *Old Babylonian Marriage Law*, 30.

67. Eckart Otto, "Rechtssytematik im altbabylonischen Codex Ešnunna und im altisraelitischen Bundesbuch," *Ugarit-Forschungen* 19 (1987): 175–97, esp. 184–85. For a discussion of Egyptian texts about adultery, see C. J. Eyre, "Crime and Adultery in Ancient Egypt," *Journal of Egyptian Archaeology* 70 (1984): 92–105.

68. Walter Kornfeld, "L'adultère dans l'orient antique," *Revue biblique* 57 (January 1950): 92–109, here 98 (my translation from the French original). Other examples are Rafael Yaron, "The Rejected Bridegroom (LE 25)," *Orientalis* 34, no. 1 (1965): 23–29, here 29. The article on adultery ("*Ehebruch*") in the German *Reallexikon der Assyriologie*, vol. 2 (1938) refers to more information about rape ("*Notzucht*"). The word *Notzucht* in vol. 10 refers readers to an article on *Vergewaltigung*, the contemporary German term for rape. The volume on words beginning with *v* has not yet been published (as of November 2009), although the publishers aim to complete the revised edition of the *Reallexikon* by 2011. For editorial comments on the new edition of the *Reallexikon*, see http://www.uni-leipzig.de/altorient/ projektrla.html (accessed November 24, 2009).

69. Landsberger, "Jungfräulichkeit," 53, 56, 63–64.

70. Biblical law does not address such a case; see the omission in Lev 18:6–18. James E. Miller, however, claims that this case is included in the law that prohibits a man from having sex with a woman and her daughter "which effectively prohibits sex with either daughter or step-daughter"; see his "Sexual Offenses in Genesis," *Journal for the Study of the Old Testament* 90 (2000): 41–53, here 42.

71. See, for example, §156 of the Code of Hammurabi, MAL 55, or Deut 22:28–29, as discussed above.

72. Harry A. Hoffner, "Incest, Sodomy and Bestiality in the Ancient Near East," in *Orient and Occident: Essays Presented to Cyrus H. Gordon on the Occasion of his Sixty-fifth Birthday*, ed. Harry A. Hoffner, Alter Orient

und Altes Testament 22 (Neukirchen-Vluyn: Neukirchener Verlag, 1973), 81–90.

73. Pritchard, *Ancient Near Eastern* Texts, 181. Roth (*Law Collections*, 282) lists MAL 9 as a rape law in the index but the meaning of this law is vague and not included here.

74. Lafont, *Femmes, droit et justice*, 137.

75. Raymond Westbrook, "Biblical and Cuneiform Law Codes," *Revue biblique* 92, no. 2 (1985): 247–64. An early publication supports the notion of rape being a problem in the ancient Near East; see Driver and Miles, *Assyrian Laws*, 37: "If it is true that so many laws argue so many sins, this offense [adultery] must have been rife in Babylonia and Assyria; for a large number of sections in the Babylonian code and in these laws are concerned with it."

76. Pritchard, *Ancient Near Eastern* Texts, 181.

77. Ibid., 182.

78. Ibid., 185.

79. Against Driver and Miles (*Assyrian Laws*, 52–53), who, on the basis of grammatical ambiguity, argue for the possibility that §55 describes either a rape or consensual sex and is followed by the law of §56 in which "the girl is the prime mover."

80. Other laws have different views about this matter; see §197 of the Hittite Laws and discussion of it below.

81. Guillaume Cardascia, *Les Lois Assyriennes* (Paris: Les Editions du Cerf, 1969), 252.

82. Driver and Miles, *Assyrian Laws*, 37; Cardascia, *Les Lois Assyriennes*, 249.

83. Pritchard, *Ancient Near Eastern Texts*, 196.

84. Neufeld, *Hittite Laws*, 194; Jost Grothus, *Die Rechtsordnung der Hethiter* (Wiesbaden: Otto Harrassowitz, 1973), 35.

85. For a similar law with a different assessment of the significance of the location, see MAL 5 and Deut 22:23–24 and the discussions above.

86. Richard Haase, "Bemerkungen zu einigen Paragraphen der hethitischen Gesetze (§§197/98, 95, 35, 37)," *Hethitica* 12 (1994): 7–10.

87. Ibid., 7.

88. *American Heritage Dictionary of the English Language*, 4th ed. (Boston: Houghton Mifflin, 2000).

89. Biblical legislation knows of incest and bestiality; see Lev. 18:6-18; 20:11-21; and Deut. 27:20-23.

90. Carol J. Adams, "Bestiality," in *Encyclopedia of Rape*, ed. Merril D. Smith (Westport, Conn.: Greenwood, 2004), 22–23.

91. Hoffner, "Incest, Sodomy and Bestiality," 83 n. 13.

92. Pritchard, *Ancient Near Eastern Texts*, 196–97.

93. Neufeld, *Hittite Laws*, 188.

94. Hoffner, "Incest, Sodomy and Bestiality," 82.

95. Neufeld, *Hittite Laws*, 53.

96. Ibid., 188.

97. Roth, *Law Collections*, 236.

98. Hoffner, "Incest, Sodomy and Bestiality," 83.

99. Ibid., 84.

100. Raymond Westbrook, "Biblical and Cuneiform Law Codes"; see also n. 37 above.

101. Other scholars also see this connection between the Christian right and the modern worldview; see, e.g., Schüssler Fiorenza, *Rhetoric and Ethic*, 42: "In spite of their critical posture, academic biblical studies are thus akin to fundamentalism insofar as they insist that scholars are able to produce a single scientific, true, reliable, and non-ideological reading of the Bible. Scholars can achieve scientific certainty as long as they silence their own interests and abstract from their own sociopolitical situation."

102. I owe the idea of connecting the epistemological imbalance in ancient rape law to the current (U.S.) sociopolitical and religious divide to Charles Nelson, professor emeritus of German at Tufts University, Boston, Massachusetts, during a conversation on November 6, 2004.

5. Gang Raping

1. Catharine A. MacKinnon, "Crimes of War, Crimes of Peace," in eadem, *Are Women Human? And Other International Dialogues* (Cambridge, Mass.: Harvard University Press, 2006), 158.

2. MacKinnon, "From Auschwitz to Omarksa, Nuremberg to The Hague," in eadem, *Are Women Human?* 178.

3. Maria B. Olujic, "Women, Rape, and War: The Continued Trauma of Refugees and Displaced Persons in Croatia," *Anthropology of East Europe Review* 13, no. 1 (Spring 1995), http://condor.depaul.edu/~rrotenbe/aeer/aeer13_1/aeer13_1.html. See also United Nations General Assembly, "Situation of human rights in Bosnia and Herzegovina, the Republic of Croatia and the Federal Republic of Yugoslavia" (55th session; 20 October 2000), http://www.unhcr.org/refworld/country,,UNGA,,HRV,4562d8b62,3b00f5 7c10,0.html (accessed November 24, 2009).

4. Joshua S. Goldstein, *War and Gender: How Gender Shapes the War System and Vice Versa* (Cambridge: Cambridge University Press, 2001), 368.

5. Human Rights Watch, "Struggling to survive: barriers to justice for rape victims in Rwanda," http://www.hrw.org/en/reports/2004/09/29/struggling-survive (accessed November 24, 2009).

6. United Nations, *Contemporary Forms of Slavery: Systematic Rape, Sexual Slavery and Slavery-like Practices during Armed Conflict*, Final Report submitted by Ms. Gay J. McDougall, Special Rapporteur (New York: United Nations, 1998), paragraphs 7–8.

7. United Nations General Assembly, "Resolution adopted by the General Assembly: 61/143 Intensification of efforts to eliminate all forms of violence against women" (30 January 2007): http://www.unescap.org/esid/GAD/Events/EGM-VAW2007/Background%20Papers/GA%20resolution%20on%20VAW.pdf (accessed November 24, 2009).

8. "Fact Sheets" are available online at http://www.un.org/en/women/endviolence/ (accessed November 24, 2009).

9. Patrick Worsnip, "U.N. Council Urges Action on Sexual Violence In War," Reuters, April 9, 2009, http://www.alertnet.org/thenews/newsdesk/N19485901.htm (accessed November 24, 2009).

10. See Point 4 of the UN Resolution 1820, http://www.un.org/Docs/sc/unsc_resolutions08.htm (accessed November 24, 2009).

11. Goldstein, *War and Gender*, 332.

12. Ibid., 371.

13. Amnesty International, "Burundi: No protection from rape in war and peace" (2007), www.amnesty.org (accessed November 24, 2009).

14. MacKinnon, "Crimes of War," 148.

15. MacKinnon, "Turning Rape into Pornography," eadem, *Are Women Human?* (see n. 1 above), 160–68. Further, in the chapter entitled "Rape, Genocide, and Women's Human Rights," she states: "Prostitution is that part of everyday nonwar life that is closest to what we see done to women in this [former Yugoslavian] war. The daily life of prostituted women consists of serial rape, recognized war or no war. The brothel-like arrangement of the rape/death camps parallels the brothels of so-called peacetime: captive women impounded to be passed from man to man in order to be raped" (ibid., 188).

16. Quoted in MacKinnon, "Genocide's Sexuality," in eadem, *Are Women Human?* (see n. 1 above), 221.

17. Ibid., 222.

18. Ibid., 225.

19. Ibid., 225–26.

20. Ibid., 226.

21. Ibid.

22. Ibid., 232.

23. So already Susan Niditch, "The 'Sodomite' Theme in Judges 19–20: Family, Community, and Social Disintegration," *Catholic Biblical Quarterly* 44 (1982): 367–69.

24. See, for example, a study guide for German theology students by Horst Dietrich Preuß and Klaus Berger, *Bibelkunde des Alten und Neuen Testaments: Erster Teil*, 3rd ed. (Heidelberg/Wiesbaden: Quelle & Meyer, 1985). In fact, in 1988, Mieke Bal stated: "The story is very little known to begin with . . ." (*Death and Dissymmetry: The Politics of Coherence in the Book of Judges* [Chicago: University of Chicago Press, 1988]: 90).

25. Phyllis Trible, *Texts of Terror: Literary-Feminist Readings of Biblical Narratives* (Philadelphia: Fortress, 1984), 65.

26. Ibid., 66.

27. Carol Meyers, Toni Craven, and Ross S. Kraemer, eds., *Women in Scripture: A Dictionary of Named and Unnamed Women in the Hebrew Bible, the Apocryphal/Deuterocanonical Books, and the New Testament* (Grand Rapids: Eerdmans, 2000), 248.

28. Mieke Bal, "A Body of Writing: Judges 19," in *A Feminist Companion to Judges*, ed. Athalya Brenner (Sheffield: Sheffield Academic Press, 1993), 208–30, here 209.

29. Ibid.

30. J. Cheryl Exum, "Raped by the Pen," in eadem, *Fragmented Women: Feminist (Sub)versions of Biblical Narratives*, Journal for the Study of the Old Testament Supplement Series 163 (Valley Forge, Pa.: Trinity Press International, 1993), 171.

31. Ibid.

32. Gale A. Yee, "Ideological Criticism: Judges 17–21 and the Dismembered Body," in *Judges & Methods: New Approaches in Biblical Studies*, ed. Gale A. Yee (Minneapolis: Fortress, 1995), 146–70, here 167.

33. J. H. Coetzee, "The 'Outcry' of the Dissected Woman in Judges 19–21: Embodiment of a Society," *Old Testament Essays* 15, no. 1 (2002): 52–63, here 59.

34. Andrew Hock-Soon Ng, "Revisiting Judges 19: A Gothic Perspective," *Journal for the Study of the Old Testament* 32, no. 2 (2007): 199–215, here 206.

35. Ibid., 201.

36. Ibid.

37. Victor H. Matthews, "Hospitality and Hostility in Genesis 19 and Judges 19," *Biblical Theology Bulletin* 22 (1992): 3-11, here 7.

38. Danna Nolan Fewell, "Judges," in *Women's Bible Commentary with Apocrypha (Expanded Edition)*, ed. Carol A. Newsom and Sharon H. Ringe (Louisville: Westminster John Knox, 1998), 73-83, here 81.

39. Pamela Tamarkin Reis, "The Levite's Concubine: New Light on a Dark Story," *Scandinavian Journal of the Old Testament* 20, no. 1 (2006): 125-46, here 129.

40. Ibid.

41. Ibid.

42. Ibid.

43. Ibid., 126.

44. Ibid., 132.

45. Ibid., 133.

46. Ibid.

47. Ibid., 136.

48. Ken Stone, "Gender and Homosexuality in Judges 19: Subject-Honor, Object-Shame?" *Journal for the Study of the Old Testament* 67 (1995): 87-107, here 93.

49. Ibid., 94.

50. Phyllis Trible, "An Unnamed Woman: The Extravagance of Violence," in *Texts of Terror: Literary-Feminist Readings of Biblical Narratives* (Philadelphia: Fortress Press, 1984), 86.

51. Ibid., 87.

52. Ibid.

53. Michael Carden, "Homophobia and Rape in Sodom and Gibeah: A Response to Ken Stone," *Journal for the Study of the Old Testament* 82 (1999): 83-96, here 85. For a similar approach, see also Ilse Müllner, "Lethal Differences: Sexual Violence as Violence against Others in Judges 19," in *Judges: A Feminist Companion to the Bible (Second Series)*, ed. Athalya Brenner (Sheffield: Sheffield Academic Press, 1999), 126-42.

54. Carden, "Homophobia," 93.

55. Ibid., 87.

56. See Gen 19:8 for a similar dynamic.

57. Carden, "Homophobia," 90.

58. Ibid., 92.

59. Ibid., 91 (emphasis added).

60. Ibid., 93.

61. Patrick S. Cheng, "Multiplicity and Judges 19: Constructing a Queer Asian Pacific American Biblical Hermeneutic," *Semeia* 90-91 (2002): 119-33, here 119.

62. Elsewhere I classify this hermeneutical strategy as an approach of "She Is Like Us"; see Susanne Scholz, "Ruth, Jezebel, and Rahab as 'Other' Women: Integrating Postcolonial Perspectives," eadem, in *Introducing the Women's Hebrew Bible*, Introductions in Feminist Theology 13 (London: T&T Clark International, 2007), 100-121, esp. 107-11.

63. Cheng, "Multiplicity," 122.

64. According to Cheng, among them are "homosexual, gay, queer, intersexed, or questioning," and "oriental, Asian, Asian American, Asian Pacific Islander, or Asian Pacific American" ("Multiplicity," 123).

65. Ibid.

66. Ibid., 124-28.

67. Ibid., 129.

68. Katharina von Kellenbach, "Am I a Murderer? Judges 19-21 as a Parable of Meaningless Suffering," in *Strange Fire: Reading the Bible after the Holocaust*, ed. Tod Linafelt (Sheffield: Sheffield Academic Press, 2000), 176-91, esp. 183-88.

69. Ibid., 180.

70. Ibid.

71. Ibid.

72. Ibid., 182.

73. Ibid., 181.

74. Ibid. Similarly, in a critique of Trible's interpretation of the Levite's action, Jan Fokkelman charges that "the two men in 19:22 are themselves driven into an appalling predicament, in the face of which the reader should refrain from passing a quick and premature [*sic*] judgment"; see Jan Fokkelman, "Structural Remarks on Judges 9 and 19," in *Sha'arei Talmon: Studies in the Bible, Qumran and the Ancient Near East Presented to Shemaryahu Talmon*, ed. Michael Fishbane and Emanuel Tov (Winona Lake, Ind.: Eisenbrauns, 1992), 33-45, here 41.

75. Von Kellenbach, "Am I a Murderer?" 183.

76. Ibid., 189.

77. Ibid., 185.

78. Ibid., 186.

79. Ibid., 189.

80. Ibid., 190.

81. Ibid.

82. Ibid., 191.

83. Ibid.

84. Erik Eynikel, "Judges 19-21, an 'Appendix': Rape, Murder, War and Abduction," *Communio viatorum* 47, no. 2 (2005): 101-15, here 113.

85. For other short references to the rape of women in war, see Deut 28:30; Judg 5:30; Isa 13:16; Lam 5:11; Amos 4:2-3; Zech 14:2. For references to the murder of city dwellers, including women and children, see Deut 2:34; Josh 6:21; 8:24-25; 1 Sam 15:3-8; Amos 7:17.

86. Eynikel, "Judges 19-21," 114: "Not one of them [women] in these . . . chapters is given a voice." This textual silencing has barely been overcome in biblical scholarship, according to Alice Bach, who writes in "Re-reading the Body Politic: Women and Violence in Judges 21," *Biblical Interpretation* 6, no. 1 (1998): 1-19, here 15-16: "While the violations of individual women in Genesis 19 and Judges 19-20 have become the subject of earnest debate in the feminist community, the carrying off of the women of Shiloh has been met with near silence. . . . Male and female commentators alike seem to identify deeply with the portrait of female victimization expressed in the narratives of violence to one woman, but silence greets the genocidal brutalization of the women of Shiloh." This article is reprinted in *Judges: A Feminist Companion to the Bible (Second Series)*, ed. Athalya Brenner (Sheffield: Sheffield Academic Press, 1999), 143-59.

87. See also 17:6; 18:1; 19:1. This is not the place to elaborate on the extensive debate about the difficulties of reconstructing Israelite history, but for further information and literature, see, for example, Philip R. Davies, *The Origins of Biblical Israel*, Library of Hebrew Bible/Old Testament Studies 485 (New York/London: T&T Clark, 2007).

88. Bach, "Re-reading the Body Politic," 17.

89. Ibid., 7, 9n, 9-10.

90. Ibid., 10.

91. Robert G. Boling, *Judges: Introduction, Translation and Commentary*, Anchor Bible 6A (Garden City, N.Y.: Doubleday, 1975), 277. For a similar approach, see also J. Gordon Harris, Cheryl A. Brown, Michael S. Moore, *Joshua, Judges, Ruth*, New International Biblical Commentary, Old Testament Series 5 (Peabody, Mass.: Hendrickson, 2000).

92. Boling, *Judges*, 279.

93. J. Clinton McCann, *Judges*, Interpretation: A Bible Commentary for Teaching and Preaching (Louisville: Westminster John Knox, 2002), 129, 133. The rape of "other" women—in this case from Babylon—is also envisioned in other biblical texts, such as Isa 13:16.

94. Ibid., 130.

95. Ibid.

96. Ibid.

97. Ibid., 139.

98. Susan Niditch, *Judges: A Commentary*, Old Testament Library (Louisville: Westminster John Knox, 2008), 185, 208.

99. Ibid., 211.

100. Tammi Schneider, *Judges*, Berit Olam (Collegeville, Minn.: Liturgical Press, 2000), 262.

101. Ibid., 282.

102. Ibid., 283. Interestingly, J. Alberto Soggin entitles Judges 21:15-25 as "The rape of the women of Shiloh"; see his *Judges: A Commentary*, 2nd ed., Old Testament Library (London: SCM, 1987). When interpreters make this point, sometimes they also refer to Deut 21:10-14. See also chapter 5 above.

103. Schneider, *Judges*, 285.

104. Ibid., 247.

105. Carolyn Pressler, *Joshua, Judges, and Ruth*, Westminster Bible Companion (Louisville: Westminster John Knox, 2002), 254.

106. Ibid., 238.

107. Ibid., 256.

108. Ibid., 257.

109. Ibid., 258.

6. Losing Power

1. Gillian C. Mezey and Michael B. King, eds., *Male Victims of Sexual Assault*, 2nd ed. (Oxford: Oxford University Press, 2000), v.

2. Susan Estrich, *Real Rape* (Cambridge, Mass.: Harvard University Press, 1987), 108.

3. Quoted in Noreen Abdullah-Khan, *Male Rape: The Emergence of a Social and Legal Issue* (New York: Palgrave Macmillan, 2008), 180.

4. Richie J. McMullen, *Male Rape: Breaking the Silence on the Last Taboo* (London: GMP, 1990), 80.

5. Abdullah-Khan, *Male Rape*, 215, 198–99, 209.

6. Ibid., 209.

7. All quotations from Abdullah-Khan, *Male Rape*, 207.

8. Mezey and King, *Male Victims of Sexual Assault*, 141.

9. Wendy Stock, "Women's Sexual Coercion of Men: A Feminist Analysis," in *Sexually Aggressive Women: Current Perspectives and Controversies*,

ed. Peter B. Anderson and Cindy Struckman-Johnson (New York/London: Guilford Press, 1998), 169–84, here 170. For one of the earliest anthropological references to this possibility, see Bronislaw Malinowski, *The Sexual Life of Savages* (London: Routledge & Kegan Paul, 1929).

10. Peter B. Anderson, "Women's Motives for Sexual Initiation and Aggression," in *Sexually Aggressive Women* (see n. 9 above), 79–93, here 79.

11. See, for example, Kate Zernike, "The Siren Song of Sex with Boys," *New York Times*, December 11, 2005; Borrie La Grange, "Man 'gang-raped' by 3 women," *News 24*, August 24, 2008.

12. Charlene L. Muehlenhard, "The Importance and Danger of Studying Sexually Aggressive Women," in *Sexually Aggressive Women* (see n. 9 above), 19–48, here 41.

13. Stock, "Women's Sexual Coercion of Men," 173.

14. Cindy Struckman-Johnson and David Struckman-Johnson, "The Dynamics and Impact of Sexual Coercion of Men by Women," in *Sexually Aggressive Women* (see n. 9 above), 121–43, here 124, 125.

15. A similarity between Ehud in Judg 3:15-22 and Joab as portrayed in 2 Sam 3:27 and 20:8-10 has been noted by Gregary T. K. Wong, "Ehud and Joab: Separated at Birth?" *Vetus Testamentum* 56, no. 3 (2006): 399–412. Wong writes: "[T]hese two accounts of Joab's assassinations seem to bear an uncanny resemblance to the account of Ehud's assassination of Eglon" (p. 400). These stories, too, are perhaps discreet hints at male rape.

16. Deryn Guest, "Judges," in *The Queer Bible Commentary*, ed. Deryn Guest, Robert E. Goss, Mona West, and Thomas Bohache (London: SCM, 2006), 168–77.

17. Quoted in ibid., 170–71.

18. Ibid., 171.

19. Timothy R. Koch, "A Homoerotic Approach to Scripture," *Theology & Sexuality* 14 (2001): 10–22, here 21.

20. Ibid.

21. Guest, "Judges," 172.

22. Ibid.

23. Susan Niditch, *Judges: A Commentary*, Old Testament Library (Louisville: Westminster John Knox, 2008), 58.

24. Guest, "Judges," 173–74.

25. Niditch, *Judges*, 58.

26. The Hebrew noun for thigh or loin (יָרֵךְ, *yārēk*) refers specifically to the "seat of procreation" in Gen 46:26 and to the "area of sexual organs" in Gen 24:2.

27. J. Clinton McCann, *Judges*, Interpretation: A Bible Commentary for Teaching and Preaching (Louisville: John Knox, 2002), 45.

28. Ibid., 44, 45.

29. See Francis Brown, S. R. Driver, and Charles A. Briggs, eds., *Hebrew and English Lexicon of the Old Testament, based on the Lexicon of William Gesenius* (1906; Oxford: Oxford University Press, 1951), 832.

30. See, for example, King James Version, New Revised Standard Version, or English Standard Version. See also J. Alberto Soggin, *Judges: A Commentary*, Old Testament Library (Philadelphia: Westminster, 1981), 52.

31. For a brief discussion, see Guest, "Judges," 173.

32. Ibid.

33. Niditch, *Judges*, 58.

34. Guest, "Judges," 174. For the suggestion that a negative view of Ehud may have intrabiblical support in 2 Sam 3:27 and 2 Sam 20:8-10, see Wong, "Ehud and Joab," 399–412.

35. See the discussion in Guest, "Judges," 174.

36. Ibid., 175.

37. Ibid., 176.

38. Ibid., 177.

39. See, for example, Athalya Brenner and Jan Willem van Henten, "Madame Potiphar through a Culture Trip, or, Which Side Are You On?" in *Biblical Studies/Cultural Studies: The Third Sheffield Colloquium*, ed. J. Cheryl Exum and Stephen D. Moore, Journal for the Study of the Old Testament Supplement Series 226 (Sheffield: Sheffield Academic Press, 1998), 203–19; C. Houtman, *Een wellustige en valse vrouw? Over een intrigerende "affaire" in Schrift en uitleg* (Kampen: Kok, 1998); Mieke Bal, *Loving Yusuf: Conceptual Travels from Present to Past*, Afterlives of the Bible (Chicago/London: University of Chicago Press, 2008).

40. Susan Tower Hollis, "The Woman in Ancient Examples of the Potiphar's Wife Motif, K2111," in *Gender and Difference in Ancient Israel*, ed. Peggy L. Day (Minneapolis: Fortress Press, 1989), 28–42, here 31–32.

41. See the comprehensive list of parallels in Hermann Gunkel, *Genesis*, trans. Mark E. Biddle, Mercer Library of Biblical Studies (Macon, Ga.: Mercer University Press, 1997; German original 1910), 406. See also the discussion of the "Tale of Two Brothers" in Hollis, "Woman in Ancient Examples of the Potiphar's Wife Motif," 33–36.

42. Bruce Vawter, *On Genesis: A New Reading* (Garden City, N.Y.: Doubleday, 1977), 403.

43. James B. Pritchard, ed., *Ancient Near Eastern Texts Relating to the Old Testament*, 3rd ed. (Princeton, N.J.: Princeton University Press, 1969), 25.

44. See also the discussions in Brenner and van Henten, "Madame Potiphar," 217; and Bal, *Loving Yusuf*, 201–5.

45. Brenner and van Henten, "Madame Potiphar," 217.

46. Ibid., 218. For a similar tradition in rabbinic literature, see James Kugel, *In Potiphar's House: The Interpretive Life of Biblical Texts* (San Francisco: HarperSanFrancisco, 1990), 29–33.

47. Susan Niditch, "Genesis," in *The Women's Bible Commentary with Apocrypha (Expanded Edition)*, ed. Carol A. Newsom and Sharon H. Ringe (Louisville: Westminster John Knox, 1998), 28–29.

48. Ron Pirson, "The Twofold Message of Potiphar's Wife," *Scandinavian Journal of the Old Testament* 18, no. 2 (2004): 248–59, here 256. See also Irmtraud Fischer, "Genesis 12–50: Die Ursprungsgeschichte Israels als Frauengeschichte," in *Kompendium Feministische Bibelauslegung*, ed. Luise Schottroff and Marie-Theres Wacker, 2nd ed. (Gütersloh: Gütersloher Verlagshaus, 1998), 12–25, here 23.

49. Pirson, "Twofold Message," 256.

50. Gerhard von Rad, *Genesis: A Commentary*, trans. John H. Marks, 3rd rev. ed., Old Testament Library (Philadelphia: Westminster, 1972), 366.

51. Gordon J. Wenham, *Genesis 16–50*, Word Biblical Commentary (Dallas: Word Books, 1994), 376.

52. Vawter, *On Genesis*, 403.

53. Von Rad, *Genesis*, 364.

54. Wenham, *Genesis 16–50*, 377; Everett Fox, *In the Beginning: A New English Rendition of the Book of Genesis* (New York: Schocken, 1983), 163; Nahum M. Sarna, *Genesis* [= *Bereshit*]: *The Traditional Hebrew Text with the New JPS Translation*, JPS Torah Commentary (Philadelphia: Jewish Publication Society, 1989), 272.

55. Victor P. Hamilton, *The Book of Genesis: Chapters 18–50*, New International Commentary on the Old Testament (Grand Rapids: Eerdmans, 1995), 461, 463.

56. Robert Alter, *Genesis: Translation and Commentary* (New York/London: W. W. Norton, 1996), 226.

57. Nelly Furman, "His Story versus Her Story: Male Genealogy and Female Strategy in the Jacob Cycle," *Semeia* 46 (1989): 141–49, here 149.

58. My translation of the Hebrew text. For the principles behind the translation, see Phyllis Trible, *Rhetorical Criticism: Context, Method, and the Book of Jonah* (Minneapolis: Fortress Press, 1994), esp. 101–6.

59. Sarna, *Genesis*, 274.

60. Esther Fuchs, *Sexual Politics in the Biblical Narrative: Reading the Hebrew Bible as a Woman*, Journal for the Study of the Old Testament Supplement Series 310 (Sheffield: Sheffield Academic Press, 2000), 146.

61. Ibid., 222.

62. Alice Bach, "Breaking Free of the Biblical Frame-Up: Uncovering the Woman in Genesis 39," in *A Feminist Companion to Genesis*, ed. Athalya Brenner (Sheffield: Sheffield Academic Press, 1993), 318–42, here 320.

63. Ibid., 321.

64. Ibid.

65. Ibid., 342.

66. Niditch, "Genesis," 28.

67. Laura E. Donaldson, "Cyborgs, Ciphers, and Sexuality: Re-Theorizing Literary and Biblical Character," *Semeia* 63 (1993): 81–96, here 85.

68. Ibid., 93.

69. Kugel, *In Potiphar's House*, 41–42; quoted in Donaldson, "Cyborgs, Ciphers, and Sexuality," 88.

70. Donaldson, "Cyborgs, Ciphers, and Sexuality," 88.

71. Ibid., 89.

72. Ibid., 90.

73. Ibid., 92.

74. Ibid., 93.

75. Walter Brueggemann, *Genesis: A Bible Commentary for Teaching and Preaching*, Interpretation (Atlanta: John Knox, 1982), 176. See also the brief discussion of this and other commentaries in J. Cheryl Exum, "Desire Distorted and Exhibited: Lot and His Daughters in Psychoanalysis, Painting, and Film," in *'A Wise and Discerning Mind': Essays in Honor of Burke O. Long*, ed. Saul M. Olyan and Robert C. Culley, Brown Judaic Studies 325 (Providence, R.I.: Brown Judaic Studies, 2000), 83–108, here 84 n. 1.

76. Martin Kessler and Karel Deurloo, *A Commentary on Genesis: The Book of Beginnings* (New York: Paulist Press, 2004), 120.

77. Bill T. Arnold, *Genesis*, New Cambridge Bible Commentary (Cambridge: Cambridge University Press, 2009), 186.

78. Hamilton, *Book of Genesis*, 51.

79. Carol Smith, "Stories of Incest in the Hebrew Bible: Scholars Challenging Text or Text Challenging Scholars?" *Henoch* 14 (1992): 227–42, here 236, 242.

80. See, for example, Hamilton, *Book of Genesis*, 51; Smith, "Stories of Incest," 237; Lester V. Meyer, "Damned If You Do and Damned If You Don't: Moral Dilemmas in the Story of Lot and His Family," *Trinity Seminary Review* 24, no. 2 (Summer–Fall 2003): 131–39, here 136; John H. Hewett, "Genesis 2:4b—3:31; 4:2-16; 9:20-27; 19:30-38," *Review and Expositor* 86 (1989): 237–41, here 241.

81. Elke Seifert, "Lot und seine Töchter: Eine Hermeneutik des Verdachts," in *Feministische Hermeneutik und Erstes Testament: Analysen und Interpretationen*, ed. Hedwig-Jahnow Projekt (Stuttgart: Kohlhammer, 1994), 48–65. See also Fischer, "Genesis 12–50," 21; and Ilona N. Rashkow, "Daddy-Dearest and the 'Invisible Spirit of Wine'," in *Genesis: The Feminist Companion to the Bible (Second Series)*, ed. Athalya Brenner (Sheffield: Sheffield Academic Press, 1998), 82–107, esp. 104–6.

82. Seifert, "Lot und seine Töchter," 64. My translation of the original German.

83. Ibid., 64–65.

84. Melissa Jackson suggests that the writers tried to "envision a new reality" in this story in which they invite us to "dream our own dreams of a world turned upside-down" and "patriarchy was not the status quo, men were seen as fools for behaving as if they were in total control, and women were valued for motherhood and also for their intelligence, courage, inventiveness, creativity." For Jackson, women's ability to trick men is the central issue of the story, not incest. See Melissa Jackson, "Lot's Daughters and Tamar as Tricksters and the Patriarchal Narratives as Feminist Theology," *Journal for the Study of the Old Testament* 98 (2002): 29–46.

85. Exum, "Desire Distorted," 87.

86. Ibid., 88.

87. Ibid., 89.

88. Ibid., 94.

89. Ibid., 91.

90. Ibid., 96.

91. For such a reading, see Guest, "Judges," 182–85.

92. Michael Carden, "Genesis/Bereshit," in *The Queer Bible Commentary*, ed. Deryn Guest, Robert E. Goss, Mona West, and Thomas Bohache (London: SCM, 2006), 21–60, here 39.

93. Exum, "Desire Distorted," 94.

94. Ibid.

95. Mieke Bal, "Delilah Decomposed: Samson's Talking Cure and the Rhetoric of Subjectivity," in eadem, *Lethal Love: Feminist Literary Readings*

of Biblical Love Stories, Indiana Studies in Biblical Literature (Bloomington/
Indianapolis: Indiana University Press, 1987), 38.

96. See, for example, the discussion by J. Cheryl Exum, "Why, Why,
Why, Delilah?" in eadem, *Plotted, Shot, and Painted: Cultural Representations of Biblical Women*, Journal for the Study of the Old Testament Supplement Series 215 (Sheffield: Sheffield Academic Press, 1996), 175–237.

97. See also Carol Smith, "Delilah: A Suitable Case for (Feminist)
Treatment?" in *Judges: A Feminist Companion to the Bible*, ed. Athalya
Brenner (Sheffield: Sheffield Academic Press, 1999), 92–116.

98. The Septuagint translates the pronoun accordingly, perhaps hinting
at the sexual nature of the moment.

99. See, for example, Arthur Cundall, *Judges: An Introduction and
Commentary* (Leicester, England/Downers Grove, Ill.: InterVarsity, 1968),
178; James L. Crenshaw, *Samson: A Secret Betrayed, a Vow Ignored* (Atlanta:
John Knox, 1978), 93; Susan Niditch, *Judges: A Commentary*, Old Testa-
ment Library (Louisville: Westminster John Knox, 2008), 161; Tammi J.
Schneider, *Judges* (Collegeville, Minn.: Liturgical Press, 2000), 220, 222;
Carolyn Pressler, *Joshua, Judges, and Ruth*, Westminster Bible Companion
(Louisville: Westminster John Knox, 2002), 220. Some ignore the signifi-
cance of this verb; see, for example, Gregory Mobley, *The Empty Men: The
Heroic Tradition of Ancient Israel* (New York: Doubleday, 2005), 191–94.

100. See, for example, Hilary B. Lipka, *Sexual Transgression in the
Hebrew Bible*, Hebrew Bible Monographs 7 (Sheffield: Sheffield Phoenix,
2006), 253.

101. My colleague Richard D. Nelson (W. J. A. Power Professor of
Biblical Hebrew and Old Testament Interpretation at Perkins School of
Theology) suggested this possibility to me in a private e-mail correspon-
dence on December 18, 2008.

102. The verb appears also in Gen 26:8, where it may connote sexual
abuse; see the discussion on marital rape in chapter 4 above.

103. Lori Rowlett, "Violent Femmes and S/M: Queering Samson and
Delilah," in *Queer Commentary and the Hebrew Bible*, ed. Ken Stone, Jour-
nal for the Study of the Old Testament Supplement Series 334 (Cleveland:
Pilgrim Press, 2001), 106–15, here 106.

104. Ibid., 109.
105. Ibid.
106. Ibid., 110.
107. Ibid.
108. Ibid., 111.

109. Ibid., 115.

110. Ibid.

111. McCann, *Judges*, 108.

112. Soggin, *Judges*, 256.

113. Rowlett, "Violent Femmes and S/M," 108.

7. Resisting the Theology of a Rapist

1. Quoted in Sally Robinson, *Marked Men: White Masculinity in Crisis* (New York: Columbia University Press, 2000), 60.

2. Tim Rohrer, "The Metaphorical Logic of (Political) Rape Revisited: The New Wor(l)d Order," *Metaphor and Symbolic Activity* 10, no. 2 (Spring 1995): 115–37.

3. Rohrer's analysis is based on the earlier one by George Lakoff, "Metaphor in Politics: An Open Letter to the Internet (1991)," http://uchcom.botik.ru/IHPCS/MET/WebLibrary/Lakoff/Metaphor-in-Politics.html (accessed November 24, 2009).

4. Ibid., 7.

5. Ibid., 8.

6. Ibid., 9.

7. Ibid., 11.

8. Perhaps Isa 3:16-17 is a preexilic text, although some commentators question an early date. For example, Joseph Blenkinsopp is uncertain if Isaiah or a later writer composed the passage (*Isaiah 1–39: A New Translation with Introduction and Commentary*, Anchor Bible 19 (New York: Doubleday, 2000), 201.

9. Johnny Miles, "Re-reading the Power of Satire: Isaiah's 'Daughters of Zion,' Pope's 'Belinda,' and the Rhetoric of Rape," *Journal for the Study of the Old Testament* 31, no. 2 (2006): 193–219, here 206.

10. F. Rachel Magdalene, "Ancient Near Eastern Treaty-Curses and the Ultimate Texts of Terror: A Study of Divine Sexual Abuse in the Prophetic Corpus," in *A Feminist Companion to the Latter Prophets*, ed. Athalya Brenner (Sheffield: Sheffield Academic Press, 1995), 326–52.

11. For another example of the poetics of rape in which the wife of a prophet is punished, see Hosea 1–3, esp. 2:3, 9-10. See also chapter 4 above, pp. 119–127.

12. Blenkinsopp, *Isaiah 1–39*, 201.

13. See, for example, Otto Kaiser, *Isaiah 1–12: A Commentary*, trans. John Bowden, 2nd rev. ed., Old Testament Library (Philadelphia: Westminster, 1983); Gene M. Tucker, "The Book of Isaiah 1–39: Introduction,

Commentary, Reflections," in *The New Interpreter's Bible: A Commentary in Twelve Volumes*, ed. Leander E. Keck et al. (Nashville: Abingdon, 2001), 6:25–305, here 81.

14. So Blenkinsopp, *Isaiah 1–39*, 201. See also J. Cheryl Exum, "The Ethics of Biblical Violence against Women," in *The Bible in Ethics: The Second Sheffield Colloquium*, ed. John W. Rogerson et al., Journal for the Study of the Old Testament Supplement Series 207 (Sheffield: Sheffield Academic Press, 1995), 248–761, here 252: "I take it as an obscene reference to the woman's vagina."

15. Exum, "Ethics of Biblical Violence," 252. See also Magdalene, "Ancient Near Eastern Treaty-Curses," esp. 333, 341–46, who links the prophetic metaphors with ancient Near Eastern treaties and the concept of divine covenant to show that the biblical metaphor originated in ancient Near Eastern treaties.

16. Miles, "Re-reading the Power of Satire," 209.

17. Ibid., 216.

18. Ibid., 215.

19. So also Christl M. Maier, *Daughter Zion, Mother Zion: Gender, Space, and the Sacred in Ancient Israel* (Minneapolis: Fortress, 2008), 108: "YHWH reveals himself as the perpetrator."

20. This translation is taken from Angela Bauer, *Gender in the Book of Jeremiah: A Feminist-Literary Reading*, Studies in Biblical Literature 5 (New York: Peter Lang, 1999), 101–2. A similar passage appears also in Jer 49:10, in which God threatens the male-personified nation of Edom with stripping him bare and uncovering his hiding places. The verb "to strip" (חשׂף) appears also in Jer 13:26 and the verb "to uncover" (גלה) appears in many rape poems, such as Jer 13:22.

21. So, for example, William L. Holladay, *Jeremiah 1: A Commentary on the Book of the Prophet Jeremiah, Chapters 1–25*, Hermeneia (Philadelphia: Fortress, 1986), 414. See also R. E. Clements, *Jeremiah*, Interpretation, a Bible Commentary for Teaching and Preaching (Atlanta: John Knox, 1988), 87: "Jerusalem is now to be faced with the inevitable fate of violence and rape that awaited a young woman captured as a prisoner of war (v. 26)."

22. Robert P. Carroll, *Jeremiah: A Commentary*, Old Testament Library (Philadelphia: Westminster, 1986), 303.

23. Miles, "Re-reading the Power of Satire," 201.

24. Ibid., 211.

25. Ibid., 209.

26. See, for example, Bauer, *Gender in the Book of Jeremiah*, 103–4; Carroll, *Jeremiah*, 303; Holladay, *Jeremiah*, 414.

27. See related but less explicit passages in Jer 2:14-25, 33—3:20; 4:18, 20; 6:8; 13:24-27; 15:15-16; 22:20-23; 30:12-15.

28. Carroll, *Jeremiah*, 303.

29. Ibid., 304.

30. Ibid.

31. Ibid.

32. Clements, *Jeremiah*, 88.

33. Miles, "Re-reading the Power of Satire," 214.

34. See Gracia Fay Ellwood, "Rape and Judgment," *Daughters of Sarah* 11 (1985): 9-13, here 13.

35. Gerlinde Baumann, *Love and Violence: Marriage as Metaphor for the Relationship between YHWH and Israel in the Prophetic Books*, trans. Linda M. Maloney (Collegeville, Minn.: Liturgical Press, 2003), 120.

36. Ibid.

37. Ibid., 134.

38. Exum, "Ethics of Biblical Violence," 253.

39. Ibid., 265. See also Christina Nießen, "Schuld, Strafe und Geschlecht: Die Auswirkungen der Genderkonstruktionen auf Schuldzuweisungen und Gerichtsankündigungen in Jer 23,9-32 und Jer 13,20-27," *Biblische Zeitschrift* 48, no. 1 (2004): 86–96, here 96: "Frauen werden hier ausschließlich über ihre Sexualität definiert, die als unkontrolliert gilt und mit dem Bösen identifiziert wird. Männliche Sexualität hingegen ist positiv konnotiert und kann, da sie als Bestrafungsmittel eingesetzt wird, für Gerechtigkeit sorgen."

40. Pamela Gordon and Harold C. Washington, "Rape as a Military Metaphor in the Hebrew Bible," in *A Feminist Companion to The Latter Prophets*, ed. Athalya Brenner (Sheffield: Sheffield Academic Press, 1995), 318.

41. The translation of this and the following passages from Ezekiel is that of the NRSV, slightly modified.

42. Mary E. Shields, "Multiple Exposures: Body Rhetoric and Gender in Ezekiel 16," in *Prophets and Daniel: A Feminist Companion to the Bible (Second Series)*, ed. Athalya Brenner (Sheffield: Sheffield Academic Press, 2001), 140.

43. Robert P. Carroll, "Whorusalamin: A Tale of Three Cities as Three Sisters," in *On Reading Prophetic Texts: Gender-Specific and Related Studies in Memory of Fokkelien van Dijk-Hemmes*, ed. Bob Becking and Meindert Dijkstra, Biblical Interpretation Series 18 (Leiden: Brill, 1996), 77. See also the imagery in Lam 1:8-10, 13, 22, which, according to F. W. Dobbs-Allsopp

and Tod Linafelt, are part of "a network of mutually reinforcing images of rape" ("The Rape of Zion in Thr 1,10," *Zeitschrift für die alttestamentliche Wissenschaft* 133 [2001]: 77–81, here 81).

44. The translation of this and the following passages from Ezekiel is that of the NRSV, slightly modified.

45. See also Jer 3:2; Hab 2:15; Zeph 2:15; 3:1. These references to Jerusalem/Zion as bringing destruction upon herself are shorter and less explicit than those in Ezekiel 16 and 23. Lamentations 1:8-10 refers to the destruction of Jerusalem as a consequence of her "grievous sin." Jerusalem even asks for divine help: "O Lord, look at my affliction, for the enemy has triumphed," but there is no answer here. For Zion gaining back her voice, see Carleen R. Mandolfo, *Daughter Zion Talks Back to the Prophets: A Dialogue Theology of the Book of Lamentations*, Semeia Studies 58 (Atlanta: Society of Biblical Literature, 2007).

46. Mary E. Shields, "An Abusive God? Identity and Power/Gender and Violence in Ezekiel 23," in *Postmodern Interpretations of the Bible—A Reader*, ed. A. K. M. Adam (St. Louis, Mo.: Chalice Press, 2001), 136.

47. Ibid., 144.

48. Shields, "Multiple Exposures," 146–47.

49. See Shields, "Abusive God?" 149–50.

50. Ibid., 148, 150.

51. Ibid., 150–51.

52. Renita J. Weems, *Battered Love: Marriage, Sex, and Violence in the Hebrew Prophets* (Minneapolis: Augsburg Fortress Press, 1995), 113; Shields, "Multiple Exposures," 152.

53. Shields, "Multiple Exposures," 153.

54. Daniel L. Smith-Christopher, "Ezekiel in Abu Ghraib: Rereading Ezekiel 16:37-39 in the Context of Imperial Conquest," in *Ezekiel's Hierarchical World: Wrestling with a Tiered Reality*, ed. Stephen L. Cook and Corrine L. Patton, Symposium Series (Atlanta: Society of Biblical Literature, 2004), 141–57, here 155.

55. Ibid., 155–56.

56. Ibid., 157. See also the discussion in Maier, *Daughter Zion, Mother Zion*, 121–24.

57. Linda Day, "Rhetoric and Domestic Violence in Ezekiel 16," *Biblical Interpretation* 8, no. 3 (2000): 205–30, here 218.

58. Ibid., 212.

59. See also Hos 2:1-23 for this pattern as it relates to the prophet/God and the prophet's wife, Gomer.

60. Day, "Rhetoric and Domestic Violence," 225.

61. Ibid., 227.

62. Ibid., 228.

63. Katheryn Pfisterer Darr, "Ezekiel's Justifications of God: Teaching Troubling Texts," *Journal for the Study of the Old Testament* 55 (1992): 97–117, here 114.

64. Ibid., 117.

65. The NRSV translates: "and their wives (will be) ravished." The Brown, Driver, and Briggs lexicon provides two translation options: "to violate, ravish" (Francis Brown, S. R. Driver, and Charles A. Briggs, eds., *Hebrew and English Lexicon of the Old Testament, based on the Lexicon of William Gesenius* [1906; Oxford: Clarendon, 1951], 993).

66. Hans Wildberger, *Isaiah 13–27: A Continental Commentary*, trans. Thomas H. Trapp (Minneapolis: Fortress, 1997), 9, 28.

67. Blenkinsopp, *Isaiah 1–39*, 279.

68. Tucker, "Book of Isaiah 1–39," 157.

69. Otto Kaiser, *Isaiah 13–39: A Commentary*, trans. R. A. Wilson, Old Testament Library (London: SCM, 1974), 19.

70. Brevard S. Childs, *Isaiah*, Old Testament Library (Louisville: West-minster John Knox, 2001), 118, 125.

71. Slightly modified translation of the NRSV.

72. Baumann, *Love and Violence*, 192.

73. Joseph Blenkinsopp, *Isaiah 40–55: A New Translation with Intro-duction and Commentary*, Anchor Bible 19 (New York: Doubleday, 2000), 280. See also Marvin A. Sweeney, *The Twelve Prophets*, 2 vols., Berit Olam (Collegeville, Minn.: Liturgical Press, 2000), 2:443.

74. Blenkinsopp, *Isaiah 40–55*, 278, 279.

75. Ibid., 280.

76. Ibid.

77. John L. McKenzie, *Second Isaiah: Introduction, Translation, and Notes*, Anchor Bible 20 (Garden City, N.Y.: Doubleday, 1968), 92.

78. Klaus Baltzer, *Deutero-Isaiah: A Commentary on Isaiah 40–55*, trans. Margaret Kohl, Hermeneia (Minneapolis: Fortress, 2001), 271.

79. Childs, *Isaiah*, 366.

80. The stem *glh* (גלה), which was used in Isa 47:2-3, appears also, for example, in Nah 2:8 and Lam 4:22 (see below).

81. See Baumann's translation of this verse in the German (*Liebe und Gewalt: Die Ehe als Metapher für das Verhältnes JHWH—Israel in der Prophetenbüchern* [Stuttgart: Katholisches Bibelwerk, 2000], 218 n. 629):

"Ich will dich schänden." The English translation of the German text offers a weak translation of v. 6 (*Love and Violence*, 209): ". . . and I will defile you. . . ." See also Gerlinde Baumann, *Gottes Gewalt im Wandel: Traditionsgeschichtliche und intertextuelle Studien zu Nahum 1,2-8*, Wissenschaftliche Monographien zum Alten und Neuen Testament 108 (Neukirchen-Vluyn: Neukirchener Verlag, 2005).

82. Slightly modified translation of the NRSV.

83. Michael H. Floyd, *Minor Prophets: Part 2*, Forms of the Old Testament Literature (Grand Rapids: Eerdmans, 2000), 71. See also Magdalene, "Ancient Near Eastern Treaty-Curses," 328–30, 333.

84. Baumann, *Love and Violence*, 52–55, 210.

85. Sweeney, *Twelve Prophets*, 2:443.

86. Baumann, *Love and Violence*, 209.

87. Elke Seifert, *Tochter und Vater im Alten Testament: Eine ideologiekritische Untersuchung zur Verfügungsgewalt von Vätern über ihre Töchter*, Neukirchener theologische Dissertationen und Habilitationen 9 (Neukirchen-Vluyn: Neukirchener Verlag, 1997), 308.

88. The repeated use of the Hebrew stem *znh* (זנה) has led interpreters to characterize woman Babylon as a prostitute. The verb is usually translated as "to play the harlot" or "to commit adultery." See Phyllis Bird, "To Play the Harlot: Inquiry into an Old Testament Metaphor," in *Gender and Difference in Ancient Israel*, ed. Peggy L. Day (Minneapolis: Fortress, 1989), 75–94.

89. Sweeney, *Twelve Prophets*, 2:24.

90. Mayer I. Gruber, "Nineveh the Adulteress," in *Prophets and Daniel: A Feminist Companion to the Bible (Second Series)*, ed. Athalya Brenner (Sheffield: Sheffield Academic Press, 2001), 220–25, here 225.

91. Baumann, *Love and Violence*, 211–12.

92. Francisco O. García-Treto, "The Book of Nahum: Introduction, Commentary, and Reflections," in *The New Interpreter's Bible: A Commentary in Twelve Volumes*, ed. Leander E. Keck et al. (Nashville: Abingdon, 1996), 7:591–619, here 615. Despite these comments, he entitles this section in his commentary as "Nahum 3:4-7, The *Humiliated* Prostitute" (emphasis added).

93. See also Erhard Gerstenberger, "עשק *'āšaq*," *Theologisches Wörterbuch zum Altes Testament*, ed. Heinz-Joseph Fabry and Helmer Ringgren (Stuttgart: Kohlhammer, 1989), 6:442–46, here 443.

94. Baumann, *Love and Violence*, 179.

95. F. W. Dobbs-Allsopp, *Lamentations: A Bible Commentary for Teaching and Preaching*, Interpretation (Louisville: Westminster John Knox, 2002), 137.

96. Adele Berlin, *Lamentations: A Commentary*, Old Testament Library (Louisville: Westminster John Knox, 2002), 114. See also Maier, *Daughter Zion, Mother Zion*, 141–60.

97. This translation is based on Bauer, *Gender in the Book of Jeremiah*, 114.

98. Abraham Joshua Heschel, *The Prophets*, vol. 1 (New York: Harper & Row, 1962), 113.

99. Holladay, *Jeremiah 1*, 552.

100. Ibid., 553.

101. Bauer, *Gender in the Book of Jeremiah*, 114.

102. Carroll, *Jeremiah*, 398.

103. Ibid.

104. Patrick D. Miller, "The Book of Jeremiah: Introduction, Commentary, and Reflections," in *The New Interpreter's Bible: A Commentary in Twelve Volumes*, ed. Leander E. Keck et al. (2001), 6:553–926, here 729–30.

105. Ken Stone, "'You Seduced Me, You Overpowered Me, and You Prevailed': Religious Experience and Homoerotic Sadomasochism in Jeremiah," in *Patriarchs, Prophets and Other Villains*, ed. Lisa Isherwood (London/Oakville: Equinox, 2007), 101–9.

106. Ibid., 106.

107. Ibid., 107.

108. Ibid., 109.

109. Ibid.

110. Robert Gordis, *The Book of Job: Commentary, New Translation, and Special Studies*, Moreshet Series 2 (New York: Jewish Theological Seminary, 1978), 325.

111. Others characterize 30:9-15 as a poem and entitle it "One Whom God Has Humbled"; see J. Gerald Janzen, *Job: A Bible Commentary for Teaching and Preaching*, Interpretation (Atlanta: John Knox, 1985), 206.

112. Samuel R. Driver and George B. Gray, *A Critical and Exegetical Commentary on the Book of Job*, 2 vols., International Critical Commentary (New York: Scribner, 1921), 1:254.

113. See Gordis, *Book of Job*, 333; Norman C. Habel, *The Book of Job: A Commentary*, Old Testament Library (Philadelphia: Westminster, 1985), 415: "God is the subject of the verb here."

114. For this translation, see Habel, *Book of Job*, 414.

115. Gordis, *Book of Job*, 326.

116. E. Dhorme, *A Commentary on the Book of Job*, trans. Harold Knight (London: Nelson, 1967), 437.

117. Driver and Gray, *Critical and Exegetical Commentary on Job*, 256.

118. Quoted in S. Tamar Kamionkowski, "Gender Reversal in Ezekiel 16," in *Prophets and Daniel: A Feminist Companion to the Bible (Second Series)*, ed. Athalya Brenner (Sheffield: Sheffield Academic Press, 2001), 170–85, here 171–72.

119. Gordon and Washington, "Rape as a Military Metaphor," 325.

120. For the discussion of the real-life implications of metaphors, see Athalya Brenner, "On Prophetic Propaganda and the Politics of 'Love': The Case of Jeremiah," in *A Feminist Companion to The Latter Prophets*, ed. Athalya Brenner (Sheffield: Sheffield Academic Press, 1995), 259: "Fantasy in pornography, as in rape, is not simply a fantasy of sex and desire. . . . Within the fantasy desire becomes a metaphor which reflects social 'reality'."

121. Athalya Brenner, "Some Reflections on Violence against Women and the Image of the Hebrew Bible," in *On the Cutting Edge: The Study of Women in Biblical Worlds: Essays in Honor of Elisabeth Schüssler Fiorenza*, ed. Jane Schaberg, Alice Bach, and Esther Fuchs (New York/London: Continuum, 2004), 79.

122. Miles, "Re-reading the Power of Satire," 215.

123. Gruber, "Nineveh the Adulteress," 224.

124. Maier, *Daughter Zion, Mother Zion*, 135, 136.

125. See Brenner, "Some Reflections on Violence against Women," 79.

126. Mandolfo, *Daughter Zion Talks Back*, 127.

127. Ibid., 127.

128. Julia M. O'Brien, "In Retrospect . . . Self-Response to 'On Saying No' to a Prophet," in *Prophets and Daniel: A Feminist Companion to the Bible (Second Series)*, ed. Athalya Brenner (Sheffield: Sheffield Academic Press, 2001), 206–19, here 218–19.

129. Miles, "Re-reading the Power of Satire," 216.

130. Majella Franzmann, "The City as Woman: The Case of Babylon in Isaiah 47," *Australian Biblical Review* 43 (1995): 119, here 19.

Conclusion

1. Marie M. Fortune, *Sexual Violence: The Sin Revisited* (Cleveland: Pilgrim Press, 2005), 237.

2. This was the subtitle of Marie Fortune's earlier book: *Sexual Violence: The Unmentionable Sin* (Cleveland: Pilgrim Press, 1980).

3. Jeffrey Gettleman, "Rape Victims' Words Help Jolt Congo into Change," *New York Times*, October 17, 2008, http://www.nytimes.com/2008/10/18/world/africa/18congo.html (accessed March 18, 2009);

idem, "Rape Epidemic Raises Trauma of Congo War," *New York Times*, October 7, 2007, http://www.nytimes.com/2007/10/07/world/africa/07congo.html (accessed March 18, 2009).

4. For more information on the problem of Christian anti-Judaism and anti–Old Testament attitudes, see, for example, Paula Fredriksen and Adele Reinhartz, eds., *Jesus, Judaism, and Christian Anti-Judaism: Reading the New Testament after the Holocaust* (Louisville: Westminster John Knox Press, 2002); Dan Cohn-Sherbok, *The Crucified Jew: Twenty Centuries of Christian Anti-Semitism* (Grand Rapids: Eerdmans, 1997); and Charlotte Klein, *Anti-Judaism in Christian Theology*, trans. Edward Quinn (Philadelphia: Fortress Press, 1978).

5. Julia M. O'Brien, "In Retrospect . . . Self-Response to 'On Saying No' to a Prophet," in *Prophets and Daniel: A Feminist Companion to the Bible (Second Series)*, ed. Athalya Brenner (Sheffield: Sheffield Academic Press, 2001), 206–19, here 218–19.

6. Johnny Miles, "Re-reading the Power of Satire: Isaiah's 'Daughters of Zion,' Pope's 'Belinda,' and the Rhetoric of Rape," *Journal for the Study of the Old Testament* 31, no. 2 (2006): 193–219, here 216.

7. Katheryn Pfisterer Darr, "Ezekiel's Justifications of God: Teaching Troubling Texts," *Journal for the Study of the Old Testament* 55 (1992): 97–117, here 117.

INDEX OF AUTHORS

INDEX OF BIBLE AND OTHER ANCIENT TEXTS

Other Ancient Sources

INDEX of SUBJECTS